Property Rights Dynamics

This volume should be a welcome addition to the bookshelf of every person interested in the function of property rights and their evolving nature. The volume contains twelve original chapters on property rights, both on their basic nature and on their application in a wide arena, including intellectual property, human tissue, and marital assets. It's a must read.

(Steven Shavell, Harvard University)

This stimulating set of essays responds to an important need. Private property increasingly extends its reach – particularly noticeable in the domain of copyright – and new property forms continually evolve. Every reader will come away from this volume with new insights and information.

(Wendy Gordon, Boston University)

This volume deals with the contemporary property rights, examining its role and effect in light of the law and economics approach, while maintaining a focus on the real world and the specificities of practical cases. In particular, this volume questions the transformation of a specific institutional remedy for a market failure – one of many available solutions – into a quasi-universal religion that dogmatically assumes property rights are always a good solution for externalities. *Property Rights Dynamics* questions why property rights have trumped other institutional devices and eroded precise evaluation according to the rule of reason, as is familiar to normative analysis where it concerns matters of economic policy.

A host of prominent contributors investigate specific milieus, support divergent theses on the effects of today's extensive propertization trend and cast new light on this crucial institution by balancing its power and its limitations.

Donatella Porrini is Associate Professor of Economics at the Università di Lecce, Italy and **Giovanni Battista Ramello** is Associate Professor of Industrial Economics at the Università del Piemonte Orientale "Amedeo Avogadro," Italy.

The Economics of Legal Relationships
Edited by Nicholas Mercuro and Michael D. Kaplowitz
Michigan State University

* The first three volumes listed above are published by and available from Elsevier.

Property Rights Dynamics

A law and economics perspective

Edited by
Donatella Porrini and
Giovanni Battista Ramello

LONDON AND NEW YORK

First published 2007
by Routledge
2 Park Square, Milton Park, Abingdon, Oxon OX14 4RN

Simultaneously published in the USA and Canada
by Routledge
711 Third Ave, New York, NY 10017

*Routledge is an imprint of the Taylor & Francis Group,
an informa business*

© 2007 Donatella Porrini and Giovanni Battista Ramello, selection and
editorial matter; the contributors, their own chapters

Typeset in Times New Roman by
Newgen Imaging Systems (P) Ltd, Chennai, India

British Library Cataloguing in Publication Data
A catalogue record for this book is available
from the British Library

Library of Congress Cataloging in Publication Data
A catalog record for this book has been requested

ISBN10: 0–415–36382–9 (hbk)
ISBN10: 0–203–01498–7 (ebk)

ISBN13: 978–0–415–36382–2 (hbk)
ISBN13: 978–0–203–01498–1 (ebk)

Contents

Contributors

Jürgen G. Backhaus holds the Krupp Chair in Public Finance and Fiscal Sociology at Erfurt University since November 2000. Between 1986 and 2000, he has held the chair in Public Economics at Maastricht University. In September 2004 he was awarded an honorary doctorate by the University of Thessaly (Greece). He has published 68 books and monographs, more than 200 articles in refereed journals and book chapters, some 30 scholarly notes and more than 60 reviews. His research interests span economics, but also neighboring disciplines such as law, fiscal sociology, and environmental sciences. In 1994 he founded (with Frank H. Stephen) the *European Journal of Law and Economics*, of which he is the managing editor.

Having edited the *Elgar Companion to Law and Economics* (Cheltenham: Edward Elgar, 1999, 2005), he has published – together with Richard E. Wagner of George Mason University – another reference work, *The Handbook of Public Finance* (Boston, MA: Kluwer, 2004).

Michele Boldrin holds a PhD from the University of Rochester (1987) and is currently a Professor of Economics at the Department of Economics, Washington University in Saint Louis. Previously, he has been on the Faculty of the University of Chicago, UCLA, Northwestern, Carlos III, Pennsylvania, and Minnesota. He is a Fellow of the *Econometric Society*, an Associate Editor of *Econometrica*, and an Editor of the *Review of Economic Dynamics*. He has served as an advisor to various international agencies and governments. His scientific work applies dynamic general equilibrium tools to real world problems, with a particular focus on economic growth, innovation, business cycles, and the welfare state. He has published multiple articles in all major economic research journals, as well as a couple of books.

Pamela Clark holds degrees in law and medicine from the University of Virginia. She is currently an Assistant Professor of Pathology and Associate Medical Director of the Blood Bank and Transfusion Services at the University of Virginia Health System.

Antony W. Dnes holds a PhD from the University of Edinburgh (1988) and is currently Professor of Economics at University of Hull, England. He is member of the Editorial Board of the *International Review of Law and Economics* and European Editor of *Managerial and Decision Economics*. He has published articles in international economic journals and is author of several books, including *Economics of Law: Property Rights, Contracts and Obligations* (2005) and *The Law and Economics of Marriage and Divorce* (2002) (also published in Japanese and Chinese).

Sophie Harnay is Associate Professor of Economics at the University of Reims Champagne Ardenne and at the Institut d'Etudes Politiques de Paris (France), researcher at the OMI – EDJ (University of Reims) and EconomiX (University of Paris 10). She received her PhD in 1999 from the University of Paris 1. Her main research interests include Law and Economics and Public Economics. She has published several articles in refereed journals. She is also the author of *R.A. Posner, l'analyse économique du droit* (2003, éditions Michalon, Paris), together with Alain Marciano. Her current research concerns judicial behaviors and corporate law.

David K. Levine holds a PhD from the Massachusetts Institute of Technology (1981) and is currently a Professor of Economics at the Department of Economics, Washington University in Saint Louis. Previously, he was the Armen Alchian Professor of Economics at the Department of Economics, UCLA, where he was also the Co-Director of CASSEL between 1999 and 2004. He is a Fellow of the *Econometric Society*, an Editor of *Econometrica*, a member of the Executive Board of *Theoretical Economics*, a past Editor of the *Review of Economic Dynamics*, of *Economic Theory*, and of the *Journal of Economic Theory*. A leading figure in the fields of game theory and general equilibrium theory, his research focuses on repeated games, reputational effects, uniqueness of equilibrium, market incompleteness and, more recently, the theory of innovation and growth. He has published multiple articles in all major economic research journals and various books in the areas of game and general equilibrium theory.

Julia D. Mahoney is Professor of Law and David H. Ibbeken Research Professor at the University of Virginia School of Law, where she teaches courses in property, non-profit organizations, and cultural property.

Alain Marciano is Associate Professor at the University of Reims Champagne Ardenne. He has published papers and edited books on law and economics, on public choice theory and also on history of economic ideas. His research interests include the nature of rules and institutions and their evolution, and the study of judicial processes and judicial decision making.

Robert P. Merges is Wilson Sonsini Goodrich & Rosati Pofessor of Law and Technology at UC Berkeley (Boalt Hall) School of Law, and a co-Director of the Berkeley Center for Law and Technology, centerpiece of the top-rated Intellectual Property program among US law schools. He is the co-author of leading casebooks on patent law and intellectual property, and has written numerous articles on the economics of intellectual property, in particular patent law. Professor Merges has worked with government agencies such as the Department of Justice and the Federal Trade Commission on IP-related policy issues. He has also consulted with leading law firms and companies. He received his BS from Carnegie-Mellon University, a JD from Yale Law School, and LlM and JSD degrees from Columbia Law School.

Ugo Mattei graduated in 1983 from the Law School of the University of Torino and he received his LLM from Boalt Hall in 1989 where he was a Fulbright Fellow. In 1985 he joined the law school of the University of Trento as an assistant professor and he received tenure as a full professor in 1990. In 1992 he was appointed as a professor in the Faculté Internationale de Droit Comparé (Strasbourg), where he served for four years. In 1994 he was appointed to the Hastings faculty as the first holder of the Fromm Chair in International and Comparative Law. In 1997 he accepted a call from the University of Turin, Faculty of Law. He is a Full Member of the International Academy of Comparative Law, a General Editor of the Series Common Core of European Private Law (Trento Project) at Cambridge University Press, A Series Editor of European Private Law in Context at Kluwer International and an Editor in Chief of Global Jurist. Ugo Mattei has published eleven books and more than one hundred other publications in English, Italian, French, Portuguese, Russian, and Chinese.

Antonio Nicita is Associate Professor of Economic Policy at the University of Siena, Italy. Graduated cum laude with a degree in Economics and Social Discipline from Bocconi University of Milan. Antonio Nicita pursued graduate studies at Cambridge and Siena where he earned his PhD in Economics. From 1997 to 2000 he served as an Economist at the Italian Antitrust Authority. In 2003 he founded with Pier Luigi Parcu a consulting company based in Rome, Italy and specialized on competition policy, antitrust and regulation advise. In 2006 he is visiting Fulbright professor in Yale, new Haven. He is one of the founders of the Italian Society of Law and Economics and he is now general secretary of the association. He has also been elected for 2006–2009 in the board of directors of ISNIE, International Society for New Istitutional Economics, Professor Nicita is the author of several publications on competition, regulation issues, economics of contracts, and law and economics.

Francesco Parisi is a Professor of Law at the University of Minnesota Law School. In 2002 he was appointed *Professore Ordinario per Chiara Fama* at the University of Milan where he holds a Chair in Economic Analysis of Private Law. From 1993 to 2006 he taught at George Mason University where he served as Professor of Law and Director of the Law and Economics Program and as an Associate Director of the J.M. Buchanan Center for Political Economy. Professor Parisi received his DJur degree from the University of Rome "La Sapienza," an LLM, a JSD and an MA degree in Economics from the University of California at Berkeley and a PhD in Economics from George Mason University. He is the author of ten books and over one-hundred and fifty papers in the field of law and economics. Professor Parisi is currently serving as Editor-in-Chief of the *Review of Law and Economics* and of the *Supreme Court Economic Review*. He is a member of the board of editors of the *International Review of Law and Economics*, the *Journal of Public Choice*, the *American Journal of Comparative Law*, and he serves on the Board of Advisors of the *Social Sciences Research Network*.

Donatella Porrini is Associate Professor of Economics at the Università di Lecce. She degreed in Law and she received the MSc in economics at QMW in London and the Doctorate in Economics in Milano. She has been researcher at the Università di Milano. She had the responsibility of teaching Law and Economics for many years. Her main research interests concern antitrust and regulation, law and economics, especially with reference to insurance and bank markets. He has participated to many international conference (i.e. presenting at the American Association of Law and Economics, 2005). She has published in the field of law and economics a number papers in national and international journals and books.

Andrea Pradi graduated in 1993/94 from the Law School of the University of Trento, where he also received his PhD in Comparative Law in 1998/99. He received his LLM from UC Berkeley Law School in fall 2002. He has been a visiting scholar at Berkeley Law School in 1993 and 2000, the Northwestern University of Chicago and a visiting professor at the University Pompeu Fabra of Barcelona in the fall 2004. In 1999 he joined the Law School of the University of Trento as a junior Professor teaching Anglo-American Law. He is in the editorial board of Global Jurist and National Reporter of the IP group of the Common Core of European Private Law Project at the Trento University. His main research topics are Comparative Law and Economics of Property, European Private Law and Intellectual Property.

Giovanni B. Ramello is Associate Professor of Industrial Economics at the Department of Public Policy and Collective Choices – POLIS, Università del Piemonte Orientale. He received an education both in economics (PhD) and in computer sciences (MSc) in Italy (Università di Torino, Università Bocconi di Milano) and in France (Université Jean Moulin–Lyon 3 and CNSM, Lyon). He has been research fellow at the Fondazione Giovanni Agnelli, Torino (Italy), at the Banff Centre for the Arts (Alberta, Canada), at SIMS-UC Berkeley, and has served as an advisor for the Forum for the Information Society, Presidency of the Italian Ministers' Council, for the Federation of the Italian Universities, for the EU Phare-Twinning Project on the Harmonization of Antitrust in the European countries and for some Italian antitrust cases. His main research interests concern industrial organization, antitrust and regulation, law and economics, intellectual property, information goods, and knowledge production. He has published in these fields a number papers in national and international journals and books and is currently member of the Board of Editors of the *Review of Economic Research on Copyright Issues* and Managing Editor of the *European Journal of Comparative Economics*.

Paul L.C. Torremans was educated at the Universities of Leuven (Belgium), Le Havre (France) and Leicester (UK). He is City Solicitors' Educational Trust Professor of Intellectual Property Law at the School of Law of the University of Nottingham and he also holds an appointment as Professor of Private International Law at the Faculty of Law of the University of Gent. His main research interests are intellectual property rights, their international exploitation and their interaction with private international law and competition law. He has published widely in these areas in scholarly journals such as the *European Intellectual Property Review*, the *Intellectual Property Quarterly*, the *International Review of Industrial Property and Copyright Law*, *IPrax*, and *Propriétés Intellectuelles*. His two main books are Intellectual Property and Private international Law, with Professor James Fawcett (1998) and Holyoak and Torremans Intellectual Property Law, Oxford University Press.

1 Property rights dynamics

Current issues in law and economics

Donatella Porrini and Giovanni B. Ramello

Introduction

This book deals with property rights, a complex institution common to all human groups. Property rights grant the holder exclusive rights over a given resource, and as such, have been a constant concern throughout the history of human societies. However, their definition, realization, and pervasiveness vary according to the specific context in which they emerge and depend largely on their function within a given society. Moreover, since social needs change over time, property rights are subject to constant evolution and transformation. This is caused primarily by group dynamics, but occasionally by the successful imposition of special interests by the major stakeholders in a particular group.[1]

In the market economy, a powerful force behind the ubiquity of property rights is the fact that clear fragmentation of the commons and the subsequent entitlement to well-defined commodities is the prerequisite for trade and market existence. Accordingly, market stimuli serve as the main impetus for change in the field of property rights in Western society.

However, if this constant change can be ascribed to the very nature of the legal institution and market needs, the increasing pervasiveness of property rights can be explained in part by influential support from the law and economics theory, which have justified them for their power to internalize externalities and promote efficiency. The domain of property rights has become so omnipresent as to create a "property rights society," where property is seen as a panacea for any type of market failure.

This point of view is often used to justify the creation of new property rights or the extension of old ones, but it disregards the fact that there is no single way to stimulate efficiency and that, in general, efficiency can be pursued only by adopting the use of reason.

In some cases, it appears that there is so much enthusiasm for the potential economic benefit of property rights that in the actual context, their effectiveness is simply overstated: a different legal institution would probably better serve the social good. On the whole, this calls for a more cautious approach when studying and applying the property paradigm.

The purpose of this book is not to dispute the usefulness and virtues of property rights. Rather, from the perspective of law and economics, and with the input of an international panel of distinguished scholars, it attempts to cast new light on this crucial institution by evaluating its power and its limitations. It also offers insights for future research.

This chapter presents the theoretical basis that contributors were given for their work, and summarizes the main topics of the book. Following this introduction the next section describes the origins of property rights. In sequence we discuss the revolutionary theory of property rights as a solution to the externality problem, and the current dynamic of the institution. The topics addressed in the following chapters, are summarized before concluding the introduction to the chapters.

The pervasiveness of property rights throughout human history

It is impossible to say exactly when and where property rights first appeared in human history. To some extent, appropriation and property rights came about as the unavoidable consequence of the exploitation by individuals of scarce resources (Demsetz, 1998). Since the beginnings of human life, hunting a wild animal or gathering fruit implied excluding other human beings from doing the same with that specific resource.

This stems essentially from the nature of wild animals, fruits, and many "subject matters" as private goods, in the sense that their consumption by an individual always entails the exclusion of someone else.

Generally speaking, a property right is the right to decide how a resource is used and, complementarily, the right to exclude someone else from doing so (Alchian, 1965). Property rights, as a *de facto* if not a *de jure* institution, have therefore existed for almost as long as human society (Bailey, 1992 and 1998).[2]

Nonetheless, at the dawn of human history, the sparse population, high fragmentation of social groups, and considerable abundance of unclaimed resources made conflicts over their consumption and use less likely and intense than today. The pivotal role of property rights was at that time barely recognized. Their importance emerged with the growing complexity of human societies and, of course, the increased scarcity of resources (Levmore, 2002).

As Demsetz writes, "In the world of Robinson Crusoe property rights play no role" (Demsetz, 1967, p. 347). The need for strong, secure property rights intensifies with the evolution and development of economic activities and their value in social contexts, driven by the concept of scarcity (Levmore, 2002).

Property rights appear recurrently in human groups – in a sense, they are a universal trait of social interaction – but their features vary so widely among social groups and from one historical period to another that no universal definition exists (Munzer, 1990). Indeed, the design, allocation, and enforcement of property rights involve a complex set of issues that different societies have managed in a variety of ways.

On the whole, a property right is a bundle of rights over the likely uses identified by the law. According to Hohfeld's paradigm of legal entitlements (Hohfeld, 1913), this bundle complies with the social organization and its values, as it defines not just what the holder can do with the right and the protected resource – his or her entitlement – but how other individuals must behave in order to preserve the holder's right, that is, the correlative obligation (others' duties).

The holder of a property right can be an individual, a group or the government. Again, there is no one solution: almost every society has designed and granted distinct property rights to different owners according to its preferences and needs (Munzer, 1990; Demsetz, 1998).

In addition, since social relationships change over time along with these preferences and needs, property rights have been continuously transformed in order to accomplish their changing roles. In other words, the history of property rights is nothing if not dynamic, and all we can do is study snapshots to understand their precise function at a given time and in a specific social context.

Property rights, therefore, are not a static ornament of human society. They are the expression of specific social groups and they play a crucial role in regulating the behavior of individuals within that group. From this perspective, the architecture of property rights speaks volumes about a society (Demsetz, 1967). Because of their idiosyncratic nature, closely related to the social dimension, they can serve as sort map through which we can infer the socially shared value system of a specific human group.

In Western culture, for instance, many scholars hold that the creation of an extended framework of property rights granted to single individuals – what is familiarly termed "private property" – is the cornerstone of the capitalist society and, to some extent, the necessary condition for freedom of its citizens and existence of the market. Today, private property is considered an irrefutable component of individual liberty. But that thesis is actually the outcome of a process several centuries long.[3]

Property rights and economic theory

A well-defined set of private property rights is central to the existence of trade. The fragmentation of the commons cannot be accomplished without a specific set of rules assigning the various fragments to individuals. Thus, the market as we define it today cannot exist without property rights. Economic theory cannot neglect this pivotal role and has always recognized the importance of property rights.

For a long time, however, economists focused their energy on understanding the price system from a micro and macro perspective. They assumed that the property rights framework was exogenously determined and, having acknowledged its value, paid it no further attention (Demsetz, 1998).

Not until the second half of the twentieth century did new thinking emerge on the subject of property rights. Rather than a simple prerequisite for the existence of markets and trade, they were now viewed as organic to economic activity and responsible for promoting efficiency.

This new awareness was driven by the seminal work of Ronald Coase (1960) and gradually extended and refined by Alchian (1965), Demsetz (1967),

Calabresi and Melamed (1972), and the proponents of the "new property rights" school (Hart, 1995).[4] The Coasean interpretation of property rights was revolutionary for both legal and economic theory. It cast new light on this apparently quiet institution that had accompanied human beings throughout their history: property rights were a crucial device for economic activity. "In all societies, primitive and modern, property rights [were and still are] an important part of social technology that helps to determine economic efficiency" (Bailey, 1998, p. 155).

Property rights achieve this goal simply by correcting market failures that arise from externalities, that is, external costs or benefits associated with the production or consumption of a specific good.[5] In other words, property rights bring back to the market exchange what has escaped from it and thus help to internalize externalities.

As a whole, the literature cited above supports the notion that if very general conditions are met – essentially the absence of substantial transaction costs – then a set of well defined property rights and the exchange mechanism are jointly able to overcome the externalities problem and promote the efficient allocation of resources, thus achieving welfare maximization.[6] Therefore, they have the additional virtue of avoiding (or at least minimizing) government intervention to foster efficiency by way of regulation. According to the Coase Theorem, once property rights are defined, their initial ownership is irrelevant since free trade will always allocate them to the most efficient user. This feature thus preserves the social value of the competitive process and the mechanism of the invisible hand, once again confirming the central role of the market in pursuing welfare and fostering economic growth.[7]

A final new characteristic of property rights had also emerged: by producing efficiency, property rights make private and public interests converge. They are no longer tools pitting individual owners against society, but devices that by means of private interests produce the public good of economic efficiency.

It is easy to grasp the revolutionary impact of this claim: new property rights could be granted and protected in light of the superior reason of efficiency, and almost everything could become "subject matter." Gone were the days when property rights were viewed as part of the endowment of the economic system. They had become a powerful tool, used extensively by economists, to solve the problem of externalities.

The enthusiasm toward property rights in recent decades has been so widespread that they are now becoming a sort of cure-all for a broad array of market failures. Indeed, the gradual wave of propertization is still very much in progress.

Property rights in the third millennium

This book expressly deals with contemporary property rights dynamics. The focal point here is the reconsideration of economic theory applied to property in light of the changes that have affected goods and society over the past century, and in light of new failures such markets have suffered.

From the recent history of property rights, we can observe that the main attitude of legal systems (justified by supportive economic theory) has been to extend the property paradigm to several new contexts, paying little heed to the nature of new subject matters or to specific features of the social context.

Once again, in other words, property rights are increasingly treated as "the solution" to every sort of market failure, and insufficient attention is paid to alternative devices proposed by economic theory, such as Pigouvian taxes or regulation.[8] The widespread acceptance of the Coase theorem – in itself not at stake here, of course – has served as an excuse far outside Coase's intentions for viewing property rights as a miraculous, quasi-universal remedy for market failures, while often totally neglecting the existence of transaction costs and additional social costs.

New or renewed property rights have recently conquered domains which can hardly be intended as "subject matter," at least within the definition of property as we have known it in the recent past. Take, for instance, the case of property rights on pollution implemented to solve environmental contamination, or the expansion of "intellectual property" to include databases, business methods, and the human genome.[9]

Over the last 50 years, property rights have also faced in several contexts an endemic difficulty of enforcement, leading one to question whether they are always the best solution to market failures or whether they are structurally weak when applied to certain domains. Let us consider, for instance, intellectual property; several recent cases are questioning the effectiveness of property rights in expressive or inventive works.

The first case in point is Napster and the dispute over copyright in the Internet domain.[10] Here, even if property infringement is evident, the broader reflection is on the conflict between a regime that rests upon exclusion of consumers and the technological changes that render communication and information sharing a crucial new phenomenon for society (Maffioletti and Ramello, 2004).[11]

The Microsoft antitrust case, which can be compared with others like Magill TV Guide or IMS Health/NDC Health,[12] has raised the question of whether the exploitation of intellectual property – intended as a remedy to avoid a specific market failure, that is, the generation of a suboptimal level of new ideas – had the unintended side effect of producing another market failure: the substantial erosion of competition and efficiency of the markets (Ramello, 2003).[13]

Again in the intellectual property domain, the issue of patent enforcement and HIV drugs in South Africa has at least raised awareness that patent rights are not always suited to by-the-book application and can, under certain circumstances, lead to an undesirable social outcome (Scherer, 2004).

In other situations, where property rights could have welfare-enhancing consequences, they are not accepted at all or are only considered in part. In the case of human transplants, for instance, clear state (i.e. public) property rights on dead human bodies could solve the market failure of the lack of organs available for transplantation. But governments reject this kind of solution, permitting the appropriability of the genome of living people but not of dead persons' organs, and implicitly accepting a *sui generis* solution that implies a parallel, illegal market of organs drawn from living people who sell or are forced to surrender parts of their body. Note that in certain cases, such as blood, private property rights are enforced and there is in fact a real market.[14]

Another point to discuss is the fragmentation of property rights, which depends on the irreversible law of entropy, and can lead to a different market failure because of the increased cost of acquiring rights (what is scholarly known as the "tragedy of the anticommons").[15]

Finally, even if property rights have their own intrinsic value, because of the market structure and the nature of the subject matters protected, they can produce an inefficient outcome. Sometimes this occurs for the simple reason that property rights are input for other activities, and a dynamic rather than static analysis can call for a different solution concept. An increasing number of scholars maintain that this is, for instance, the case for knowledge, based on an idiosyncratic productive process that strong propertization can significantly affect (Ramello, 2005).[16]

In this vein, there are streams of new literature supporting the idea that property must sometimes be bounded and even weakened. In antitrust law, for instance, the essential facility doctrine holds that under certain circumstances, a right holder may be forced to allow other individuals to access his or her property by virtue of the welfare-enhancing effects of competition. Such a case is now at the center of a lively debate between the United States and Europe.[17]

In short, the above suggests the need for a different normative policy toward property rights. If the implementation of such rights can, in specific cases, promote economic efficiency – and we do not contest this trait – then they are no more than useful institutional devices that compete with other solutions, produce their own inefficiencies, and require the case-by-case evaluation typical of economic analysis.

Critical issues of the property rights society

The chapters of this book constitute an essay on the role and effects of property rights in light of law and economics, while maintaining a focus on the real world and the specificities of practical cases. The book is not meant to dispute or even challenge the ability of property rights to promote efficiency under many circumstances. Rather, it questions the transformation of a specific institutional remedy for a market failure – one of many available solutions – into a quasi-universal religion that dogmatically assumes property rights are always a good solution for externalities. It questions why property rights have trumped other institutional devices and eroded precise evaluation according to the use of reason, as is familiar to normative analysis where it concerns matters of economic policy.

In the following chapters several prominent authors, investigating specific milieus, support divergent theses on the effects of today's extensive propertization trend. As a whole, they maintain the impression that case-by-case evaluation cannot be avoided for this presumedly infallible solution.

We are convinced that property rights are still a valuable resource for legislators and policy makers in several situations, and that they can play a significant role in promoting efficiency in economic systems. But they are no more than this – one of a range of valuable solutions. Only the daily use of human intelligence can transform them into a powerful tool, whereas any dogmatic assumption is likely to produce nothing but inefficiency.

The book is in three parts that address complementary subjects. Part one offers a theoretical perspective, focused on the evolution of property, its functional role in society and its dynamics. Part two discusses three case studies on the extension of property rights, and part three deals with ambiguities in existing institutional frameworks that involve or avoid property rights.

Origins, development, and theoretical paradigms: main issues

The debate in part one is opened by Francesco Parisi, author of two thoughtful contributions on the dynamic nature and effects of the property rights system. His work supports the premise that these elements should be considered carefully to understand the role and consequences on efficiency of the institutional framework. Next, Ugo Mattei and Andrea Pradi contribute additional food for thought by examining the traditional law and economics theory of property under the lens of comparative analysis. Then, Antonio Nicita challenges the traditional idea that property rights can always be easily designed and implemented, by introducing the concept of property incompleteness.

More specifically, in Chapter 2 Francesco Parisi starts with the study of property in Western culture, discussing its functional and dynamic evolution in the social milieu. The property framework, he writes, is created and designed to satisfy specific needs of the society in which it is rooted. From the history of property through modern law, Parisi traces the origin and evolution of property rights systems in light of changes in Western economies. The path of civilization, from the age of hunters through the age of pastures and shepherds to today's market society, has been paralleled by constant changes in property rights that have essentially served to keep the legal institution in tune with its evolving function in society.

Indeed, the link between functional role and dynamic is so tight in the property domain that it seems impossible to look at the property rights system without a clear understanding of the societal needs that generated the institutional framework.

In Chapter 3, entitled "Property Rights: A Comparative Law and Economics Perspective in the Global Era," Ugo Mattei and Andrea Pradi – in a similar vein – alert the reader to pay attention to the real-world complexity of human relationships. Although property rights can play a pivotal role in the market society, their extension to all aspects of that society can backfire in particular scenarios.

The authors' main criticism regards the quasi-dogmatic adoption of the Coase theorem to internalize externalities in a variety of settings, even where other, possibly more efficient solutions are affordable. They argue that the historical contingency of the Coase theorem as an attempt to overcome the dominant approach to externalities by taxes, since Pigou (1932), has produced a misleading ideological conflict between property rights and regulation as models of market governance, by considering the former as the sole institutional alternative that can efficiently tackle the problem of externalities. By contrast, a quick look at the real world – and at much of law and economics literature (Shavell, 1984; Kolstad *et al.*, 1990; Boyer and Porrini, 2002) – shows that property rights and regulation, rather than being in conflict, most often serve the same purpose.

Mattei and Pradi also question the Cosean concept that when transaction costs are low enough, the legal system cannot impact efficiency. Adopting a comparative legal approach, they outline a different conception of property rights and of their exploitation inside markets and society. The challenge for future research is to construct a theory of property rights that properly considers the complexity generated by legal, institutional, and social changes.

Francesco Parisi addresses that complexity in depth in Chapter 4, discussing the entropy produced by the property dynamic and generating a sort of asymmetric Coase theorem. According to Parisi, a close look at real life shows that the transfer of rights, necessary for the existence of trade, is likely to produce a one-way bias that leads to property rights fragmentation. Reunification involves higher transaction costs than those paid in the original deal, and increase monotonically according to the extent of the fragmentation, putting the reversibility of the process at stake. This inertia, so far neglected by economic theory, may possibly favor the tragedy of the anti-commons, thus affecting the pro-efficiency role of property rights.[18] Furthermore, it produces two distinct externalities conflicting with the one that justified the design of a property rights system: on the one hand, the owner's exercise of the exclusionary right, given the highly fragmented property regime and absence of a coordination mechanism, reduces the value of complementary rights held by other individuals. On the other, the withholding of productive resources may generate future externalities "because the underuse of productive inputs today has consequences for the future, as standard growth theory suggests." Legislators have sometimes been able to introduce "gravitational forces" that can control and reduce the entropy/inertia, which must, however, be properly taken into account in order to attain the efficient solution originally pursued by property rights.

In Chapter 5 Antonio Nicita extends the concept of incompleteness from contracts to property. The main challenge here is toward the assumption that property rights are always and easily well-defined. Precisely, the puzzling point under analysis is an ambiguity emerging in economics: on one hand the *homo oeconomicus*, as extensively discussed by the literature on contractual incompleteness, is pervasively bounded in the capacity to *ex ante* define all the contingencies that may affect the content of bilateral contractual agreement; on the other society – intended as a sum of *homini oeconomici* – is always able to define a "social contract" in which the institution of property is a fully defined object whose primary characteristics are that of securing full control over resources, thus promoting stability of expectations and incentives' alignment.

Accordingly, Nicita investigates the specific problem of *ex ante* defining a property right over entitlements perceived as a presumptive rights by at least two alternative claimants. This situation, associated with what he defines as *ex ante* transaction costs, determines the emergence of the property incompleteness problem. In such a case property rights cannot be the efficiency enhancing devices.

The extension of property: field investigations

The second part of the book address the extension of property rights within an already protected domain and to new subject matters. Again, it highlights how a property regime can only be evaluated in its specific context. The three chapters – by Michele Boldrin and David Levine; Robert Merges; and Pamela Clark and Julia Mahoney – deal respectively with the current extension of copyright, the patentability of business methods, and the privatization of human tissues. Taken as a whole, their detailed results confirm the "rule of reason" approach as the only reasonable normative method for managing the extension of property rights.

The US Copyright Term Extension Act of 1998 is the provocative basis from which in Chapter 6 Michele Boldrin and David Levine challenge the traditional argument in favor of copyright. That argument, of course, rests heavily on a metaphor from the Chicago school of law and economics:

> [t]he process of securing intellectual property over ideas is logically and eco-nomically equivalent to the establishment of well defined property rights on parcels of unowned land. Without well defined and secure property rights, the fertile lands of the Western frontier could not be efficiently cultivated or put to pasture, greatly reducing economic development. Similarly, if ideas are not the exclusive private property of someone, they cannot be developed and brought to fruition.[19]

By this reasoning, copyright is granted so that creators will reap sufficient revenue from their creative effort. Conversely, consumers benefit indirectly from copyright, since by paying a monopoly price to creators they receive the creation in exchange, while without copyright they would receive nothing. Much literature based on these premises has supported the incentive theory with the argument that creations of any kind should not be left in the public domain.

Boldrin and Levine reject the notion that this foundation of intellectual property is a given, irrefutable truth. They strongly dispute the current trend toward extending intellectual property rights – what they term the creation of Universal Intellectual Property, which has acquired the status of a public religion – based on the questionable "and shockingly profound revelation [that] anything that can be monopolized ought to, by whoever lays claim to it first."

Their main argument relies on the idiosyncratic character of ideas, whose natural and logical ecosystem is the public domain, which in knowledge produc-tion is a necessary but not sufficient requisite for competition (hence efficiency). Indeed, the public domain is not a commons of unowned ideas or public property available for the plundering, but a productive resource, vitally needed to foster invention and the competitive process (Ramello, 2005). In short, Boldrin and Levine suggest that the economics of knowledge be viewed from a distinct perspective "grounded on different premises and adopt[ing] different modeling strategies than the rest of economics."

A different conclusion is reached by Robert Merges in the chapter "The Uninvited Guest: Patents on Wall Street." Merges discusses the extension of patent protection to business methods, a specific step in the current trend toward "propertization of just about everything," to the financial services industry: banking, investment banking, and stock brokerage. The chapter is a sort of a field investigation of the newly created property rights framework in an economic area that has long existed – and flourished – without it. The main concern here is the potential long-term effect on the financial world and on financial innovation of the new privatization, which is obviously motivated by rent seeking. In the past, information on new business methods was disseminated from innovators to other firms in the relatively closed circle of experts in each area, but with the advent of patents, such innovations can now be "codified" and exploited in a way not previously possible. Since it is difficult to predict the future, the author relies on examples from nineteenth-century railroad development and from the modern software industry, where early concerns that patents would fundamentally undermine innovation were proven to be quite wrong.

Merges's conclusion is semi-positive: patents on Wall Street may well be uninvited guests, but something good may come of it. Old practices will have to be examined, implicit routines made more explicit, and received wisdom questioned. "After all, nature teaches that regular events like this are good – that the uninvited guest is sometimes the most interesting one of all."

Chapter 8, by Pamela Clark and Julia Mahoney, addresses property rights in relation to human biological materials such as organs, blood, gametes, and other tissues. The debate here is whether legislators should recognize property rights over parts of the human body and, if so, what kind of property rights should be recognized and who should be their holders.

In this case, welfare maximization assumes the contours of the development and dissemination of life- and health-saving technologies. The authors begin by acknowledging the crucial role property rights have played in medical sciences: organ transplantation, fertility treatment, anatomical education, biomedical research, and therapeutic activities have depended and still depend on the enforcement of existing property rights over human tissues. Nonetheless, although property rights are a necessary condition for allowing modern medical practices to exist, this does not necessarily imply that the market should govern the exchange of such rights. Generally speaking, for example, the force of donors and altruism has proved to be superior in a number of cases, while the typical pricing system of the market sometimes hurts the quality of the "commodities" produced and exchanged. Thus, the typical economic solution of privatization does not work *per se*, and complementary devices, based essentially on regulation and in part on non-economic motivations, are equally important.

Considering other areas of controversy as well, the authors conclude that, given the acceptability of private property rights to human tissue, these rights cannot be treated as an universal remedy and must be specially designed and controlled in order to further the goal of public health. The challenge for twenty-first-century legislators, courts, regulators, and other decision makers is thus to define a property rights setting that encourages innovation and facilitates access to the benefits of biomedical technologies, while adequately protecting the interests of tissue sources. This implies many difficult choices about the scope of the public domain in human genetic information, the opportunities for tissue sources or their survivors to receive compensation, and the extent to which traditional property rights require change.

Insights from ambiguous cases

The chapters in the third section of the book deal in various manners with ambiguous cases. Sometimes the property rights framework has been developed so extensively that it overlaps different legal bodies, producing regulatory interplay whose outcomes are unpredictable. This appears to be the case with copyright and antitrust laws, as discussed by Paul Torremans. As a variation on this theme, the incomplete definition of property rights and access to alternative legal systems can lead to rent-seeking behaviors that, once again, may have consequences unintended by the law. Property rights, therefore, cannot be designed without considering all feasible alternatives for individuals. The treatment of marital assets in the UK and the EU, investigated by Antony Dnes, is an interesting example of this issue. Sophie Harnay and Alain Marciano go further in this direction, showing that – contrary to expectations – there are areas in which the usual propertization trend is simply not applied. The likely explanation is that legislators have taken into account the specificity of the subject matter and decided that the openness of the system is more important than the typical incentives and effects brought about by property rights. This is precisely what accounts for the lack of intellectual property rights in judge-made law. Finally, Jürgen Backhaus deals with the intriguing case of *sleeping owners*, that is, economic agents who own property but has no incentive to use it. Also in this case property rights fail to reach an efficient outcome.

In Chapter 9 Paul Torremans focuses on the *liaisons dangereuses*[20] between copyright and competition laws, on the basis of what can be termed a modern European saga: the IMS Health/NDC Health antitrust case and the decision to enforce the essential facility doctrine, a *de facto* infringement on the exclusive right granted by property.

Once again, ambiguity and conflict are produced by friction between two legal systems, both designed to prevent specific market failures and ultimately to promote efficiency. However, whereas antitrust law seeks to achieve this by eliminating behaviors and practices that restrict competition, copyright takes the opposite approach, creating legal monopolies and altering the competitive paradigm.

Torremans attributes this ambiguity to the specific model of competition in information markets, which is unlike that in markets for tangible goods. Because copyright grants an exclusive right, it can potentially be used to restrict competition, raising a conflict between the two laws. Antitrust enforcement can overcome the problem, but since copyright is a property right, permitting its infringement more than sporadically via the essential facility doctrine or whatever norm will significantly affect the property rights bundle and the outcome of the legal framework in a way unintended by lawmakers (Ramello, 2003).

The author concludes that although the IMS saga is over and several copyright matters seem to have been clarified in relation to the essential facilities doctrine, many issues call for further illumination – as evidenced by the controversial European Microsoft decision.

Antony Dnes, in Chapter 10, discusses another intriguing case: the treatment of marital assets. He views the measures proposed in the EU Draft Constitution to harmonize family law as an opportunity to correct some problems with English laws on property division in the event of divorce. Particularly, Dnes writes, harmonization at the EU level is desirable in order to prevent forum shopping, expensive conflicts and opportunistic behavior. People may shop around in order to circumvent threats implied by the legal system under which they were married. By creating a degree of uniformity across member states, such opportunism within the EU can be prevented.

By contrast, the negative benchmark is the current system in the UK, where courts enjoy broad discretion that heavily affects incentives for divorcing parties and their legal counsel. This discretion is an element of uncertainty for the parties and does not produce optimal deterrence, intended as an institutional device set up to save marriages. It is worth noting that from an economic point of view, reducing the incentive to cheat on marriage vows might be expected to enhance the attractiveness of marriage compared with a less reliable environment, and to reduce uncertainty over the value of marriage (Dnes, 1998).

A well designed set of property rights will give equal weight to the rules by which these rights and the related subject matters are divided if a marriage contract is cleared. Various solutions are theoretically feasible: enforceable prenuptial agreements, or equal share by default. Although different, both solutions will produce transparent incentives, avoid rent-seeking behaviors and generate efficiency, if courts are firm in their enforcement of the fledgling property rule.

Dnes thus gives further support to the notion that a property rights system needs to be as carefully designed as possible in order to generate efficient results. Even in the domain of love and emotion, where economics would indeed seem to be an uninvited guest, solid property rules are crucial for governing expectations and efficient behaviors.

In Chapter 11, Sophie Harnay and Alain Marciano raise the interesting question of why, if judges are rational, utility-maximizing agents (as extensively supported by law and economics theory [Posner, 1994]), they do not adopt the propertization paradigm under intellectual property laws for the production of information.

The authors, while accepting the interpretation of judges as economic agents, argue that the "market analogy" is misleading. The doctrine of precedent, which governs the common-law system but plays an important role in civil law systems as well, relies on the intertwining of private and collective dimensions in judicial innovation, which is peculiar to collective invention.

In this perspective, judge-made law, as recognized by mainstream law and economics theory (Landes and Posner, 1976), presents an analogy with capital formation: the set of existing precedents is a stock of capital goods, and precedents themselves are informational goods conveying low-cost information to judges as well as to litigants. Thus, a precedent has collective advantages, such as indivisibility, non-rivalry, and non-excludability of the beneficiaries; the incremental cost of an additional user is very low; and the body of precedents constitutes a pool of shared information.

Of course, judicial institutions are specifically designed to overcome the lack of classic forms of compensation for individual contributors, and to promote the production and diffusion of precedents. Particularly, the system of reciprocal disclosure of court decisions enables all members of the community to screen and evaluate input, which promotes the incremental refinement and critical evaluation of decisions. The judicial community collectively assesses contributions to the body of precedent and determines which are valuable to the entire community, and should therefore be incorporated into judge-made law, laying the basis for a cumulative shift toward higher quality.

Harnay and Marciano provide valuable insight by demonstrating that the externality problem does not always require the solution of property rights. In the case of knowledge production, where, as increasingly argued (see also Boldrin and Levine in this book or Ramello, 2005), externalities are organic to the productive process, propertization should not only be avoided but is likely to determine inefficient outcomes.

Jürgen Backhaus in Chapter 12 concludes by offering an interesting cameo on the gaps in urban and rural development caused by what he defines as "sleeping owners," that is to say individuals who have acquired property rights through unification (i.e. the unification treaty and subsequent legislation) but have no incentive to make use of them. Sleeping owners either do not exercise their property rights, because transactions costs exceed the conceivable benefits (*usus fructus*), or are interested solely in speculating on them as surrounding property values raise their own. A joint analysis of property rights, land rents, and opportunity costs is needed to explain this phenomenon. Backhaus concludes with suggestions for relief and policy alternatives. His provocative conclusion is that in this particular case, the Coase theorem is wrong in claiming the irrelevance of property distribution.

Conclusions

The study of property rights is a formidable journey into human history, human cleverness in organizing social relationships and exploiting resources, and the limits and contradictions of society.

The nature of private good of many resources has driven human beings to create a specific institutional device for their exploitation and exchange.

Economic theory has discovered that this institutional product is so well designed that in many cases, it has the "last but not least" effect of promoting the efficient economic use of those resources. This finding explains to some degree the almost blind support for property rights and their extension to all aspects of society.

However, blank checks are not the usual remedy for economic problems, and the pages of this book recommend a more cautious approach to the creation and exploitation of property rights.

Property rights are a powerful device for stimulating efficiency and overcoming market failures. But they have no supernatural virtue, and must be carefully designed and weighted in order to produce the desired outcome.

This chapter has surveyed the main role of property rights and introduced critical points for study by scholars, legislators, and policy makers. For in-depth discussion, read on.

Acknowledgment

We are grateful to the colleagues who participated in this project and who otherwise inspired our research into property rights dynamics. In particular, we are indebted to Alberto Cassone, Wendy Gordon, Nicholas Mercuro, Francesco Silva, three anonymous referees for their helpful suggestions, and to the publisher and Università Carlo Cattaneo LIUC for their support. This publication is part of a PRIN 2005 research project. Although the joint editorship, Giovanni Ramello is the author of this chapter. The usual disclaimer applies.

Notes

1 Known as "regulatory capture," a significant component of public choice theory.
2 Naturally, we can expect that different mechanisms of transfer – combat, theft, etc. – played a more important role in early history than today's familiar market exchange.
3 It has roots in Lockean theory of property rights as natural rights (1690) and has extensively permeated Western legal theory (see Munzer, 1990). On the evolution of property in Western society, see Chapter 2 by Francesco Parisi.
4 See also Colombatto (2004) regarding a survey on property rights in economic theory.
5 As is well known in economic theory, externalities exist because of the interdependence between production and/or consumption of sets of economic agents. Generally speaking, an externality is a commodity produced during the consumption or production of another good that affects other producers or consumers (see Jha, 1998).
6 See Chapter 3 for an extensive discussion of this point.
7 For a survey from this perspective see, for example, Barzel (1997). However, this virtue of property rights appears not always to work (see Chapter 12).
8 See Jha (1998), Porrini (2005) and Chapters 3 and 11.
9 On environmental regulation in general, see Boyer and Porrini (2002). The extension of intellectual property to business methods is discussed in Chapter 7 and to human tissues in Chapter 8. For further critical discussion see Nicita *et al.* (2005).
10 A&M Records, Inc. vs Napster, Inc., 114 F. Supp. 2d 896 (N.D. Cal. 2000); A&M Records, Inc. vs Napster, Inc., US Court of Appeals (9th Circ., 2001). For an economic discussion see Ramello (2001).
11 See also Chapter 6.

12 Case T-69/89 Radio Telefis Eireann vs Commission (Magill TV Guide Ltd intervening) [1991] 4 CMLR 586; case T-70/89 British Broadcasting Corporation and BBC Enterprises Ltd vs Commission (Magill TV Guide Ltd intervening) [1991] 4 CMLR 669 and case T-76/89 Independent Television Publications Ltd vs Commission (Magill TV Guide Ltd intervening) [1991] ECR II-575, [1991] 4 CMLR 745; Commission Decision 2001/165/EC, 3 July 2001 in Case COMP D3/38.044 – NDC Health/IMS Health: Interim Measures [2002] OJ L59/18- C-481/01 IMS Health v NDC Health [2004] 4 CMLR 1543.
13 See Chapter 9 of this book.
14 See Chapter 8.
15 On property fragmentation, see Chapter 4.
16 See Chapters 6 and 11.
17 See Chapter 8.
18 On the tragedy of the anti-commons see Heller (1998).
19 See, for example, Landes and Posner (2003).
20 A catchy definition by Pardolesi and Granieri (2003).

References

Alchian, A.A. (1965), "Some Economics of Property Rights," *Il Politico*, 30, 816–829.
Bailey, M.J. (1992), "The Approximate Optimality of Aboriginal Property Rights," *Journal of Law and Economics*, 35, 183–198.
Bailey, M.J. (1998), "Property Rights in Aboriginal Societies," in Newman, P. (ed.), *The New Palgrave Dictionary of Economics and the Law*, 155–157, London: Macmillan.
Barzel, Y. (1997), *Economic Analysis of Property Rights*, 2nd edn, Cambridge: Cambridge University Press.
Boyer, M. and Porrini, D. (2002), "The Choice of Instruments for Environmental Policy: Liability or Regulation?," in Swanson, T. and Zerbe, R. (eds), *An Introduction to the Law and Economics of Environmental Policy: Issues in Institutional Design*, Research in Law and Economics, 20, Oxford: JAI-Elsevier, 247–269.
Calabresi, G. and Melamed, A.D. (1972), "Property Rules, Liability Rules, and Inalienability: One View of the Cathedral," *Harvard Law Review*, 85, 1089–1128.
Coase, R. (1960), "The Problem of Social Cost," *Journal of Law and Economics*, 3, pp. 1–44.
Colombatto, E. (ed.) (2004), *The Elgar Companion to Economics of Property Rights*, Cheltenham, UK, Northampton, MA: Edward Elgar.
Demsetz, H. (1967), "Toward a Theory of Property Rights," *American Economic Review*, 57, 347–359.
Demsetz, H. (1998), "Property Rights," in Newman, P. (ed.), *The New Palgrave Dictionary of Economics and the Law*, London: Macmillan.
Dnes, A. (1998), "The Division of Marital Assets Following Divorce," *Journal of Law & Society*, 25, 336–364.
Hart, O. (1995), *Firms, Contracts, and Financial Structure*, Oxford: Oxford University Press.
Heller, M.A. (1998), "The Tragedy of the Anticommons: Property in the Transition from Marx to Markets," *Harvard Law Review*, 111, 621.
Hohfeld, W.N. (1913), "Some Fundamental Legal Conceptions as Applied in Judicial Reasoning," *Yale Law Journal*, 23, 16–59.
Jha, R. (1998), *Modern Public Economics*, London: Routledge.
Kolstad, C.D., Ulen, T.S., and Johnson, G.V. (1990), "Ex post Liability for Harm vs ex ante Safety Regulation: Substitutes or Complements," *American Economic Review*, 80, 888–901.

Landes, W. and Posner, R. (1976), "Legal Precedent, A Theoretical and Empirical Analysis," *Journal of Law and Economics*, 249–313.

Landes, W. and Posner, R. (2003), *The Economic Structure of Intellectual Property Law*, Harvard University Press.

Levmore, S. (2002), "Two Stories about the Evolution of Property Rights," *Journal of Legal Studies*, 31, 421–451.

Locke, J. (1690), *Second Treatise on Government*, URL: http://www.ilt.columbia.edu/academic/digitexts/locke/second/locke2nd.txt

Maffioletti, A. and Ramello, G.B. (2004), "Should We Put Them in Jail? Copyright Infringement, Penalties and Consumer Behaviour: Insights from Experimental Data," *Review of Economic Research on Copyright Issues*, 1, 81–95.

Munzer, S.R. (1990), *A Theory of Property*, Cambridge: Cambridge University Press.

Nicita, A., Ramello, G.B., and Scherer, F.M. (2005), "IPRs and the Organization of Industries. New Perspectives in Law and Economics," *International Journal of Economics of Business*, 12, 289–296.

Pardolesi, R. and Granieri, M. (2003), "Proprietà Intellettuale e Concorrenza: Convergenza Finalistica e 'Liaisons Dangereuses'," *Il Foro Italiano*, 10, 193–215.

Pigou, A.C. (1932), *The Economics of Welfare*, 4th edn, London: Macmillan.

Porrini, D. (2005), "Environmental Policies Choice as an Issue of Informational Efficiency," in Jurgen, G. and Backhaus, II (eds), *The Elgar Companion to Law and Economics*, Cheltenham, UK and Northampton, MA: Edward Elgar, 350–363.

Posner, R. (1994), "What do Judges and Justices Maximize? (The Same Thing Everybody Else Does)," *Supreme Court Economic Review*, 3, 1–41.

Ramello, G.B. (2001), "Napster et la musique en ligne. Le mythe du vase de Pandore se répèterait-il ?," *Réseaux*, 19, 131–154.

Ramello, G.B. (2003), "Copyright and antitrust issues," in Gordon, W.J. and Watt, R. (eds), *The Economics of Copyright: Developments in Research and Analysis*, 113–147, Cheltenham, UK and Northampton, MA: Edward Elgar.

Ramello, G.B. (2005), "Private Appropriability and Sharing of Knowledge: Convergence or Contradiction? The Opposite Tragedy of the Creative Commons," in Takeyama, L., Gordon, W., and Towse, R. (eds), *Developments in the Economics of Copyright: Research and Analysis*, 120–141, Cheltenham, UK and Northampton, MA: Edward Elgar.

Scherer, F.M. (2004), "A note on Global Welfare in Pharmaceutical Patenting," *World Economy*, 1127–1142.

Shavell S. (1984), "Liability for harms versus regulation of safety," *Journal of Legal Studies*, 13, 357–374.

Part I

Property rights and law and economics theory

Justifications and main issues

2 The fall and rise of functional property

Francesco Parisi[1]

All societies recognize private property, to a greater or lesser extent. The content of property and its entitlements, however, varies substantially across societies, both historical and contemporary. The comparative and historical study of the concept of property reveals a close relationship between the structure of an economic system and the structure and content of property rights. In this essay, I shall consider the origins and the main stages in the evolution of property and elaborate an economic explanation of the evolved conceptions of property.

Property rights emerge and grow in societies in relation to the cost/benefit calculus regarding the establishment and protection of such rights. Economic change creates new cost–benefit relationships, giving rise to modifications in property regimes (Posner, 1998; Rose, 1998).[2] This gives rise to a ground-up conception of property, in which the legal notion of property reflects the localized and evolving function performed by property in society. The natural propensity of humans to possess productive and scarce resources and the social acceptance of this human attitude gives origin to the institution of property and its regulation. This functional and dynamic evolution of property is the object of this study.

A sketched history of property

The institution of property is nearly as old as recorded history. In spite of its stability as a fundamental institution of human society, the concept of property and the privileges, obligations and restrictions that govern ownership have undergone substantial change throughout history.

The history of property is illuminated by economic theory. The concept of scarcity – which some notable authorities believe is at least a necessary condition for the establishment of enforceable property rights – is valuable in explaining the limited domain of property in early societies and the changing contours of property protection as a result of changes in the economic structure of society.[3] As pointed out by Demsetz (1967), property rights develop to internalize externalities in the use of scarce resources. However, there are costs associated with the establishment of property. While scarcity may be necessary for giving objects value and prompting the desire to have property rights, the establishment of such rights also requires that their protection be economically efficient from a societal standpoint, in the sense that the marginal benefit of protection (internalization) exceeds the marginal cost of protection. Property rights emerge only when the gains of internalization become larger than the cost of internalization. The study of the historical evolution of property confirms these economic propositions and reveals that changes in the economy often trigger changes in the social and legal conception of property.[4]

A large number of anthropologists and legal historians have come to agree on the identification of some general patterns in the evolution of property, as I shall now describe.

Hunters and shepherds: the rise of functional property

The age of hunters was perhaps one of the first stages in which humans appeared to assert property claims over physical resources. In a hunter's society, property consisted mostly of what hunters could kill for their own consumption or trade. At this stage, there was no need to define property rights over other resources, such as land or stock of wild animals and consequently little need for institutional protection of property rights.

During this era, the social structure was characterized by the presence of tribes, or clans. The modes of production in this phase were hunting and fishing, and joint production and equitable sharing governed the distribution of the bounty.[5] The clan, which was a group of several families, acted, in effect, as a family-based firm.[6] This segment of the tribal property stage appears to correspond closely to Adam Smith's ([1776] 1986) description of the first stage of development in human society (the age of hunters).[7] Smith observes that, at this stage, abundance of unclaimed resources made establishment of property rights unnecessary, as negative externalities from overuse were unlikely. Any property claim beyond what the hunters' clan could use for their own consumption would in fact impose prohibitive monitoring and enforcement costs.[8]

Quite interestingly, Bouckaert (1999) points out that, even when property rights to a stock cannot be established, property rights to its flow still might be created.[9] Such a regime of property claims over flow, rather than stock, of resources, seems to characterize this first stage in the evolution of property.

Economic historians generally identify the second stage in the evolution of human economy as the age of pasture and shepherds. During this period, people began asserting property claims over animal herds and grazing lands. Property claims were still asserted by the tribe, rather than by individuals within the group. In most early societies, population increase and gradual competition for the use of land for grazing required that land to be divided among tribes: 'The earliest distribution of the land was into pasture and territories of chase common to the tribe, for the idea of individual ownership of the land is of ulterior and tardier growth' (LaFargue, 1975, p. 36). Such claims were initially asserted by means of occupation, use or accession. In this phase, tribal property was non-transferable.

As people appropriated herds and flocks, the supply of available animals became scarce, such that the remaining individuals were unable to gain their subsistence from hunting. The property owners consequently grew fearful that the poor would attempt to appropriate their property. This was the stage during which greatly unequal distribution of property first arose. The extremely unequal distribution of claimed resources and subsequent scarcity of unclaimed resources were each necessary, and the combination of them sufficient, for establishment of property rights. Smith ([1776] 1986) argues that individuals thus first gained the right to exclude others from their property.

Agriculture and the rise of spatial property

In subsequent times, agriculture and management of farm animals gradually became the predominant modes of production. Pipes (1991) focuses on resource depletion as the primary genesis of the human notion of property, noting above all else that communal ownership is inefficient. He writes:

> [I]n all primitive societies and most non-Western societies in general, land was not treated as a commodity and hence was not truly property, which, by definition, entails the right of disposal.... The transformation of land into tribal, family, or individual ownership seems to occur, first and foremost, in consequence of population pressures which call for a more rational method of exploitation, and it does so because the unregulated exploitation of natural resources leads to their depletion.[10]

The transition from hunting and gathering to agriculture around 10000 BCE made land use more efficient and increased the value and resulting social appreciation of property.[11] This change in the economy was accompanied by a gradual gain in the importance of the family. Family units gradually acquired interests that were different from those of the clan at large. In this context, the tribal land of the pastoral communities was gradually partitioned among the families that constituted the clan or tribe and what was the communal territory of the tribe was gradually parcelled out to become the collective property of individual families.[12] Still, the property rights of the family were subject to regulation by the tribe.

The assignment of land to the family units did not take place in what modern scholars would consider full property. Instead, limited property rights were assigned to family units in order to allow them to carry out more effectively the specific agricultural activity that they intended to perform. The land assigned to family units remained subject to other property claims held by the tribe at large. These included rights for hunting and also compatible grazing uses of the land. The territorial scope of the partial property rights depended on the nature of the rights involved. Thus, for example, the pasture of lands was originally the joint property of all the members of the clan. This was so because given the structure of the economy no single individual or family could have optimally exploited such right to pasture. As LaFargue (1975) points out, the unit of the economy gradually changed from the tribe or clan to the smaller family unit. Gradually, the parcels of land were cultivated by each family under the direction of its chief and the supervision of the village council. The resulting crops were the property of the family, and would not become the property of the tribe or clan collectively, as it was the case in earlier periods.

In these societies, relatively simple rules governed land ownership. The character of property rights allocated to the family unit was related to the prospective functional use of the land. Other tribe members outside the family could continue to use the land for non-agricultural purposes. For example, those who used the land to hunt continued to hold hunting privileges, and those who raised livestock could hold grazing rights in the same geographic area. Such functional conceptions of property were the natural consequence of the derivation of property from actual use and possession of the land. Over time, the way in which the land was used determined the kinds of possession possible.[13] This system often resulted in multiple property claims coexisting on the same land. Customary rules then regulated the possession, use and transfer of such functional rights. Such functional divisions often made good sense because different owners could undertake specialized activities over the same territory with little encroachment on one another.

Given the low population density and the limited rate of exploitation of natural resources, functional partitions of property were often efficient. They provided an opportunity to allocate the same land towards multiple privately held use rights, allowing an optimal level of exploitation, as all parts of the property could be used.[14] Detailed customs, based on past usage and historic rights, determined what was considered acceptable conduct with respect to the interaction (natural externalities) between the various activities. Early societies thus embraced a 'functional' conception of property, in which property rights were related to specific uses of the land, rather than a spatial conception of property in which the confines of property were determined by physical boundaries. Property was not divided along spatial lines, as in the modern world, but through horizontal functional partitions, in which different individuals or families would own specific rights over the land related to specific uses (e.g. farming, fishing, hunting, etc.).

As time progressed, however, agricultural societies developed a more complex conception of property in which functional partitions of rights survived as exceptions to a regime of unified ownership.[15] This paradigmatic shift is under-standable, given that in an agricultural economy the coexistence of multiple rights over the same land created conflicts and increased opportunities for wasteful externalities. Furthermore, functional partitioning of land, while efficient in a stable economy, became unsustainable in conditions of rapid economic change. Moving from pastoral to agricultural economies, many societies thus changed their property systems, abandoning functional property in favor of spatial prop-erty (i.e. making their property systems more similar to those we are accustomed to observing in the modern Western world).

This transition has an economic explanation. With a rapidly changing economy, optimal uses of land were also subject to rapid flux. Multiple functional claims impeded the implementation of new, more efficient uses of the land. It was also more difficult for agriculture to coexist with other functional uses. Spatial property, with its defined boundaries, was better suited to accommodate the rise of agriculture and its need of hegemony over the use of land.

In spatial property regimes, a single owner generally holds all rights pertaining to a defined tract of land. Such unified ownership better served the needs of a changing economy that wished to harness the economic power of agriculture. The division of property along functional lines, while allowing the optimization of property with respect to all of its potential uses, did not provide sufficient flexibility to accommodate structural transformations over time. The Romans recognized this, and made absolute ownership rights the cornerstone of Roman property law.[16]

Feudalism and medieval land law

The historical evolution of property led to the emergence (and gradual dominance) of spatial conceptions of property, with absolute property regimes as the default legal rule in all established agricultural societies. During the feudal era, a new array of functional and legal limitations on the use and disposition of land encroached on the Roman conception of absolute property. Although the foundations of the medieval law of property were unquestionably Roman, the feudal system gradually transformed the accepted social conception of property.

In the feudal world, rights and duties were based on land tenure and personal relationships, and this conception of property was instrumental in maintaining feudal social and economic structure. The early types of land licenses resembled grants of full ownership, but in later times the kings and the lesser lords kept the ownership of the land to themselves and granted only partial rights of use and exploitation.[17] Land was held in fief by vassals as a result of a grant by their lords in exchange for a variety of services and vows of personal loyalty.[18] These grants of fragmented ownership gradually became hereditary holdings.[19] Customary norms prevented the unilateral abrogation of these grants, except as a result of legal forfeiture and seizure.[20] This resulted in a multi-layered, and potentially irreversible, fragmentation of property.

In this feudal system of land tenure, each individual was defined by his hierarchical status and relationship to land. With the sole exception of the king, every individual was subservient to another. According to the well-known feudal pyramid, only the lesser tenants ('tenants in demesne') had possessory use of the land, and all the others served as intermediaries in the collection of fees and granting of services and protection. The king stood as the ultimate residual claimant. Through this process, feudal property became quite distinct from the Roman paradigm of property, as feudal grants were always limited by the act of license and title; possessory interests never resided in the same hands. Property ownership was neither unlimited nor absolute; interests were not enforceable *erga omnes*, but rather consisted of a bundle of rights and duties, partially applicable to the whole community and partially determined by the specific contractual relationship between the grantor and the grantee. A complex system of political and social control reinforced this transition from the Roman system to the feudal regime of dispersed ownership (and property fragmentation).

Feudalism was inextricably linked to agricultural life. In an agricultural economy, functional forms of fragmentation are generally not problematic, as long as the physical unity of land is preserved. In this respect, feudal legal systems were designed to limit the risk of excessive fragmentation.[21] Rules of primogeniture[22] and prohibition of subinfeuds[23] are examples of the attempts of feudal law to constrain entropy in property.

The hierarchy of services from the tenants in demesne all the way up the chain of ownership to the king also served to structure the agricultural economy in order to support the military, which was of chief importance to a regime constantly on the verge of war. As Dukeminier and Krier (2002) point out, the king originally demanded the service of knights from the lords under him to constitute the military. Those lords, beset with this requirement, would ensure that the knights would be provided by requiring the appropriate services (such as horses, food, etc.) from the vassals beneath them, who in turn would demand from the tenants in demesne the raw materials needed to fulfill the vassal's obligations. In this way, the king, by establishing an ultimate societal goal – a military – and charging others with the task of providing that product, could organize the use of land to meet that goal in a way that Roman property rights would not allow.

The peculiar coexistence of physical unity and legal disunity in feudal property worked in an agricultural economy, but proved problematic in any other kind of economic context. Indeed, feudal arrangements, which generally flourished in closed agricultural economies, did not take root in urban environments, which were not as integral to the military effort.[24] The cities of the Roman empire, in as far as they survived at all, did not have a parallel feudal structure,[25] with the exception of some urban areas in Italy and southern France.[26]

The modern conception of absolute property

With the approach of the modern era came another paradigmatic shift in the conception of property. Just like the transition from pastoral to agricultural economies rendered the so-called functional conceptions of property impracticable, the gradual growth of the economy made the feudal dispersion of control over property highly problematic.

As generally recognized in the literature, the abolition of feudalism was a necessary precondition for the shift to a modern market in land, in which individuals can transfer full ownership and development rights to third parties through contracts or testamentary dispositions. The transition back from the relativistic and contractual basis of property to the Roman absolute conception of ownership was not gradual and smooth, however.[27] The historical events surrounding the end of the feudal era demonstrate the power of the irreversible dynamics of entropy in property, a theme of this essay.

Both a political and ideological revolution was required to reshape the dominant conception and content of property. The French revolution marked a critical turning point. In a vain attempt to stave off serious political and social upheaval, the French nobles and clergymen renounced some of their feudal privileges at the first session of the *Estates General* in over 200 years on 4 August 1789. The theoretical significance of this action was great, as it freed the land from a multitude of personal servitudes (e.g. hunting rights and labour services). Other feudal burdens (e.g. seigneurial fees) could be extinguished by paying a lump sum amount to the lords (generally corresponding to 20 to 25 times the value of the annuity). In practice, the peasantry was unable to pay the large amounts required to obtain release from the feudal servitudes. The French Revolution brought with it the collapse of the feudal regime, with the outright abolition of all burdens and seigneurial fees without compensation.

During the eighteenth century, it had become fashionable to point to the feudal tradition as the root of the inefficient property fragmentation and to rebel against the feudal heritage by proclaiming a new paradigm of absolute and unified property. Historically, feudal land systems imposed positive obligations on landholders that were not part of the Romanistic bundle of rights and duties of property holders, mixing absolute and relative rights in a hybrid property relationship. Hegel's ([1821] 1942) philosophical version of this history has influenced the legal conceptions of property around the world. Hegel purports that the standardization of property interests is a movement that is related to the difficult struggle to free property from the pervasive feudal encumbrances, suggesting that individual freedom closely depends on the freedom of property.[28]

In this setting, the Roman approach became the model for bourgeois property, conceived as an absolute private right to the enjoyment of one's land. This renewed conception is at the origin of much theoretical work in legal theory and philosophy. One can think of John Austin's ([1832] 1885) premise that the right of property consists of two main elements: the right to use the property and the power to exclude others.[29] Most importantly, eighteenth- and nineteenth-century-theorists specified the structural attributes of a property right. Among others, we find the Kantian notion that universal norms must be negative in content, that is, they 'must command individuals as *not* to do something' and that 'the correlative of a real right cannot require action...'.[30]

This conception of absolute property contrasted dramatically with the concept of feudal property as a bundle of rights and duties that mixed relative and absolute relations in both private and public spheres. Although, in many respects, such a unified conception of property was already present in the pre-feudal world, the intellectual reaction against the old regime led to a more nuanced articulation of this ideal.[31] This theoretical evolution culminated in the revolutionary events of the 1790s that marked the beginning of a new era in the property regimes of France and the rest of Europe. This new legal approach, in order to meld successfully the concepts of functional unity with the revived absolute conception of property, had to have substantive rules to foster functional, physical and legal unity in property. These principles of unitary property are embodied in several important rules that characterize modern property law, which I shall consider next.

Unity in property

As a reaction to the feudal tradition, the Rationalist jurisprudence of the eighteenth century and the modern codifications of the nineteenth century revived the various important Roman rules of property, recasting them as general principles of civil law. The principles of unity in property can be tentatively grouped under the headings of (i) functional, (ii) physical and (iii) legal unity. As more extensively discussed in prior work (Parisi, 2002a) these related principles contribute in different ways to control the problems of entropy in property.

Functional unity

Under classical Roman law, the property owner (*proprietarius*) was not allowed to transfer anything less than the entire bundle of rights, privileges and powers that he had in the property. Conveyances of rights in a lesser measure than full ownership were only permitted on an exceptional basis and in a limited number of cases.[32] Thus, for example, the creation of legally binding restrictions on property was limited to situations in which the dominant estate could demonstrate a perpetual need for the arrangement. In the Roman Digest we read that servitudes necessitate a *causa perpetua*.[33] In other passages, the Roman sources explicitly indicate that the servitudes created for the transitional benefit of the owner of a neighbouring lot (as opposed to the perpetual benefit of the land itself) were not valid.[34]

As I have discussed above, the notion of absolute ownership underwent a substantial change in feudal law, but eventually regained popularity at the time of the modern European codifications. The modern codes limit the permissible level of functional property fragmentation and further provide property-type protection only for specific, socially desirable, property rights.[35] This favouring of certain property arrangements is known as the *numerus clausus* principle, and is an important expression of the fundamental principle of unity that underlies modern property law. The purpose of this principle is to forestall private individuals from creating property rights that differ from those that are expressly recognized by the legal system.[36]

The early formulations of the *numerus clausus* lacked a well-articulated rationale, especially striking because it contrasts sharply with the doctrine of freedom of contract, namely that two parties to a private contract may agree on virtually any arrangement without government limitations.[37] The dichotomy between these contract and property paradigms results in a general tension between the principle of freedom to contract and the societal need for standardization in property law. The modern European codifications all reflect this tension. They promote freedom of contract by recognizing and fully enforcing both nominate and innominate forms of contract. Yet at the same time they limit private autonomy in property transactions and only enforce transactions pertaining to standardized (or nominate) forms of property.[38]

Although in many ways the intellectual product of the French revolution, the influence of the *numerus clausus* principle has lasted well beyond the post-revolutionary codes, and can be found in most of the modern European codes. The Napoleonic Code of 1804,[39] the German Civil Code (BGB) of 1900[40] and several other codifications[41] contain provisions that restrict the creation (or at least withhold the enforcement) of atypical property rights. As Rudden (1987, p. 243) aptly put it, 'in very general terms, all systems limit, or at least greatly restrict, the creation of real rights: "fancies" are for contract, not property'.

These limits on the creation of atypical property rights eventually emerged as a general principle of modern property law. Even jurisdictions that have not formally codified the doctrine adhere to its strictures.

The requirement that the transfer of immovable property be recorded in a public registry enforces the *numerus clausus* principle because only nominate property rights can be duly registered, thereby ensuring the intelligibility of public records for notice and publicity purposes.[42] It follows logically that any contract that constitutes or modifies a property situation in disregard of the taxonomy of real rights recognized by the legal system is only a source of contractual obligations.[43] But Gambaro (1995, p. 67) illustrates the paradox of allowing parties to enter into binding contractual obligations, yet preventing them from enjoying the benefits of those agreements. If the public record system does not allow atypical property rights to be recorded, freedom of contract is itself undermined, because the system withholds the mechanism – namely the recording system – that could transform an atypical property agreement between the parties from a personal obligation into a real right enforceable against third-party purchasers.

Physical unity

Other basic principles of modern property law demonstrate the general tendency of legal systems to combat entropy and promote unity in property. In dealing with the physical partition of property, the rules of civil law systems symbolize the ideal of physical integrity of property. For instance, a large number of civil law systems jurisprudentially or legislatively recognize the owner's right to fence property as a symbolic prerogative of his sovereignty.[44] Furthermore, civil law systems address the problem of physical unity with rules restricting horizontal partitions of property building on the heritage of Roman legal systems that generally limited recognition of subsoil real rights, as suggested by the Latin maxim: '*Cuius est solum eius est usque ad coelum et usque ad inferos*' (whoever owns the land owns the property all the way to heaven and all the way to the centre of the earth).[45]

The theory and practice of property law regarding physical unity has undergone several changes over the centuries. Whenever recognized, the *ad coelum* rule presumes that someone who buys property unaware of any obstacle to its free use (*bona fide* purchaser) acquires priority over other claims on the land, be they for underground or surface resources.

In spite of the medieval departures from unified conceptions of property, most of the modern civil codes of the nineteenth century reinstated the Romanistic conception of property disallowing horizontal forms of property fragmentation.

In both the French Code of 1804 and the Italian Code of 1865 land could not be horizontally severed into multiple surface and subsurface estates, and legal title to the various land strata had to vest in a single owner. Early common law erected similar obstacles to the horizontal fragmentation of property[46] and, thanks to the work of Lord Coke in the early seventeenth century, the abbreviation '*ad coelum*' became a term of art in English law.[47]

These constraints on the freedom of the parties were an important corollary of the principle of physical unity in property that led to the eighteenth-century intellectual reaction against feudal property fragmentation, but they did not shape the ultimate approach to property that emerged in Continental Europe. In spite of the *numerus clausus* principle and the other formulations of the ideal of unitary property, the explicit prohibitions of the modern codes proved ineffective.[48] Property owners continued to partition their land into multiple surface and subsurface estates. Originally such agreements could not convey real title to the various land strata, but parties occasionally attempted to bypass this impediment by agreeing not to invoke accession rules against the titular owner of surface rights, should the informal surface owner decide to erect a building on the land.[49] The courts were initially reluctant to enforce the parties' agreements, which they found in open contravention of the unity rule. Over time, however, civil courts developed a more accommodating attitude and allowed such atypical forms of property fragmentation to survive in the shadow of the law.

The twentieth-century codes eventually abandoned the rule prohibiting the horizontal fragmentation of property. Starting with the German BGB of 1900[50] and the Italian Civil Code of 1942,[51] civil law moved away from applying the principle of physical unity, reverting to the standards in effect prior to the modern codifications.

Any one or more of three practical reasons discussed below reversed the trend. First, horizontal fragmentation became so commonly tolerated that it no longer was exceptional, and unity became a symbolic legal fiction. Enforcing a rule of unity under such circumstances risked disrupting a peaceful status quo in order to confront the unavoidable dilemma of deciding which of the two good faith parties should acquire title to the property.[52] Second, the risks of horizontal forms of property fragmentation are limited: few parties engage in such partitions, and in practice no more than two layers – surface and subsoil – are likely. This limited form of fragmentation does not raise serious strategic problems or enforcement costs, given the bilateral monopoly of the two fragmented owners under the circumstances. Third, the practical need for regulating mineral rights and rights in the exploitation of underground resources, as well as increased value for their exploitation, prompted the gradual abandonment of the older dogma.

Mid-twentieth century civil law scholars criticized abandoning the rule of physical unity because doing so violated the modern ideal of unified property. Horizontal property fragmentation appeared antithetical to traditional notions of property ownership that created in a landowner absolute, indivisible rights to a vertical space extending *usque ad coelum, usque ad inferos*, as well as creating mutual constraints on surface and subsurface ownership.[53]

Legal unity

A third principle of Western law – granting the owner absolute power to dispose of his property – is also closely related to the concept of unity in property, although with quite different implications. All the main European codes enunciate this principle. For instance, Article 544 of the French Civil Code states, 'Ownership is the right to enjoy and dispose of things in the most absolute manner', a provision included almost verbatim in the Italian Civil Code of 1865. Similarly, Paragraph 903 of the German BGB affirms that the owner of an object 'may deal with the thing as he pleases and exclude others from any interference'.

While these statements appear uncontroversial on their face, they become difficult to implement with joint ownership. The principle of absolute disposition indeed becomes an oxymoron when two or more individuals jointly hold decision rights. In addressing this problem, legal systems have historically adopted rules that facilitated the reunification of use and placed exclusion rights in the hands of a single individual. The common law achieved these two objectives by making it difficult to create joint tenancy (a legal fiction in which two or more people are regarded as a single owner) and relatively easy to destroy the arrangement. A joint tenancy required the owners to demonstrate the four 'unities', namely: (a) time (they acquired the property at the same time); (b) title (they all signed the same instrument); (c) interest (they owned identical rights); and (d) possession. If any of these elements were missing, then the joint tenancy could not be created.

Along similar lines, anyone who found himself owning something jointly with others could cause the common property to be divided, in keeping with the Latin maxim *'nemo invitus ad communionem compellitur'* (no one can be forced to have common property with another). Division could be done unilaterally. All one joint tenant had to do was convey his interest to a third party and the joint tenancy was severed, reverting to a tenancy in common and allowing owners to convey or devise their interests to third parties. Some early cases found that merely expressing the intent to sever the joint tenancy was sufficient to do so. If the tenants could not agree on the management of the property, another option was to petition for partition, in which case the court would either divide up the property or order it sold and divide the proceeds among the owners. Very similar rules are present in civil law jurisdictions to minimize the hold-up power of joint owners in the use of the joint property. In application of the principle of legal unity in property, these systems introduced mechanisms that were easily triggered to allow owners greater autonomy in disposing of their property, even when others had rights over the same land.

Variations in modern property law

As discussed in Parisi (2002a), legal systems around the world have in different ways manifested a general reluctance to recognize atypical property agreements as enforceable real rights.[54] In recent decades, however, courts and legislatures in both civil and common law jurisdictions, attuned to the modern needs of land developers and property owners, have recognized new property arrangements.[55]

The clearest example of this gradual expansion of standard property arrangements in civil law jurisdictions can be found in the area of covenants that attach to the title of property ('run with the land') and that occasionally create new *sui generis* real rights. A real covenant is a promise to do, or refrain from doing, something that is connected to land in a legally significant way.[56] Under traditional common law, the rights and duties associated with contracts were not assignable (Corbin, 1926) because parties to the original agreement did not have the right to bind third parties to adhere to their arrangement. Accordingly, the benefits and burdens of the original covenants did not transfer with the interest in the land. In many situations, this frustrated the purpose of creating a real covenant in the first place.

Due to the perceived net benefits in having the rights and burdens of a real covenant run with the land, courts gradually created a new body of law to overcome the obstacles posed by traditional property and contract theories.[57] Almost without exception, however, legal systems implementing these innovations have created atypical regimes to govern remedial protection and regulate these new rights – rules that diverge substantially from the traditional principles governing property or contracts. Commentators generally attribute these divergences to mere historical accidents (Yiannopoulos, 1983; Dwyer and Menell, 1998, p. 760). Contrary to the common wisdom in the literature, I suggest that these anomalies are not haphazard.

In order to protect these newly recognized real rights, courts have developed an elaborate set of requirements to minimize the long-term effects of the non-conforming fragmentation of property, adopting a set of rules that differ from traditional property or contract law. Legal systems instead balance the need to mitigate entropy in property by creating perpetual restrictions on the use and alienability of property with the demands of landowners and property developers wishing to exercise their contractual freedom to dispose of their property as they deem appropriate. Various legal traditions have employed different instruments to achieve this goal. For example, under modern French law, courts do not recognize atypical property covenants as sources of real rights, though they allow parties to approximate a real right by drawing upon the notion of transferable obligations. Thus, French cases have construed contracts between property owners as sources of obligations that are effective against third persons.[58] In Germany and Greece, atypical property covenants are also not enforced as real rights, but, as Yiannopoulos (1983) points out, allowing the contractual remedies to extend beyond the original parties to the covenant produces similar effects.

Interestingly, legal systems often encourage open access to common property (e.g. roads, navigation, communications, ideas after the expiration of intellectual property rights, etc.),[59] and in other cases the legal system creates and facilitates fragmentation. For instance, the social planner uses entropy to his benefit by using conservation easements and the fragmentation (e.g. multiplication) of administrative agencies overseeing of land development to slow the pace of suburban development.[60] In yet other instances, the owners themselves structure the non-conforming property arrangements.[61]

Although problematic as a rule, non-conforming partitioning of property rights may be somewhat sensible in achieving specific policy goals or other objectives that property owners desire. These idiosyncratic arrangements are both a reflection of the individual's right to freedom of contract and a legitimate policy instrument for the urban planner. In sum, respecting individual autonomy while minimizing the undesirable deadweight losses that could result from these arrangements is the critical goal.

Conclusion

In this essay, I have traced the origin and evolution of property rights regimes in light of the changes to economic systems since the earliest days of human civilization. The foundations for this study lay to a certain extent in the work of Demsetz (1967) and other philosophical minds such as Hegel ([1821] 1942) and Smith ([1776] 1986), who recognize that when resources are scarce, human societies formulate property rights to allocate use and regulate production. The development of property rights over time is nothing if not dynamic. The early stages of property – the ages of hunters, pastures and shepherds and agriculture – reveal the origins of some central tenants of modern property such as commonality (i.e. sharing mechanisms), the right to exclude, customary restrictions and spatial property notions. In the feudal era, the juxtaposition of physical unity and legal disunity allowed for a primitive form of centralized planning for agricultural resources, but then rapidly propelled Western societies towards revolutionary changes in property rights as economies became more complex with changing needs. Absolute rights emerged from the feudal era as individuals gained rights to use and transfer land. However, in the pre-modern era, Western societies struggled with the extent to which functional, physical and legal unity ought to restrict an individual's bundle of rights in property.

Finally, in modern times, economics remains useful to examine the continuing changes in property rights regimes. Covenants, used frequently by land developers, have emerged as a medium for owners to exercise contractual freedom yet preserve unity. As the modern economy changes, so too will Western systems of property.

Notes

1 Professor of Law and Director Law and Economics Program, George Mason University. An earlier version of this study was published as an entry in the Elgar Companion to Property Rights edited by Enrico Colombatto (2005). I would like to renew my thanks to Lee Istrail and Peter Irvine for their valuable research and editorial assistance.

2 Posner (1998, p. 40) points out that, at common law, domestic animals are owned like any other personal property, whereas wild animals are not owned until caught or killed. This is because the cost of enforcing private property rights over wild animals outweighs the value of the animals.

3 Smith ([1776] 1986); Demsetz (1967). Rose (1985) similarly suggests that in addition to scarcity, 'we need the capacity to shut out others from the resources that are the objects of our desire, at least when those objects become scarce' and that 'by allocating

exclusive control of resources to individuals, a property regime winds up by satisfying even more desires, because it mediates conflicts between individuals and encourages everyone to work and trade instead of fighting, thus making possible an even greater satisfaction of desires' (Ellickson *et al.*, 1995, p. 22).

4 Economists have rationalized the conditions for the emergence of property rights. Demsetz (1988, p. 107) pointed out that 'Increased internalization, in the main, results from changes in economic values, changes which stem from the development of new technology and the opening of new markets, changes to which old property rights are poorly attuned'.

5 LaFargue (1975, pp. 22–24) uses data from Lewis Henry Morgan's (d. 1881) famous anthropological studies to suggest that a similar phase of evolution characterized the social setting of Native American tribes. These clans shared in the product of each producer, distributed meals equitably, ate moderately and that the tribe's life could be characterized as 'primitive communism'.

6 LaFargue (1975) defines a family as a 'consanguine collective', or a group of blood relations.

7 Adam Smith ([1776] 1986, pp. 69–70) identifies four stages in the development of civil society, two of which are closely tied to the origins of property. The first stage, according to Adam Smith is the age of hunters.

8 Maine ([1861] 2000) examined whether the property regimes that preceded the modern individual property system evidenced a predominantly communal or individual character. The results of his investigation led him to criticize other theorists' emphasis on the role of individual property. Even when human societies came to accept the idea that the majority of objects can be subjected to private ownership, the holders of such property rights were often family and groups, rather than single individuals. Maine likens the early regimes of property to systems of joint ownership, not separate ownership. Looking at the origins of property in Chapter 8 of his book, Maine ([1861] 2000) thinks a major flaw in the occupancy theories of the origin of property is that they look at individuals rather than families and groups. He says it is likely that property originated as a communal claim. He looks at the village communities in India to support this theory. In these communities, as soon as a son is born, he acquires a vested interest in his father's property (the family estate). The property remains undivided for several generations.

9 Bouckaert (1999) discusses various property rules that maximize societal utility, drawing a distinction between a property right to a stock and a right to its flow. For example, assigning property rights to own a herd of wild animals would be prohibitively expensive but rights to captured and killed game can be created efficiently.

10 Pipes (1991, p. 89).

11 'Hunting and gathering, though involving relative little effort, is exceedingly wasteful of land' Pipes (1991, pp. 92–93).

12 In addition to parents and their children, the family unit also included the father's 'concubines...his children, his younger brothers, with their wives and children, and his unmarried sisters'. LaFargue (1975, p. 50). 'The arable lands, hitherto cultivated in common by the entire clan, are divided into parcels of different categories, according to the quality of the soil...the number of lots corresponds to that of the families' (Ibid., p. 52).

13 No single act of possession can encompass all potential forms of land use, meaning that the system of deriving ownership from possession generates limited (or 'functional') property rights, see Rose (1985) and Parisi (2002a).

14 For an application of this framework to modern settings, see Banner (1999) and Henry Smith (2000).

15 Absolute property rights can be observed only as an exceptional category in most non-Western societies while they represent a default property regime in modern Western legal systems. Historically, the absolute Western conception of property is not universal.

16 Obviously, if a single owner can claim tract of land, a different fragmentation problem may take place: excessive spatial fragmentation, leading to inefficiencies of scale. Western agricultural societies dealt with this problem in a variety of ways. In Roman law, the head of the household (*paterfamilias*) had concentrated authority over the property. An elaborate system (*peculium*) mitigated this concentrated legal capacity as with other members of the family group, such as slaves and sons, authorized to make binding legal transactions relating to property. In later times, when legal capacity was extended to every individual of majority age within the group, the fragmentation of property was prevented though other rules and social customs, such as succession rules (e.g. rules of primogeniture), and institutional arrangements (e.g. feudal hierarchies) resulting in the concentration of land in the hands of a few individuals.

17 Other privileges of the lord included the so-called feudal incidents, which, among other things, gave the lord right to possess the land.

18 Over time, the services, which were originally related to supporting and defending the lord in time of war through military service were gradually converted into pecuniary obligations. It is impossible to understand the developments of medieval society without realizing that the crown and the nobility (and within each major feudal manor the lord and his vassals) were power centres that were always potentially in conflict. The famous feudal pyramid (king, nobility, lords, vassals) depicts a dynamic society that was often on the verge of disintegration. On the personal level, the loyalty agreement between a lord and his vassal always tended to mask that same kind of unstable relationship and, likewise, the property ties attempted to create a bonding mechanism that would foster stability.

19 If a tenant died without heirs, the land returned to the lord: a form of residual claim of the sovereign that survives, under different name, in the modern law of successions.

20 Forfeiture and seizure were remedies that allowed the lord to regain possession of the land if a tenant had breached his oath of loyalty or failed to perform the applicable feudal services. Similar remedies applied in the case of high treason in favour of the king. For further discussion, see Dukeminier and Krier (2002).

21 Even the feudal law of property – often presented as the paradigm of entropic property – conceived remedies to combat excessive property fragmentation. Indeed, while some functional forms of fragmentation of property were instrumental to the stability of the feudal society, others could be easily prevented.

22 In the Western legal tradition, laws forbidding the partitioning of land and establishing the succession to land in favour of the youngest or eldest son have often been utilized to preserve the unity of land. These rules often had customary origins and enjoyed a large degree of voluntary compliance, given the interest of most landowners in protecting the power and prestige of the family, which was traditionally linked to the size of land holdings. In this context, priority in succession was traditionally given to the eldest son (primogeniture) or to the youngest son (ultimogeniture). The principal effect of these rules has been the maintenance of unity in the estate of the deceased.

23 Rules emerged to prevent the further fragmentation of possessory interests even in feudal times. The tenants in demesne could not subcontract their rights and obligations through the creation of a lower rank of feudal agents. The practice of subinfeudation has provided much of the intellectual justification for the modern constraints on functional property fragmentation. Rudden (1987) refers to this idea as the 'pyramiding' rationale: if each succeeding owner of a property interest has the power to intertwine the land with the performance of a fancy, then the land will be encrusted with a pyramid of obligations not unlike those that were associated with the practice of subinfeudation. Rudden acknowledges the weight of this argument, but makes three objections. First, he thinks that the historical objection to subinfeudation did not primarily concern the layers of obligation. Second, he thinks that a legal mechanism could check the excesses of a wider system of property interests. Third, market mechanisms rather than legal mechanisms may better solve such pyramid problems.

24 According to Monateri (1996), it is not coincidental that the rebirth of Roman legal studies began at a time of revival of urban life in northern Italy. Southern France was the centre of a code-oriented legal system, as the Roman law remained in force. In contrast, a more complete feudal system in northern France led to the development of customary law under the Carolingian Franks. The cities were not centres of feudal, but rather ecclesiastical, power, so that canon law took precedence, although the merchant law was an important component of the *ius commune* at least in localities with active commercial markets. Parisi and O'Hara (1998) and Parisi (1998) observe that although jurisdictional conflicts were possible, feudal law harmoniously coexisted with the merchant law, given the different focus on property and contract issues (i.e. feudal law generally covered property and status issues, while the latter was mostly dealt with contract and commercial issues).

25 The feudal system did not form the base of jurisdiction in cities, where canon and Roman laws took precedence. Feudal law was not congenial to the dynamic needs of the emerging mercantile class. As a result of the commercial revolution brought about by the medieval mercantile class, the large cities of the former Roman empire became attractive localities for the development of active commercial markets, and most second-generation medieval merchants relocated their centre of activity in large cities. At this point, the law merchant became an increasingly important component of the *ius commune*. For further analysis, see Galgano (1976).

26 Feudalism spread from France to northern Italy, Germany and Spain and, later, into some of the eastern Latin territories of Europe. Most of the other great civilizations of the world have gone through periods resembling the feudal arrangements.

27 The feudal property arrangements characterized much of the customary law of property, but medieval academic jurists continued to utilize the Roman categories of property in their scholarly writings. This facilitated the return to the Roman categories that were eventually reinstated as part of the opposition to feudalism that helped lead to the French Revolution.

28 Rudden (1987, p. 250) keenly points out 'the word "servitude" covers both slavery and easements'.

29 John Austin ([1832] 1885, p. 808).

30 Rudden (1987, p. 249) thinks that these logically relate to Austin's premise, citing Immanuel Kant ([1797] 1887, p. 14) in support of these propositions.

31 Mattei (2000, p. 14) observes that the modern unitary theory of property rights is indeed the intellectual product of the French Revolution. Along similar lines, the extensive work of Rodota' (1990) demonstrates the limits of the analogies between the Roman notions of absolute property and the modern restatement of such notion contained in Article 544 of the French Code of 1804. For further historical analysis of this important transition in the conception of property, see Monateri (1996).

32 Thus, for example, use and exploitation rights divorced from ownership (*usufructus*) could be given only to a living person for the duration of his lifetime; the creation of legally binding restrictions on property (*servitudes*) was sharply limited.

33 Paulus Book 25 *ad Sabinum* in D. 8.2.28: '*omnes autem servitutes praediorum perpetuas causas habere debent*' (all servitudes must have a perpetual cause).

34 Paulus Book 15 *ad Plautium* in D. 8.1.8: '*ut pomum decerpere liceat et ut spatiari et ut cenare in alieno possimus, servitus imponi non potest*'. (Servitudes cannot be created to grant rights for harvesting fruit or to have meals or merely to walk on another's property.) Such atypical arrangements – it was understood as an implicit corollary – could however, be created as a matter of personal obligations.

35 European scholars also refer to this principle by invoking the concept of nominate property rights. Merrill and Smith (2000, p. 69) have recognized that, although the *numerus clausus* principle is mostly a Roman law doctrine followed and enforced in most civil law countries, the principle also exists as part of the unarticulated tradition

of the common law. The authors illustrate the many ways in which common law judges are accustomed to thinking in terms comparable to the civilian doctrine.

36 For a modern challenge to the *numerus clausus* principle, see Rudden (1987) who critically analyses the legal, philosophical and economic justifications for limiting the types of legally cognized property interests to a handful of standardized forms.

37 Merrill and Smith (2000, pp. 68–69) note the peculiar dichotomy between property and contracts, observing that while contract rights are freely customizable, property rights are restricted to a closed list of standardized forms.

38 This implies that property rights are only enforced with real remedies if they conform to one of the 'named' standardized categories. Conversely, the presumption is the opposite in the field of contracts: the legal system enforces all types of contracts unless they violate a mandatory rule of law concerning their object and scope.

39 Several articles of the French Civil Code embrace the concept of 'typicality' of real rights and articulate principles of unitary and absolute property. See, for example, Article 516 on the differentiation of property; Article 526, enlisting the recognized forms of limited real rights (usufruct, servitudes and mortgages); Articles 544–546 on the definition and necessary content of absolute ownership, etc.

40 BGB Paragraph 90, by providing that 'Only corporeal objects are things in the legal sense' can be seen as a substantial departure from the feudal conception of property, where most atypical rights had an intangible nature.

41 Practically all important modern codifications – not all of which were directly influenced by the French and German models – embrace a similar principle of unity in property. Rudden (1987) provides a comparative survey of the *numerus clausus* principle in the modern legal systems of the world, reporting that many Asian legal systems have adopted a basic rule according to which 'no real rights can be created other than those provided for in this Code or other a legislation', for example, Korean CC 185, Thai CC 1298 and Japanese CC 175. Similar provisions exist in other systems of direct European derivation such as Louisiana CC 476–8, Argentine CC 2536, Ethiopian CC 1204 (2) and Israeli Land Law 1969 sections 2–5.

42 The 'absence of notice' legal rationale purports that it would be difficult for a purchaser to know about 'fancies', or non-*numerus clausus* property interests. Rudden (1987) objects to this rationale. He thinks that a functioning recording system could reveal fancies to a purchaser. Further, notice is neither necessary nor sufficient to create valid property interests. For further analysis of this point, see Mattei (2000, pp. 91–92), who observes that the same restriction on the admissibility of recordable instruments does not exist in common law jurisdictions, where parties can create property rights with a much larger degree of autonomy (e.g. by means of the creation of a trust instrument).

43 Rudden (1987, p. 243) notes that Argentina is the only country that articulated this important logical corollary in the form of a code provision: Argentine CC 2536.

44 Paragraph 903 of the German BGB, granting the power of absolute disposition, similarly recognized by other codes and civilian courts. See also Mattei (2000, p. 123).

45 The '*ad coelum*' rule was first found in Gaius's Institutiones, and later reproduced in Justinian's Digest and Institutiones. The basic concept is that real property extends vertically all the way to hell (*inferos*) and heaven (*coelum*). Already in the Republican era of Roman law, however, the so-called grants *ad aedificandum* (which were later given full remedial protection through the *actio de superficie*) allowed the creation of horizontal surface rights that could be held by subjects other than the owner of the subsurface estate.

46 Wenzel (1993) points out that the horizontal fragmentation of property was not permitted in early common law. She attributes this to two main reasons: (a) the popularity of the *ad coelum* rule in medieval English thinking and the dominance of absolutist theories of property; and (b) the practices of land transfer that, through the ritual of

'seisin' (resembling the *traditio simbolica* of the Roman law), required the symbolic conveyance of possession via the manual delivery of a stone or clump of soil taken from the land. The ritual of the *traditio simbolica*, Wenzel suggests, was not suitable to symbolize the transfer of title to subsurface rights or undiscovered mineral rights.

47 The '*ad coelum*' doctrine is still used in modern law in two main settings: one being in property law, to approach questions of adjoining ownership (e.g. cases of constructions hanging over the neighboring land, etc.); and in international law, to approach issues of territorial sovereignty over airspace. Most recently, the doctrine has been revived in public international law through the claims of equatorial states for their rights over the geostationary orbit (for satellites). Obviously, non-equatorial states oppose the applicability of the '*ad coelum*' rule and invoke the application of a rule of first possession.

48 As to the vertical limits of property, even in the early times, the appeal to the *ad coelum* rule was mostly symbolic and subject to several exceptions. The value of such symbolism, however, should not to be underestimated, given the interpretive force that is often associated with general principles in civil law systems.

49 According to the accession rule, *superficies solo cedit*, in the absence of such agreement, the owner of title could claim ownership to any construction erected on the land by third parties.

50 BGB, Paragraphs 1012–17, which were later replaced by a special law of 15 January, 1919, which provided a more explicit regulation of the matter.

51 Article 952 of the Italian Civil Code of 1942 recognizes surface rights as an enforceable real right.

52 Conflicting claims of building and land owners would have been resolved according to the civilian rules of accession, according to which the owner of the land would acquire title to the building erected by third parties (i.e. *superficies solo cedit*) with a duty to compensate the latter for the lesser amount between the incremental value of the property and the cost of the building. The default solution under the code may have occasionally proven unfair, given the greater subjective value of a building for those who designed and built it, compared to the average market value or the subjective valuation of the unwilling owner of the land.

53 Horizontal partition may prevent valuable improvements, such as levelling the ground for agricultural or construction purposes, excavating for proper drainage, or simply creating a well or a wine cellar, etc. For a historical survey of the evolving conceptions of physical unity in property, see also Bianca (1999).

54 Recently, common law courts have been relatively creative in figuring out ways to enforce contracts that create covenants designed to protect existing amenities in residential areas. Furthermore, legal systems occasionally will invent a new form of property. Despite these periodical innovations, this area of the law remains the most archaic. Rose (1999, pp. 213–214) observes that the common law system of estates in land now seem almost risibly crude and antiquated. As the author ironically points out, references to the 'fee tail' seldom fail to bring a smile.

55 Yiannopoulos (1983) notes the inadequacy of building and zoning ordinances to satisfy the needs of local property owners (e.g. for the preservation of the subdivision style, etc.). He also mentions that land developers have, since the turn of the century, imposed contractual restrictions limiting the use of property to enhance property values (e.g. restricting use to certain specified purposes, prohibiting the erection of certain types of buildings or specifying the material or the colors that may be used in the construction). Rudden (1987) observes, along similar lines, that although standard possessory interests involve exclusive and continuous possession, individuals may seek to acquire alternate interests such as a time-share, which is exclusive possession for repeated, short intervals. He thinks that servitude interests have seen the most innovation of late, and that security interests have seen the least innovation.

56 Real covenants and easements differ from one another in various respects. An affirmative real covenant is a promise to do an affirmative act (e.g. a landowners' agreement with her homeowner's association to pay yearly fees, or a landowner's agreement to keep his lawn well trimmed). An affirmative easement, by contrast, is a right held by the owner of the benefiting land, called dominant estate, to use another party's land, called servient estate. There is no affirmative obligation for the servient estate owner to do anything. As it is generally explained, the servient owner only has a 'negative duty' to refrain from interfering with the other party's rights.

57 Under the modern contract doctrine, an assignee is liable for pre-existing contractual obligations only if he or she expressly assumes those obligations. The problem of the law of real covenants is thus principally concerned with situations where the assignee has not expressly agreed to assume the covenants of the previous owner. Enforcing these real covenants as mere contracts would often frustrate the goals pursued by the parties, given the frequent objective to allow the burdens and benefits of real covenants to pass to the successive owners of the underlying estates.

58 Yiannopoulos (1983) observes that the French Supreme Court (e.g. Civ. 12 Dec., 1899, D. 1900.1.361, with a note by Gény) recognized the effect against third parties of a property covenant relieving the operator of a mine from liability for damage to the surface. See also Bergel (1973).

59 See Rose's seminal 'Comedy of the Commons' (1986), describing the origins of, and justifications for, common law doctrines and statutory strategies that vest collective property rights in the 'unorganized' public as a means of optimal resource management. Most recently, Henry Smith (2000) introduced the notion of semi-commons. These are property arrangements consisting of a mix of both common and private rights, with significant interactions between the two, observing that this property structure allows the optimizing of the scale of different uses of the property (e.g. larger-scale grazing, smaller-scale grain growing, etc.).

60 The idea of the anticommons in environmental regulation is explored further in Mahoney (2002).

61 Most recently, Dagan and Heller (2001) present the case of the liberal commons as a compelling illustration of efficient commons. Less obviously, we could imagine cases of purposely chosen anticommons. Examples of purposeful dysfunctional property fragmentation can be found in situations where unified property owners want to generate anticommons problems as a way to control the use of their property beyond the time of their ownership. An interesting real life example is offered by the case of nature associations and mountain-hiking clubs that utilize anticommons-type fragmentation as a way to ensure long-term or perpetual conservation of the land in its current undeveloped state.

References

Austin, John (1832), *Lectures on Jurisprudence*, 5th edn (1885), ed. R. Campbell, 2 vols, London: J. Murray.

Banner, Stuart (1999), 'Two properties, one land: law and space in 19th-century New Zealand,' *Law and Social Inquiry*, December, 807–852.

Bergel, Jean-Louis (1973), *Les Servitudes de Lotissement à Usage d'Habitation*, Paris: Librairie Générale de Droit et de Jurisprudence.

Bianca, Massimo C. (1999), *La proprietà*, Diritto Civile, 6, Milano: Giuffre.

Bouckaert, Boudewijn (1999), 'Original assignment of private property', 1100 *Encyclopedia of Law & Economics*, Cheltenham, UK and Northampton, MA: Edward Elgar.

Corbin, Arthur L. (1926), 'Assignment of contract rights', *University of Pennsylvania Law Review*, 74(3), 207–234.

Dagan, Hanoch and M.A. Heller, (2001), 'The liberal commons', *Yale Law Journal*, 110(1), 549–623.

Demsetz, Harold (1967), 'Toward a theory of property rights', *American Economic Review*, 57(2), 347–359.

Demsetz, Harold (1988), *Ownership Control and the Firm: The Organization of Economic Activity*, Vol. I, Oxford: Basil Blackwell.

Dukeminier, Jesse and Krier, J.E. (2002), *Property*, 5th edn, New York: Aspen Law & Business.

Dwyer, John P. and Menell, P.S. (1998), *Property Law and Policy: A Comparative Institutional Perspective*, New York: Foundation Press.

Ellickson, R.C., Rose, C.M. and Ackerman, B.A. (eds) (1995), *Perspectives on Property Law*, 2nd edn, Boston, MA: Little Brown.

Galgano, Francesco (1976), *Lex Mercatoria*, Bologna: Il Mulino.

Gambaro, Antonio (1995), *Il Diritto di Proprietà*, Milano: A Giuffre.

Hegel, Georg Wilhelm Friedrich ([1821] 1942), *Philosophy of Right*, tr. T.M. Knox, Oxford: Oxford University Press.

Kant, Immanuel (1797), *Philosophy of Law*, tr. W. Hastie, Edinburgh [1887].

LaFargue, Paul (1975), *The Evolution of Property: From Savagery to Civilization*, Chicago: Charles H. Kerr.

Maine, Henry (1861), *Ancient Law*, (2000 edn), York, PA: Beard Group.

Mahoney, Julia (2002), 'Perpetual restrictions on land and the problem of the future', *Virginia Law Review*, 88(4), 739–787.

Mattei, Ugo (2000), *Basic Principles of Property Law*, Westport, CT: Greenwood Press.

Merrill, Thomas and Henry Smith (2000), 'Optimal standardization in the law of property: The *numerus clausus* principle', *Yale Law Journal*, 110(1), 1–70.

Monateri, Piergiuseppe (1996), *Il Modello di Civil Law*, Torino: Giappichelli Editore.

Parisi, Francesco (1998), 'Customary Law', in P. Newman (ed.), *New Palgrave Dictionary of Economics and the Law*, London: Macmillan Reference Ltd, pp. 572–579.

Parisi, Francesco (2002a), 'Entropy in property', *American Journal of Comparative Law*, 50, 595–622.

Parisi, Francesco (2002b), 'Freedom of contract and the laws of entropy', *Supreme Court Economic Review*, 10, 65–90.

Parisi, Francesco and Erin O'Hara (1998), 'Conflict of laws', in P. Newman (ed.), *New Palgrave Dictionary of Economics and the Law*, London: Macmillan Reference Ltd, pp. 387–396.

Pipes, Richard (1991), *Property and Freedom*, New York: Alfred A. Knopf.

Posner, Richard A. (1998), *Economic Analysis of Law*, 5th edn, New York: Aspen Law & Business.

Rodotà, Stefano (1990), *Il Terribile Diritto*, 2nd edn, Bologna: Il Mulino.

Rose, C.M. (1985), 'Possession as the origin of property', *University of Chicago Law Review*, 52(1), 73–88.

Rose, C.M. (1986), 'The Comedy of the commons: custom, commerce, and inherently public property', *University of Chicago Law Review*, 53(3), 711–781.

Rose, C.M. (1998), 'Canons of property talk, or, Blackstone's anxiety', *Yale Law Journal*, 108(3), 601–632.

Rose, C.M. (1999), 'What government can do for property (and vice versa)', in Nicholas Mercuro and Warren Samuels (eds), *The Fundamental Interrelationship between Government and Property*. Connecticut: JAI Press Inc., pp. 209–222.

Rudden, Bernard. (1987). 'Economic Theory v. Property Law: The *Numerus Clausus* Problem', in John Eekelaar and John Bell (eds), *Oxford Essays on Jurisprudence*, 3rd edn, 239–263.

Smith, Adam (1776), *An Inquiry into the Nature and Causes of the Wealth of Nations*, reprinted in Robert Heilbroner (ed.) (1986), *The Essential Adam Smith*, New York and London: W.W. Norton.

Smith, Henry E. (2000), 'Semicommon property rights and scattering in the open fields', *Journal of Legal Studies*, 29, 131–169.

Wenzel, Michelle Andrea (1993), 'Comment: the model surface use and mineral development accommodation act: easy easements for mining interests', *American University Law Review*, 42(2), 607–681.

Yiannopoulos, Athanassios N. (1983), *Civil Law Property Coursebook: Louisiana Legislation, Jurisprudence, and Doctrine*, 3rd edn, Baton Rouge: Claitor's.

3 Property rights

A comparative law and economics perspective in the global era

Ugo Mattei and Andrea Pradi

A story of cultural imperialism

This paper deals with the global diffusion of property rights theory used in the economic analysis of the law. By discussing the reasons of its international success, one becomes aware of the simplifications brought about by such theory and of the political consequences of its widespread adoption. The result of its diffusion is a poor understanding of the real-world complexity of human relationships and a naturalized conservative political platform. The extension of economic theory of property rights in to domains where the economic logic poorly reflect the real life complexity of individual motivations and of political platforms rises serious question in need of answer by legal and political institutions.

Private property has always been considered the foundation stone of capitalism, and no ambitious political philosophy can be developed without approaching this fundamental legal, cultural, and economic institution. Nevertheless, property rights have been object of systematic legal and economic inquiry within a fairly recent tradition of thought, coinciding with the economist's takeover of US legal thought in the second half of last century. It is only in the last third of the twentieth century, after Coase's investigation on the problem of social cost, appeared in the Journal of Law and Economics in 1960 (Coase, 1960), that we can establish the starting point for the current mode of legal and economic analysis of property rights. From Coase onward, we assume that the primary function of property law became the reduction of transaction costs in order to let individuals bargaining to reach the efficient allocation of resources. This theoretical achievement has encouraged widespread efforts to use property rights to solve problems of externalities in a variety of situations, even in domains that might appear governed by forces and feelings other than economic rationality.

However, the very narrow and technical nature of law and economics scholarship, has hidden the real revolutionary change in the conception of property rights, more generally in the relationship between the market and the law, produced by the Coase theorem. In receiving the Coase theorem, lawyers found themselves faced with clear evidence that liability rules, whose impact was limited by Coase to the domain of distribution rather than of efficiency, could, nevertheless, be used as a means to equalize private and social costs, by compelling a property right holder to internalize his or her costs. This observation represented a real paradigmatic shift from the natural law model of property still assumed by traditional economic analysis (property as sovereignty). Unfortunately, this view of the Cathedral has been obscured, because the idea of liability is antithetical to that of property as a domain of unrestricted idiosyncratic freedom. Thus, the message received from Coase, short from being the possibility of usefully incorporating liability in the economic theory of property (in order to search for a more social model of capitalism), has been that, when transaction costs are low enough, the legal regime cannot impact efficiency, so the law should refrain from messing with the market its role being to "mimic" it rather than to attempt controlling its distortions.

Law and economics expansion has thus been achieved on this simplified, irresponsible, and unrealistic institutional background, whose policy conse- quences are the writing of a blank check to corporate capitalism (Hertz, 2001, p. 7). Moreover, the historical contingency of the Coase theorem as an attempt to over- come the dominant approach to externalities (taxes and bounties), championed by Pigou since the thirties, has produced a misleading ideological conflict between property rights and regulation as models of market governance, considering the former as the sole institutional alternative able to efficiently tackle the problem of externalities even though this has never been the point of Coase's theory on Property rights (Coase, 1996). A comparative legal approach, nevertheless, shows that in the real life of the law most often property rights and regulation, rather than conflicting, serve the same purpose (Mattei, 1997, p. 115). Different legal systems handle externalities problems by complex institutional mixtures, that we need to carefully analyze and understand rather than concluding that a certain abstract model is better than another only because sponsored by mainstream economists.

In front of the simplified models promoted by economists, the real intellectual challenge, for legal scholarship, is to construct a theory of property rights able to take into account the complexity of the real world, in order to establish a genuine commitment of law and economics to progressive, more civilized, law reform, and social change. The narrow and materialistic form of human relationship that law and economics carries with its bias in front of a neo-liberal model of capitalism, should than be resisted.

The economic foundation of property rights

As it is well known, the most common justification of property rights is today to remedy the so-called tragedy of the commons (Hardin, 1968). This parable exposes the tragic outcomes of the overuse of scarce resources caused by the absence of restrictions over their consumption. In a well-known version, one should imagine three communities living on the shores of a lake in a rather primitive state of development. Fishing is the only activity and the fish in the lake currently reproduce enough to feed all the three communities. From the economic perspective, an efficient equilibrium exists because the three communities live on the income from the capital, rather consuming the capital itself. Suppose now that a more efficient fishing technique has been invented allowing for more fishing in less time. Even if the communities were aware that increasing fishing causes adverse impacts on the fishing environment, the invisible hand will lead them to over-fishing. In fact, if one community self-restrains, in order to maintain the equilibrium, it will not capture the benefit of this responsible effort, as the other two will fill the space that it has left. Rather, every community has a strong incentive to fish extensively, because it will keep all the gains of the fish it captures, while the cost of the excessive use of the resource in common are shared by all the three communities. Thus, it makes than little sense for one community to worry about the long-term effects of over-fishing, without being sure that the others will act in the same way. Unless the communities find some sort of binding agreement, the outcome will be a tragic rush to over-consumption that ends up in complete fish depletion.

A global approach to property law should consider the world as a gigantic commons to be divided up in order to avoid tragic outcomes. The division of such a complex common between so many communities, and further between so many individuals within the community, is made possible through the development of fundamental political institutions such as markets, property rights, and other legal institutions (Rapaczynski, 1996) either formal or informal (Rose, 1986; Ostrom, 1990). Economists, lawyers, and political scientists generally agree that the way to avoid the tragedy is to develop techniques that, rather than allowing free exploitation of scarce resources, are able to determine "prices" that correspond to the social cost of the consumption. Naturally, there is much political disagreement on how to fix such prices and particularly who is entitled to fix them. Nevertheless, in every legal system, one technique, although by no means the only one, is a system of property rights.

Going back to our story, suppose that the need for fish in one of our three communities increases because, for example, a doctor has invented a medicine that decreases the rate of infant death and the community experiences an unexpected growth. Its demand for fish will increase together with the price of the fish since we can assume supply immutable. By splitting up the lake and allocating exclusively one parcel to each community, each one is forced to face the long-term effects of the use of its resources. Each community will then avoid over-fishing, because it will bear all the costs of it. Each community will consequently invest its limited resources in the most efficient way to maintain the natural equilibrium. Granting property rights over scarce resources, allows individual owners to gain the benefits from the appropriation of the utility stemming from their goods and, at the same time, to face the long-term costs of their action.

According to the usual reading of the parable, ownership of goods is thus allocated to private individuals because of the benefit that they are able to gain from the appropriation. Work and investment are thus stimulated, with benefit for society. As an exclusive power to rule over commodities, private property prevents individuals from consuming resources without the owner's consent, and gives them incentives to bargain an efficient resources allocation. In fact individuals are willing to acquire a resource through a market transaction only if the resource is worth to them more than to its present owner.

It is worth noting that the "Tragedy of the Commons" actually conveys the much more limited idea that, for the sake of the common good, scarce resources need regulation rather than unrestricted freedom. In global perspective it is thus compatible with many models of capitalism and even with communism, since individual ownership is only *one of the possible ways to regulate the commons*, actually a quite dangerous one, since it opens the way to waged labor, human exploitation and alienation, all forms of externalities that, in the real world, are produced rather than cured by individual ownership (Stiglitz, 2003). In fact, it is not always the case that individuals can consent to costs and benefits being passed upon them. In our crowded world, due to the difficulty to completely separate property rights, let alone exploitive and/or opportunistic behavior, rarely does the behavior of one owner fail to affect others. Whenever one individual imposes the costs of his action upon another, outside a voluntarily agreement, we are facing "negative externalities" or "external diseconomies," wealth transfers taking place, outside of the marketplace (Davis and Hullet, 1977). The clearest example is the problem of industrial pollution. One party (the polluting factory) consumes a scarce resource (peace and quiet, clean air, fresh water) without bearing the costs of this consumption. On the other hand, an externality may be positive. For example, whenever a private party beautifies a landfill, transforming it into a garden, it renders a benefit to all the owners of property nearby, which will enjoy a new beautiful environment without having borne the costs and thus having the value of their property "freely" increased. Both in the case of positive and negative externalities, a transfer of wealth between two or more individuals has taken place, outside of the marketplace. The marketplace fails in its primary function of efficiently allocating resources, inasmuch as the system of prices transmits incorrect information. The ultimate result of this failure is that there will not be enough, or that there will be too much of a given commodity than the efficient amount. In our example, without a system of property law able to avoid externalities, there will be too much pollution and too little beautiful gardens.

Economists are concerned with both types of externalities, because both produce inefficiency. Lawyers more commonly focus on negative externalities, the ones that are likely to produce social conflicts and need to be restrained.

The Coase theorem as a paradigm of law and economics

Within the Coase theorem, scholars did approach the problem of externalities in the framework of property rights (Demsetz, 1998, p. 144). By demonstrating his theorem, Coase concluded that whenever the parties have the possibility to negotiate without being restricted by excessive costs, they reach efficient solutions independently of the legal rules, governing their relationship (Cooter, 1982). After bargaining, property rights will be so framed to cover exactly the particular activity of the property owner who values them more. Consequently, in a costless negotiation, no costs are imposed on anyone else. In the apologetic vision following the dominant read of the theorem, property rights indisputably become a market institution able to channel individual greed to the benefit of the community (Barzel, 1997). Indeed, in the absence of transaction costs, property rights, by themselves, are able to create both the incentives to negotiate and the restrictions capable of making individuals pay for the consumption of scarce resources without passing the cost among others.

Born as a simple attempt to challenge the Pigouvian tax-based approach as a primary tool to internalize externalities, the Coasean approach to property rights rapidly became the paradigm of law and economics, seizing the tremendous opportunity open to interdisciplinary work in US law schools by dominating legal realists (Gilmore, 1977, p. 80). After Coase, the problem deserving attention became that of the correct allocation of "transaction costs," that are part of the real world. Transaction costs, have been seen as wastes that efficiency suggests reducing, as much as possible, for the sake of future social interaction (Williamson, 1995). The law should thus be structured in order to remove the impediments to bargaining, so as to create incentives for individuals to bargain over resource allocation. In this vision the law, constitutes a program of social allocation of resources from which the parties should be, in principle, able to negotiate alternative, more efficient solutions. With Coase we assist the triumph of default law over mandatory rules. When bargaining is costless the law becomes part of the problem rather than of the solution, because individuals can reach a more efficient resources allocation than the one the legal rules suggest. Accordingly, the parties should be left free to change legal rules that allocate property rights in case they reach an agreement to do so (Mattei, 2000).

However it is not always the case that negotiation is successful. Often individuals encounter serious problems of communication that prevent them to reach an agreement over a resource allocation. Sometimes, such problems arise from the distance the parties must travel to communicate in person, and the high costs of such travel. Sometimes, communication problems may derive from one party's hostility toward the other. Sometimes, it is costly to get enough information either about the trustworthiness of the other party to the bargain or the object about which we are bargaining. Many times, fundamental problems are created by a severe unbalance of power between the parties. Due to lack of information or excessive cost of obtaining information, one or both parties might lack confidence to enter into a bargain, or many times might enter into bargains that are neither efficient nor fair because of power differences.

Whenever bargaining is prevented by these reasons, the law should be a part of the solution to these problems, so that transaction costs are reduced or allocated to the party that is in the best position to face them (Cooter and Ulen, 2003). The rules of property that legal systems employ to settle conflicts can move in the direction of an efficient solution by lowering transaction costs. In this vision, the efficiency of property law is thus a function of the costs of the enforcement of property rights (Ellickson, 1991). The more a system of property law is self-enforcing, the more it is efficient. In order to make property law as self-enforcing as possible, economic analysis offers a clear and quite simplistic suggestion: property rights should be clearly separated and the rules of property law should be as clear as possible. Confusion and doubt in the rules of property create incentives to litigate, because each conflicting individual hopes that he will end up being favored by the judicial decision. Clear-cut property rights, to the contrary, reduce litigation because the parties will already know who will lose and who will win so that they will avoid wasting money in litigation. Clear-cut property rights, in other words, do create incentives to negotiate (and find an efficient agreement) rather than litigate (and waste resources).

Coase and the real life of the law

As the work of an economist able to use private law categories, the Coase theorem offers to lawyers few clearly spelt out concepts, making the problem of externalities approachable in terms of legal concept, familiar to first-year law students. Thus highly simplified legal notions find their way into legal scholarship. To follow Bruce Ackerman's jargon, the simplifiers take over the complexifiers in the law (Ackerman, 1984). From Coase onward many believe that a well-defined system of property rights will take care of externalities, because individuals will bargain to reach an efficient result (Demsetz, 1967; De Alessi, 1969; Libecap, 1986). This wonderful achievement not only has encouraged widespread efforts to use property rights to solve problems of externalities in a variety of situations (Furubton and Pejovic, 1972), but has also represented a fundamental paradigmatic shift in legal reasoning, challenging the hierarchical relation between the legal system and the market (Kelsen, 1934) in favor of an understanding, globally much admired by the "Washington consensus," of the market determining and controlling the law by promoting efficiency as a sort of constitutional value. Property rights are, indeed, able to align private and social cost whenever bargain succeeds, so that there is no *prima facie* necessity of state regulation with respect to the problem of externalities. The burden of proof is thus shifted. The need of regulation must be shown, a very difficult task given the dominating idea of efficiency.

The very special institutional position seized by property rights does not necessarily imply neglecting other institutional alternatives (Komesar, 1994). But the bias in favor of a self-regulating market is quite obvious, given the natural law conception of property that serves as institutional background for law and economics. Because of such obsolete and self-serving conception of ownership (refurbished by Coase), the rights of an individual naturally end at the beginning of those of another, so that the false dichotomy between property rights and regulation ends up reinforced. Indeed regulation, almost redundantly limits ownership, "naturally" free, until its intrinsic structural limits (provided by opposing property rights). The natural law school considers ownership a zone of individual sovereignty over resources as the most effective barrier against the power of the state. This ideology has always perceived limits, by means of public regulation, as something to be avoided, as authoritarian restrictions over a proprietary freedom already naturally limited in the interest of other owners. However, the natural law conception of property is an intellectual category that is not, and has never been, reflected as law in action in any legal system: neither in common law tradition, in which historically, the separation between property and liability has never been experienced (Lawson and Rudden, 2002) nor in the civil law tradition in which the naturalistic model posed by the Napoleonic civil code has always been accompanied by public law regulation in order to limit it (Gambaro, 1994). In the real life of the law, moreover, owners very rarely self-limit, the trend actually being for bigger interests to always prevail on smaller ones. The recent US case Kelo vs City of New London, where small residential ownership has been expropriated in favor of commercial developments, is the best example of law and economics of property in action.

Since Coase, we have full knowledge of two alternative models of institutional control of externalities, the Pigouvian model, based on centralized regulation and the Coasean decentralized model, based on the enforcement of property rights. Economists tend to compare these abstract models, almost invariably concluding in favor of the latter. Nevertheless, modern legal systems show significant complexity in taking care of externalities, both because of the number of individuals or organization that compete for scarce resources, and because of the number of institutional actors that are enabled to make proprietary choices. In the real world externalities are handled by a mixture of Pigouvian and Coasean approaches. Sometimes public law directly tackles some externalities (e.g. the many regulations regarding nuclear plants and related activities or the many inalienability rules). Sometimes private law is called upon to react against them. In the civil law tradition private law rules are usually found in civil codes, while in the common law tradition they are contained in the general common law of property, contracts, and torts.

Usually the economic literature describes the public law model as a collective control of externalities, while the private law model is conceived as decentralized (Calabresi, 1970). Collective controls are carried on by a process of decision-making, which is brought to life collectively by professional or quasi-professional politicians, through political institutions and the democratic process. Collective choices tend to reflect the variable power structure characterizing political organizations, and often redistribute resources with no attention to internalization of externalities, because of rent seeking of progressive and many times of reactionary political platforms.

The private law rules, on the other hand, are administered by the courts, and are the product of professional lawyers. They thus follow a decentralized logic different from that of the political process. In practice, such arrangement means that property rights confer upon every citizen some power in his dealings with others. This power becomes effective in court whenever the property right holder claims to be victim of negative externalities. For example, if I own an apartment, I may complain in court against my neighbor's noisy use of his apartment at night. The rules of property law that derive from resolutions of these conflicts (e.g. absolute quiet use after midnight) are not choices made directly by a collective political body (such as letting or forbidding nuclear plants to operate). They are the result of a series of incremental and independent decisions made by the courts in the resolution of a number of different conflicts between individuals. In this sense, the power of the owner is decentralized, carried on outside collective political institutions, and exercised by every owner in relation to some decision making related to the scarce resource allocated to her.

A very clear bias in favor of the efficiency of the common-law adjudication process promotes the courts of law as the most important actors of the legal system (Posner, 2003, p. 529). The decision of the judge, in US legal system, is particularly important for the future, since it creates the structure of property rights on which future transactions might rely. Courts faced with a claim of a plaintiff claiming to be a property owner will find themselves confronted with the choice between: (a) protecting the owner by means of a full proprietary protection (property rule); (b) granting the plaintiff damages which compensates him for the externality affecting his economic interest, denying the protection of his right (liability rule); (c) finding for the defendant, thus reallocating property rights or considering the resource part of the public domain.

According to economists, efficiency considerations offer clear guidelines for such a choice by looking on transaction costs that might preclude the possibility of the parties from finding an efficient agreement between them. When transaction costs are low, the property rule protection, enjoining any action contrary to the will of the owner, should be favored. When transaction costs are high, the liability rule, compelling internalization by granting damages, is the best remedy (Calabresi and Melamed, 1972).

Just because in theory the judge has no power to enter political judgments aimed at redistribution, only the struggle against externalities, and not redistribution, should guide the courts in their work of conflict resolution. For this reason much less economists can tell us on the decision to reallocate property rights or to keep the commodity in the public domain in the hypo sub (c). While the first choice might depend on unbalances of power between the parties (that economists traditionally disregard), the second usually depends on the particular nature of the contested commodity (e.g. human genes, natural resources, kidneys, etc.) that makes it more problematic to apply standard economic theory.

Simplistic models and the denial of real distributional stakes

Whichever solution the law appears to prefer in terms of substantive law, economic analysis suggests to look at the problems of its implementation. Property law, far from being confined to an abstract set of principles and rules, is rooted in institutions that may or may not be able to enforce a given social plan of resource allocation. Clearly, in the absence of effective institutions, it is only the rule of the stronger that prevails. The social signals contained in substantive law are able to create effective incentives only if made credible by an effective legal process. Applied law knows more complex forms of property rights, so that the notion assumed by neo-classical economics, is only a pale reflection of the reality. Real life property rights are based on a variable mixture of property and liability rules, allocated in different ways to different individuals, by different institutional agencies in different legal systems.

The increase of social complexity also increases the complexity of the legal process that frames property law. Consequently, in all modern legal system, property law is not limited to private law but rather involves also the public law. It is a complex aggregate of political, professional, and private decision making, involving an always increasing number of resources that markets construct as scarce (different recent examples: domain names in the internet or human genome). Property law is thus the product of the relationship between individual power and legal restrictions in the use of scarce resources.

Modern legal systems depart from each other on their framing property rights, even if the neo-classical economic model of property claims a global universal status. Some legal systems may be more willing than others to maintain the Pigouvian model of central control of externalities. To give account of this complexities, every theory of property rights, claiming global status, should at least acknowledge the following central point: in the real world there cannot exist a system that deals with externalities using a pure decentralized model, nor can exist a fully centralized way. This consequence of the impossibility of the a "pure" and of a "pure absence" of the market (Calabresi, 1978) shows how, in practice, a fully decentralized system of externality control corresponds to no control at all. Each legal system necessarily uses, together with aspects of the Coasean solution, a larger or smaller centralized system of collective control of externalities.

Because of its non-acknowledgment of variations, due to imperialism and universalism of neo-classical economic theory, law and economics theory of property is thus grounded in an institutional background that is either an abstract natural law model, or a simplified version of the modern institutional setting of US law. Economists tend to disregard the contribution of the public law in the development of an efficient human organization, because they consider regulation affected by rent seeking and capture (Rice and Ulen, 1981). Nevertheless, public regulation of scarce resources, including the political choice to allocate them in the public rather than in the private domain, is crucial for lawyers that see private law and public law as cooperating in defining and limiting property rights. To the contrary, economists develop models in which the private law creates property rights as zones of individual freedom and self-interested appropriation of wealth, while the public law limits property rights, lowering their value and thus impairing the efficient use of resources. Indeed, in the standard neoclassical economic approach, private law is the province of the market, while public law is the province of the government. Economists are biased in favor of markets and thus of the common law process administered by the courts that they consider "efficient," "neutral," or "objective," thus naturalizing the status quo against redistribution (with the exception of that in favor of the stronger).

However, as we have seen before, courts are ill-equipped to taking care of situations in which the particular nature of the contested commodity suggest to keep it into the public domain, so that their decision making is always biased in favor of the private sector. In particular, when transaction costs cannot be lowered because of the number of individuals involved, or where there is a case for the public domain, government regulation is a valid institutional alternative in order to allocate resources outside of market transactions (Komesar, 1994).

The necessary attention for the complexities of the legal process, particularly when approached with transaction costs in mind, suggests carefulness in generalizations. Considering courts as one of the institutional alternatives available in framing property rights, one can see that most often it can cost a lot more to resolve the dispute in court rather than by means of an administrative agency or some other *ex ante* institutional alternative. For example, in the case of urban land use, transaction costs suggest the superiority of zoning ordinances supervised and enforced by administrative agencies over private law alternatives administered by courts. Litigation is expensive, time-consuming, and piecemeal, and it is not wise to leave to judges' decisions about urban planning, which they are not equipped to take (Komesar, 2001).

Universalism and double standard in action: intellectual property

The contribution of law and economics to the study of property law can be seen mainly as the development of a relatively simple framework in which a variety of legal institutions find a common logic in the attempt to remedy externalities and to create proper incentives for individuals to negotiate. The expansionistic and universalistic blend of neoclassical economic analysis, together with the thick layer of ideological assumptions that are embedded in such economic reasoning, lie behind the intellectual success of this approach to law (Kennedy, 1998).

Its universalistic approach that makes this brand of jurisprudence easy to apply in contexts different from those of its production (the United States) and the relative simplicity of its basic assumptions have determined the success of the property rights paradigm and the seeds of its diffusion (Kennedy, 2003). In comparative law it has been clearly explained that the success of an academic paradigm in the law is strictly connected with its apparently easy adaptability in different context, which is mostly due to universalism and relative independence from a given textual legal background (Watson, 1994). More generally, it has been observed that circulation of a legal approach is inversely proportional to the degree of legal positivism of the legal culture that has generated it (Mattei, 1994). For these and other reasons linked to its dominating political conservatism, the economics of property rights has become crucial for policy analysis, legal drafting, and legal interpretation of property law and it has been applied to an ever-increasing area of human relationships. Clearly the so-called institutions of the Washington consensus (WB, IMF, WTO, etc.) have leveraged its diffusion, by making neoclassical and supply side economics the backbone of global development.

Furthermore, efficiency reasoning has represented a new strong source of legitimacy for lawyers, that decades of dominant legal realism required to be reconstructed, providing the degree of neutrality and objectivity that is crucial to the pursuit of any hegemonic or imperialistic scheme. Further, incidentally to the conservative neo-liberal project, efficiency ideology has produced the most important cultural stream diffusing tacit assumption of US-based legal consciousness (Mattei, 1997, p. 226). Naturally, the globalization of economy proved to be the ideal promoting environment for the world-wide achievement of hegemony by the economics of property rights theory. Privatizations and structural reforms propagated by mighty institutions of the global governance, such the World Bank, the IMF, and the WTO, through the endorsement of the most simplistic ideas of law and economics rendered the property rights paradigm the only legal platform for the governance of the global economy. Needless to say, this platform is very business friendly, as the example of intellectual property makes quite clear.

The non-territorial nature of intellectual property, as symbolized by the Internet, and the claim of universality and of objectivity of its justification show how simplicity transforms into hegemony and domination. The pure individualistic rhetoric of Intellectual Property (IP), reinforced by crude neo-classical economic models, has lead toward the creation of legal monopolies. Such monopolies are justified by the "necessity" to grant incentives to creativity. They are enforced world-wide by the most powerful global institutions (WTO, WIPO) and their regulations (Trade Related aspects of Intellectual Property Rights – TRIPS) (Blakeney, 1997). It is almost universally recognized that the TRIPS Agreements have driven humankind into a new era of global property relationships, in which the corporate capital, controlling intellectual property, is much stronger than national governments and actually expropriates them of sovereignty. TRIPS Agreements have created a new uniform property rights legal environment, framed after the legal and economic model discussed above. The TRIPS Agreements (and other multilateral agreements) institute a hard compilation of principles for an international, uniform, property law (Ginsburg, 2000) based on a simplified legal notion and political idea of property rights.

As it has always happened in "revolutionary moments," also in front of the technological revolution there is a need of institutional answers to new problems. The technological revolution has changed radically the traditional idea of property. By detaching the object of ownership from the physical reality (the so-called dematerialization), the traditional defining ground of property law, it has conveyed different forms of expression than the ones we have normally dealt with. This state of affairs calls for an intellectual effort in order to develop legal categories able to reflect the nature of the new property relationships. In order to answer the issues that the techological revolution has given rise to, legal institutions have found it easier to reshape traditional concepts and categories, to adapt them to the evolving reality. Intellectual Property law has been framed around the ancient notion that individual labor (creativity) deserves a prize, and that the recognition of exclusive property rights constitutes such a prize. We are thus back to Locke and to other natural law rhetoric of individualistic ownership. Within this rhetoric, exactly as nobody would farm without guarantee of exclusive property on the outcome of his/her labor, nobody would have incentives in developing ideas without protection granting a monopoly on his/her creativity. The logical consequence of this assertion is that nobody would carry on a study of genetical modification of corn unless there is a guarantee that the legal system helps imposing such technology to all corn farmers, driving them to growing practices different from their traditional communitarian ones (Aoki, 1998).

The Western paradigm of intellectual property has been developed along the natural law model of property, the very same that earlier on in history legitimized colonization and appropriation of indigenous land, on the theory that the savages did not know ownership and thus could not efficiently farm their land. Such natural law conception, based as it is on physical possession, focuses the final product of the creative process, the physical thing (suffice to think about the major requirement for copyright protection is still the fixation in a tangible thing: book, magnetic support like CD, or other), even though, clearly, "digital goods" are public goods, sharing many of the very characteristics pointed out by economics: non-rivalry of consumption and high costs of exclusion.

Even from the perspective of law and economics, there is a need to distinguish public goods from private goods. The former, characterized by rival consumption, must be objects of private property, while the latter, whose consumption is not rival, should be object of public property and remain in the public domain. The classic example used by economists to show that sometimes property law is not enough to introduce proper economic incentives is that of the lighthouse. Like no one would cultivate in order to give away the harvest to the first person that passes by, similarly, no one builds a lighthouse, thus assuming the costs of construction and maintenance, without the promise of future profits. Since it is impossible to exclude any sailor from enjoying the lighthouse, and it is also impossible to charge ships passing by in the high ocean for the use of it, no lighthouse would be built unless the government intervenes directly, for example, by power to levy taxation like charges on boats in nearby ports. The lighthouse, as well as the protection against enemies' air force attacks, is a "public good" by its nature and private property in the case of public goods is not an efficient institution.

Intellectual categories, such as the natural law concept of property, used in TRIPS Agreements is thus incompatible with the intrinsic nature of information as a public good, and, in a different perspective, with some fundamental communitarian values of non-Western societies. We are thus facing a sort of technological crisis of legal institutions regarding property over immaterial goods, such as ideas, inventions, and, generally speaking, information (Hirshleifer, 1971).

In front of this scenario, rather than using a double standard that protects monopoly in the hands of corporations while at the same time imposing free competition as the global, "naturalized" rhetoric, the intellectual challenge is to construct a theoretical model of property rights able to take into account the complexity of the real word. Only by such effort of institution building there might be some hope to use law and economics to achieve much needed legal and social change, in an era in which progress and civilization are frustrated by rampant corporate capitalism, of which too often law and economics is only an apologetic chorus. Globally applying the economic logic to property law, means buying into conservative biases against redistribution of resources and government intervention.

Such risk particularly materializes when the notion of property is extended far beyond the limits of an economic institution, into domains of human relationship in which the economic logic poorly reflects the real life complexity of individual motivations. If such imperialism of economics, powerfully leveraged by institutions of global governance (IMF, WB, WTO, etc.) is not *globally exposed and resisted now*, it will only offer to humankind of deadly reactionary political platforms (such as the Structural Adjustment policy) under the ideology of efficiency, rather than progress and civilization through law.

References

Ackerman, B.A. (1984), *Reconstructing American Law*, New Haven, CT: Yale University Press.

Aoki, K. (1998), "Neocolonialism, Anticommons Property and Biopiracy in the (not so brave) New World Order of International Intellectual Property Protection," *Indiana J. Global Legal Studies*, 6:11.

Barzel, Y. (1997), *Economic Analysis of Property Rights*, 2nd edn, Cambridge (UK): Cambridge University Press.

Blakeney, M. (1997), "Trade Related Aspects of Intellectual Property Rights: A Concise Guide to the TRIPS Agreements," London: Sweet & Maxwell.

Calabresi, G. (1970), *The Cost of Accidents. A Legal and Economic Analysis*, New Haven, CT: Yale University Press.

Calabresi, G. (1978), "Tort. The Law of the Mixed Society," *Texas L. Rev.*, 96:519.

Calabresi, G. and Melamed, D. (1972), "Property Rules, Liability Rules, Inalienability: One View of the Cathedral," *Harv. L. Rev.*, 85:1089–1128.

Coase, R.H. (1960), "The Problem of Social Costs," *Journal of Law and Economics*, 3:1–44.

Coase, R.D. (1996), "Law and Economics and A.W. Simpson," *Journal of Legal Studies*, 25: 103–118.

Cooter, R.D. (1982), "The Cost of Coase," *J. Leg. Stud*, 11:1.

Cooter, R.D. and Ulen, T. (2003), *Law and Economics*, 4th edn, Boston, MA: Addison-Wesley Series in Economics.

Davis, J.R. and Hylett, J.R. (1977), *An Analysis of Market Failures: Externalities, Public Goods and Mixed Goods*, Gainesville: Edward Elgar.

De Alessi, L. (1969), "Implication of Property Rights for Government Investment Choice," *Am. Econ. Rev.*, 59:13.

Demsetz, H. (1967), "Towards a Theory of Property Rights," *American Economic Review*, 57:347–359.

Demsetz, H. (1998), "Property Rights," in P. Newman (ed.) New Palgrave Dictionary of Economics and the Law London: Macmillan Reference; New York: Stockton, 3:144.

Ellickson, R.C. (1991), *Order Without Law: How Neighbors Settle Disputes*, Cambridge, MA: Harvard University Press.

Furubton, S. and Pejovic, E.G. (1972), "Property Rights and Economic Theory: A Survey of Recent Literature," *J. Econ. Lit.*, 137.

Gambaro, A. (1994), "The Abuse of Right in the Civil Law," in A. Rabello (ed.) *Aequitas and Equity*, 375.

Gilmore, G. (1977), *The Ages of American Law*, New Haven, CT: Yale University Press.

Ginsburg, J. (2000), *International Copyright: From a "Bundle" of National Copyright Laws to a Supranational Code, J. Copyr. Soc.*, 47:265.

Hardin, G. (1968), "The Tragedy of the Commons," *Science*, 162:1243–1248.

Hertz, N. (2001), *The Silent Takeover: Global Capitalism and the Death of Democracy*, New York: The Free Press.

Hirshleifer, J. (1971), "The Private and Social Value of Information and the Reward to Innovative Activity," *Am. Econ. Rev.*, 61:561.

Kelsen, H. (1934), *Pure Theory of Law*, translated by M. Knight, University of California Press edition, 1967.

Kennedy, D. (1998), "Law-and-Economics from the Perspective of Critical Legal Studies," in P. Newman (ed.) New Palgrave Dictionary of Economics and the Law London: Macmillan Reference; New York: Stockton, 2:465.

Kennedy, D. (2003), "Two Globalizations of Law & Legal Thought: 1850–1968," *Suffolk U. L. Rev.*, 36:631.

Komesar, N. (1994), *Imperfect Alternatives: Choosing Institutions in Law, Economics, and Public Policy*, Chicago, IL: The University of Chicago Press.

Komesar, N. (2001), *Law's Limits: The Rule of Law and the Supply and Demand of Rights*, Cambridge (UK): Cambridge University Press.

Lawson, F.H. and Rudden, B. (2002), *An Introduction to the Law of Property*, 3rd edn, Oxford: Oxford University Press.

Libecap, G. (1986), "Property Rights in Economic History: Implications for Research," *Exploration in Economic History*, 23:227.

Mattei, U. (1994), "Why the Wind Changed: Intellectual Leadership in Western Law," *Am. J. Comp. L.*, 42:195.

Mattei, U. (1997), *Comparative Law and Economics*, Ann Arbor: The University of Michigan Press.

Mattei, U. (2000), *Basic Principles of Property Law: A Comparative Legal and Economic Introduction*, Westport, CT: Greenwood Publishing Group.

Ostrom, E. (1990), *Governing the Commons: The Evolution of Institution for Collective Action*, Cambridge (UK): Cambridge University Press.

Posner, R.A. (2003), *Economic Analysis of the Law*, 6th edn, New York: Aspen Law & Business.

Rapaczynski, A. (1996), "The Roles of the State and the Market in Establishing Property Rights," *Journal of Economic Perspective*, 10:87–103.

Rice, E. and Ulen, T. (1981), "Rent-Seeking and Welfare Loss," *Research in Law & Econ.*, 3:53.

Rose, C. (1986), "The Comedy of the Commons: Custom, Commerce and Inherently Public Property," *U. Chi. L. Rev.*, 53:711.

Stiglitz, J.E. (2003), *Globalization and Its Discontents*, New York: Norton & Company Inc.

Watson, A. (1994), "The Importance of 'Nutshell'," *Am. J. Comp. L.*, 42:1.

Williamson, O.E. (1995), *Transcation Cost Economics*, Brokfield, Vt.: Edward Elgar.

4 Entropy and the asymmetric Coase theorem

Francesco Parisi[1]

Property division creates asymmetric transaction costs: unlike ordinary transfers of rights from one individual to another, reunifying fragmented property rights usually involves transaction and strategic costs higher than those incurred in the original deal (Parisi *et al.*, 2000). Such costs increase monotonically with the extent of fragmentation.

Building upon such intuition, this article suggests that property is subject to a fundamental law of entropy.[2] In the property context, entropy induces one-directional bias which leads toward increasing property fragmentation. The laws of entropy further indicate that only in the purely abstract limited case of (both internally and externally) reversible transformations will the overall net change in entropy be zero. As applied to our property context, this further indicates that only in a world of zero transaction costs would there be no such tendency toward fragmentation.

The economic forces that induce entropy in property are quite straightforward.[3] Property division creates one-directional inertia.[4] Even reversing a simple property transaction can result in monopoly pricing by the buyer-turned-seller; reunifying property that has been split among multiple parties engenders even higher costs given the increased difficulty of coordination among the parties and the increased opportunity for strategic pricing by the multiple sellers.

The comparative and historical analysis of the law of remedies offers a fertile ground for examining the role of legal rules in minimizing the potential welfare losses resulting from the impediments that force certain transactions to be unidirectional. This paper revisits the implications of the normative Coase theorem (e.g. Calabresi and Melamed, 1972; Ayres and Talley, 1995; Kaplow and Shavell, 1996) and considers the choice of optimal rules and remedies to combat entropy in property. I formulate an efficiency hypothesis, suggesting that legal systems address problems arising in a positive transaction cost environment by developing rules that closely approximate the results the parties would have reached in a zero transaction cost world. I compare the ideal choice of remedies with the reality of property law. Entropy creates one-directional transactional impediments that explain several apparent anomalies in the law of remedies. This paper formulates an efficiency hypothesis pertaining to property: Given the greater difficulty of reaggregating property once fragmentation is allowed, legal systems adopt legal mechanisms to combat entropy. Furthermore, they provide less extensive property-type (in the Calabresi sense) protection to atypical property arrangements.

This paper proceeds as follows. To start with I briefly refer to the recent literature showing that dysfunctional dismemberment of property often leads to suboptimal utilization of resources and suggest that fragmentation leads to an asymmetry in the positive-transaction-cost environment of the normative Coase theorem. Hold up problems and asymmetric transaction costs create one-directional stickiness in the reallocation of property rights.[5] The strategic behavior of the owners of the divided property often results in asymmetric transaction costs. As an illustration, I refer to the models of fragmented property presented by Buchanan and Yoon (2000) and Parisi *et al.* (2000), in which property owners are faced with an anticommons problem. In that setting, externalities and strategic behavior produce deadweight losses and transaction costs that increase monotonically depending on the extent of fragmentation and the forgone complementarities between the property fragments. An important implication of such monotonicity is the fact that it is easier to fragment property than to rebundle it.

Subsequently, I posit that courts and legislators, consciously or unconsciously, take the asymmetric effects of property fragmentation into account when considering the best legal rules to apply in a given situation. This efficiency hypothesis further predicts the emergence of a dual regime of remedies to compensate for the one-directional stickiness in the parties' exchanges in several situations related to contract and property law. According to this hypothesis, when transaction costs are asymmetric, legal systems take into consideration their "direction" (i.e. the relative cost of reallocating entitlements from one party to the other), rather than the total transaction costs faced by all the parties. This is done in order to minimize the welfare losses occasioned by such asymmetric stickiness. On the basis of this hypothesis, I formulate an asymmetric version of the normative Coase theorem, evaluating (a) the optimal initial assignment of rights, and (b) the most desirable choice of remedies for situations characterized by the asymmetric frictions identified in the earlier section.

Finally, I illustrate this efficiency hypothesis with examples from comparative property law, specifically comparing the ideal choice of remedies with those that are granted in situations of asymmetric transaction and strategic costs. I look at several apparent anomalies in property law through the lens of asymmetric transaction cost minimization. Examples from both Common law and Civil law systems reveal the robustness of the efficiency hypothesis in different legal environments.

Fragmented property and asymmetric transaction costs

Asymmetric transaction costs characterize a variety of legally relevant relationships, including the case of dysfunctional fragmentation of property, which has been considered by recent research in law and economics (Heller, 1998;

Buchanan and Yoon, 2000; Parisi *et al.*, 2000). The qualification of "dysfunctional" in the present context refers to the cases where closely complementary fragments of property are attributed to different owners.[6] The reunification of these kinds of fragmented rights usually involves transaction costs greater than those incurred during the original fragmentation of the right. In spite of the complementarities between those fragmented rights, it is often harder to reunite separated property bundles than it is to break them apart.

Surmising the reason for such asymmetry is quite straightforward. A single owner faces no strategic costs when deciding how to partition his property. Conversely, as shown in Parisi *et al.* (2000), multiple non-conforming co-owners are faced with a strategic problem in their unification decisions. These strategic impediments increase the transaction costs of any attempted reunification of the original property, now diffusely controlled by a group of non-conforming owners. Reunification costs increase monotonically depending on both (a) the extent of fragmentation; and (b) the synergies and complementarities between the property fragments.

Once fragmentation takes place, reunification requires the involvement of multiple parties, with transaction and strategic costs increasing with the number of parties. This creates one-directional stickiness in the process of reallocating property among different levels of fragmentation.[7] Likewise, the resulting level of deadweight losses is a function of the degree of complementarity between the property fragments. In the presence of strategic hold-up problems, valuable synergies may remain unexploited.

The problem of fragmented property

In the traditional law and economics literature, the expression "partitioning of property rights" refers to both spatial and functional forms of fragmentation, but during the last couple of years the interest in atypical forms of property fragmentation (Merrill and Smith, 2000; Smith, 2000; Parisi, 2001) has grown. The simple intuition developed in these studies can be summed up as follows: unlimited access to a commons results in over-consumption, and, conversely, multiple exclusion rights result in too little use of a resource. Subsequent extensions of this insight have focused on the efficiency of the commons and on examples of successful coexistence of common and private property regimes (Smith, 2000). Other scholars have shown that functional and spatial partitioning of property lead to different results with respect to deadweight losses due to under exploitation (Heller, 1998; Banner, 1999). A final group has considered the role of legal doctrines in limiting the extent of property fragmentation (Heller, 1999; Merrill and Smith, 2000).[8] The main conclusion of these recent contributions is that atypical forms of property fragmentation can result in the inefficient use of resources, unless the costs of dividing the property in question are less than the possible externalities that the concentrated use of the property would create.

Subsequent models of the anticommons (Buchanan and Yoon, 2000; Parisi *et al.*, 2000) have further shown that anticommons deadweight losses result from a lack of conformity between use and exclusion rights or, more generally, from splitting two or more complementary elements of a property right. A dysfunctional fragmentation of property, in which different agents hold complementary fragments of the original right, always cause the risk of inefficiencies. The nature of the fragmentation, rather than its mere extent, has a direct impact on the resulting deadweight loss.[9]

In search of a unified conception of property

The natural structure of a property right aptly illustrates the essence of the problem of dysfunctional property fragmentation. According to the traditional conception of property, owners enjoy a bundle of rights over their property which includes, among other things, the right to use their property and to exclude others from it. In such a framework, the owner's rights of use and exclusion are exercised over the same domain. The right to use and the right to exclude are complementary attributes of a unified bundle of property rights.

A model of fragmented property allows us to link the welfare losses due to the lack of unity in the internal content of property. For example, a dismemberment of property with a resulting discrepancy between the rights of use and exclusion held by the various owners produces welfare losses. Such problems are not confined to situations of insufficient or excessive physical fragmentation of ownership (such as those considered in the traditional economic literature), but also result from the dismemberment – and resulting non conformity – between the internal, functional, or legal entitlements of the property.

As shown by Parisi *et al.* (2000), the qualitative results of the commons and anticommons models represent limit points along a continuum, each characterized by different levels of discrepancy between use and exclusion rights, with welfare losses varying accordingly.

Rational owners and property fragmentation

Given an array of exploitation opportunities, a single property owner will choose the optimal level of fragmentation that maximizes the discounted present value of property; in contrast, the model of fragmented property highlights the cost of dispersed decision-making power and exclusion rights. If each property owner has exclusive authority to decide whether to contribute his or her property fragment to a joint value-enhancing project, then these uncoordinated decision rights create a problematic friction in the reallocation of resources, and, consequently, a suboptimal level of reunification.

Each of the owners of the fragmented property rights wants to maximize his total revenue from participation in the joint project. By pursuing this goal, each person does not fully consider the effect of his participation choice on the other owners, leading to an overall under-exploitation of the joint investment opportunity.[10]

Even though in the present papers I focus on examples of functional or legal fragmentation of property, there are some interesting similarities between situations of fragmented ownership and situations of joint ownership. In the usual joint ownership situation (e.g. joint ownership of a parcel of land), either owner can exclude, with an effect that may be likened to the anticommons problem of fragmented ownership. This similarity is interesting, considering that joint ownership and fragmented ownership seem superficially opposite. But, from the point of view of asymmetric transaction costs, there are some significant economic differences between joint ownership and fragmented ownership that should be anticipated explicitly at this point.

For this purpose, it is important to observe that the strategic impediments to property reunification are the result of a "veto" power held by property owners.[11] Whenever joint owners are subject to a unanimity rule for deciding on the use of their jointly held property, the veto problem arises, in spite of the different apparent structure of joint and fragmented ownership. But important differences remain, due to the different incentives of joint versus fragmented owners in the face of a value-enhancing use opportunity.[12]

This logic rests on the tragedy of the anticommons. Like for a typical anticommons case, none of the parties has an opportunity to internalize the full benefit and costs of his control over the common resource, leading to an inefficient result. As pointed out by Parisi *et al.* (2000), if individual co-owners, acting under conditions of individualistic competition, have concurrent controls on entry, they will exercise exclusion rights, even when the use of the common resource by one party could yield net social benefits. To put it differently, some common resources will remain idle even in the economic region of positive marginal productivity[13] because the multiple holders of exclusion rights do not fully internalize the cost created by the enforcement of their right to exclude others.

A fragmented property problem leads to two kinds of externalities. First, the exercise of a right of exclusion by one member reduces or eliminates the value of similar rights held by other individuals, causing static (or current) externalities. In price theory terms, one can think of this externality as the cross price effect of the various exclusion rights. Second, withholding productive resources may create dynamic (or future) externalities, because the underuse of productive inputs today has consequences for the future, as standard growth theory suggests.

The analysis of these conditions reveals that the uncoordinated choices and the strategic costs faced by the fragmented property owners lead to under exploitation of the joint project opportunities, compared to the unified ownership alternative.

The asymmetric Coase theorem

In a world of zero transaction costs, an efficient allocation of resources occurs regardless of (a) the initial allocation, or degree of fragmentation, of the legal entitlement and (b) the choice of remedies to protect the resources in question. The Coase theorem suggests that if all rights are freely transferable and transaction costs are zero, an inefficient initial partitioning of property rights will not prevent an efficient final use of the resources. If the property is inefficiently divided, the owners of the various property fragments will reunify them, automatically maximizing the total value of the resource.

Once the ideal conditions of the positive Coase theorem are relaxed, however, the efficiency of the final allocation depends on the initial division of resources and on the availability of remedies that facilitate the reunification of fragmented property, when necessary. As for the general case, the dual objective is to allocate entitlements initially in a way that minimizes the effects of the positive transaction costs and, if the rights and entitlements are already assigned, choose legal rules to reduce the social welfare losses by facilitating optimal levels of reunification.

I will proceed by considering the related questions of (a) optimal allocation of rights; and (b) optimal remedial protection, given asymmetric transaction costs.

Allocating entitlements in the presence of asymmetric transaction costs

The social problem of optimal allocation of rights in a situation with asymmetric transaction costs is qualitatively similar to the single owner's dilemma of dividing his property among different uses when he faces subsequent reallocation costs.

In a world with perfect information, the single owner would always select an initial allocation that results in an efficient final use of the resource. With perfect foresight and information, the single owner would thus be able to optimize the use of his property, in spite of the positive transaction (or transfer) costs, reaching the same equilibrium that could be achieved in a world of zero transaction costs. Under these ideal conditions, transaction (or transfer) costs do not impede the optimal final allocation of resources.

Not surprisingly, this result changes if we introduce imperfect information. With uncertainty, the efficiency of the final allocation will in fact depend on (a) the likelihood that any feasible initial assignment coincides with the optimal final allocation, and (b) the costs of reallocating rights in the event of an initial mistaken allocation.

From a policy perspective, the central lawmaker will use the one-agent equilibrium as a benchmark for the optimal allocation of resources. According to this simple extension of the normative Coase theorem, the optimal allocation of rights under: (i) imperfect information, and (ii) asymmetric transaction costs would follow the logic, as follows.

Assume a finite set of possible initial allocations, I, and a finite set of possible final allocations, J. For the sake of this qualitative argument, allocations of rights will be mapped into unique integers i and j, represented in the sets I and J respectively. $P(i)$ is the exogenous frequency with which allocation i is the most efficient final allocation. $\phi(i)$ is the endogenous frequency with which allocation i is chosen as the initial allocation (i.e. our policy control variable). The notation C_{ij} denotes the cost of moving from allocation i to allocation j. More generally, let reallocation costs vary from case to case. I allow for one-directional stickiness in the reallocation costs generating asymmetric transaction costs.

The reallocation cost function can thus be defined as

$$C_{ij}(\phi, \rho, p) = K(1 - \delta_{ij}) \cdot g(\rho, Np(j) \cdot \phi(i))$$

$$C_{ii} = 0, \quad \text{as} \quad \delta_{ij} = 0, \quad i \neq j, \quad \delta_{ij} = 1, \quad i = j$$

$$C'_{\phi} > 0, \quad C''_{\phi} > 0; \quad C'_{\rho} > 0, \quad C''_{\rho} > 0 \tag{4.1}$$

The index δ_{ij} is Kronecker's delta function; there are no costs when reallocating a right to its current use. C, the reallocation costs, are assumed to be an increasing function, g, of the level of property-type protection, ρ. As usual, I assume that there are increasing marginal costs for reallocating rights. Marginal administrative costs thus increase with the total expected number of the mistaken allocations requiring judicial intervention, $N_p(i) \cdot \phi(j)$. This implies that marginal costs increase with an increasing frequency of *ex post* reallocations.[14] The function g has therefore positive second derivatives in both arguments.[15]

The factor K captures the one-directional stickiness of the allocation process so that different costs C_1 and C_2 will be faced when reallocating from i to j and from j to i, respectively:

$$K = \begin{cases} C_1 \, \forall \, (i \to j) \\ C_2 \, \forall \, (j \to i) \end{cases} \quad \text{and} \quad C_1 < C_2 \tag{4.2}$$

For any initial allocation i, the expected cost of moving to the efficient outcome, at any given level of property right protection, ρ, is:

$$E(i|\bar{\rho}) = \sum_{j \in J} p(j) C_{ij} \tag{4.3}$$

Faced with a choice among alternative allocations of limited resources, a benevolent policymaker would carry out the same cost–benefit analysis that would be undertaken by the single owner of multiple entitlements. In selecting the optimal allocation, any rational agent would estimate the expected values of the n alternative allocations, $E(i)$, and would select the initial allocation yielding the highest net value.

In order to minimize the expected costs of future transfers, the optimal initial allocation minimizes equation (4.1) with respect to the control variable $\phi(i)$. The minimization of the expected costs will inform the selection of an initial allocation designed to minimize both the expected aggregate cost of its potential inefficiency and the transaction costs of changing to a more efficient allocation.

For a multidimensional problem with asymmetric transaction costs, the optimal social allocation is the one that maximizes the expected value of the final allocation at the net of the expected transaction costs, if reallocation is necessary.

$$\underset{i}{\text{Min}} E(i|\bar{\rho}) = \sum_{i \in I} \left\{ \phi(i) \sum_{j \in J} p(j) C_{ij} \right\} \quad C_{ij} \neq C_{ji} \tag{4.4}$$

This minimization requires the estimation of $p(j)$, that is, the respective probabilities that each alternative allocation may coincide with the desired final allocation, and C_{ij}, that is, the directional reallocation costs among different uses.

It is worth noting that this optimization process requires both the assessment of the likelihood of different situations arising in the future, and the evaluation of the impact of asymmetric transaction costs in the context of the uncertainty over the optimal final allocations. To solve the allocation problem under uncertainty in our case, it would be necessary to consider: (a) the relative cost of reallocating from the initial allocation i to the efficient allocation j, which we have denoted C_{ij}; and (b) the probability $P(i)$ that allocation i is the most efficient final allocation, among the n possible alternative allocations.

The presence of asymmetric transaction costs renders the present optimization problem different from the usual case of the normative Coase theorem. In the usual formulation of the Coase theorem under symmetric transaction costs, $C_{ij} = C_{ji}$, the optimization problem is simplified and ends up with an optimal choice determined by the respective probability of alternative efficient final allocations. The optimal initial allocation coincides with the most likely efficient final allocation (i.e. $i^* = \text{Max}\ \{P(i)\}$).

In the presence of asymmetric transaction costs, $C_{ij} \neq C_{ji}$, the optimal initial allocation is derived considering the costs and benefits of alternative allocations, taking such asymmetry into account.

Choosing the optimal remedy

According to the well-known normative formulations of the Coase theorem, if the initial allocation of rights and resources has already been made, deadweight losses depend on the choice of remedial protection for such rights. Most notably, Calabresi and Melamed (1972) point out that, in the presence of positive transaction costs, the choice between property-type and liability-type remedies has important efficiency consequences. When an entitlement is protected by a property-type remedy, its transfer can only occur with the owner's consent, at the price he demands, creating the conditions for hold-up problems. In the presence of high transaction costs, liability rules are thus more likely to induce efficient reallocations of rights and resources.

These well-known considerations have provided the basis for much of the common wisdom during the last 25 years in the law and economics profession. Over the same period, however, several scholars have challenged the validity of the Calabresi and Melamed framework, pointing to the limitations of liability-type protection.[16] These critiques have led to various refinements of the original Calabresi and Melamed (1972) framework, which shall be taken into consideration in the present analysis.

In studying the design of optimal remedies in cases of asymmetric transactions costs, one must recognize that the law and economics literature identifies several arguments to refute the hypothesis that liability-type and property-type remedies are equivalent in low transaction cost environments. Most recently,

Kaplow and Shavell (1996, 768ff.) have identified several factors, each casting doubt on such equivalence.[17] These scenarios include: (a) the threat of sequential takings under a liability rule to undermine the owner's bargaining power, as his remaining entitlements would be vulnerable to attack; (b) the risk of reciprocal takings, leading to a destructive contest between owner and the taker to retain final control of the asset; (c) the rent dissipation that will result from costs that both owners and takers would incur in both protecting their property and in an attempting to acquire control of their opponent's assets; (d) inefficiencies resulting from the limited liability, and resulting suboptimal incentives, of judgment-proof takers; and (e) the increased administrative costs of enforcing a liability-type rule.

The alternative remedies force the parties involved to reveal different amount of information. As property-type and liability-type remedies have different effects on the incentives of the parties to reveal information in the bargaining process. Under a property-type remedy, the owner will never receive less than the value he places on his entitlements and will on average be able to extract part of the buyer's surplus. In contrast, under a liability-type remedy, the owner will not be able to extract the taker's surplus. Kaplow and Shavell (1996, p. 771) mention this issue when discussing the causes of differential distribution of income under the two remedies. The different mechanisms at work, however, have more than merely distributional consequences, given the inability of liability-type remedies to capture the owner's subjective value of the entitlement. Transfers under a liability rule do not guarantee the efficiency of the final allocation, because it is impossible to know for certain that the taker actually values the entitlement more than the original owner, who may have unquantifiable sentimental value in the property.[18]

As a result, non-consensual transfers further reduce an owner's incentive to undertake specific investments that would increase his subjective value of the property. Most liability rules, in fact, do not compensate the sunken costs or owner-specific investments, increasing the victim's subjective loss, but rather base payment on average market values and so partially ignore the forgone consumer surplus of the victim. Threatened by a non-consensual takings, an owner is unlikely to make specific investments in his property. The same is true of the forgone "endowment effect" of the current owner (Kahneman and Tversky, 1979; Hanemann, 1991). In as much as the risk of non-consensual takings results in a non-compensated loss of "endowment valuation," a liability rule would create a reduction in bondage opportunities with a loss of consumer surplus.

Finally, as pointed out by Krier and Schwab (1995) liability rules tend to reduce the incentives of people to learn how to bargain through property rules.

Optimal remedies in the presence of asymmetric transaction costs

In light of the previous considerations, I now consider the optimal choice of remedies in the context of asymmetric transaction costs. I assume that, *ceteris paribus*, property-type remedies encourage owner-specific investments, thereby increasing the value of the entitlement for the current owner and producing a socially preferable result to liability-type responses. In order to maintain the general applicability of the analysis, I consider the property-liability nature of the remedy as a continuous variable, denoted as ρ. I model the value of property entitlements for the owner, V_i, as an increasing function of the property-type protection, ρ, granted to those rights. This assumes that the private and social value of the entitlement is a monotonically increasing function of the property-type remedial variable, ρ, with decreasing marginal benefits (i.e. $V_i' > 0$ and $V_i'' < 0$).

Following the traditional wisdom in the law and economics literature, I recognize that property-type remedies increase the transaction costs whenever a reallocation of resources is necessary. I assume the usual cost curvature, $C_{ij}' > 0$ and $C_{ij}'' > 0$. Given the continuous remedial variable, ρ, I model the choice of property protection as an optimization problem that changes the remedy both in terms of (a) the value of property in its status quo allocation, and (b) the transfer costs and possible allocational inefficiency, if a different allocation becomes necessary. Such optimization problem can be formulated as follows:

$$\operatorname*{Max}_{\rho} W(\rho | N\phi(i) \cdot p(j)) = \sum_{i \in I} \sum_{j \in J} \{V_i(\rho) - \phi_i \cdot p_j C_{ij}(\rho)\}$$

$$V_i' > 0, \quad V_i'' > 0; \quad C_{ij}' > 0, \quad C_{ij}'' > 0 \qquad (4.5)$$

The *ex ante* choice of an optimal remedy should balance the expected marginal costs and benefits of alternative levels of remedial protection, taking into account the effect of asymmetric transaction costs. For the reasons expressed above, the value of the current property allocation, $V_i(\rho)$, increases with the level of property-type protection. An increase in property protection, however, increases the expected costs of reallocating the use of fragmented property, $C_{ij}(\rho)$. Such *ex post* reallocations become necessary with frequency $\phi_i \cdot p_j$, that is, the product of the probabilities of the respective initial and final allocations for all $i \neq j$.

Comparing the first order conditions of the optimal remedies for the realloca-tion of rights between i and j, we can see that, given the one-directional stickiness in the exchange process, asymmetric remedies are desirable. For example, if the transfer cost from allocation i to allocation j is lower than the cost of the transfer back from j to i, allocation j may be granted a lower level of property-type protection, ρ, compared to allocation i. This result can be easily confirmed by inspection of the first order conditions of the social value function (4.5):

$$\sum_{i \in j} \sum_{j \in J} \left(\frac{\partial V_i}{\partial \rho} - p_J \frac{\partial C_{ij}}{\partial \rho} \right) = 0 \quad \text{at} \quad \rho^* \qquad (4.6)$$

For (4.6) to characterize a maximum, the first order conditions should be inter-preted to require a balancing of the marginal benefit of a change in ρ (i.e. the marginal increase in the value of property in its current allocation) with the discounted marginal cost of such increased protection (i.e. the marginal change in reallocation costs). Optimization thus requires:

$$\frac{\partial V_i}{\partial \rho} = p_j \frac{\partial C_{ij}}{\partial \rho} \; \forall i \tag{4.7}$$

It is possible to note from (4.7) that any change in costs $C_{ij} \neq C_{ji}$ requires a change in the value of ρ, for the equality to hold. The solution of our optimization problem thus implies that asymmetric optimal remedies $\rho_{ij}{}^* \neq \rho_{ji}{}^*$ are necessary for all cases of asymmetric transaction costs $C_{ij} \neq C_{ji}$. Optimal remedies are thus determined by the expected directional costs in the contractual or property relationship, as opposed to the average or total transaction costs in the relationship.

The dilemma of fragmented property

By articulating the problem of non-conforming property rights in terms of choosing the optimal remedy, we can revisit the three commonly enlisted solutions. Entitlements can be protected by property rules (transfer of the entitlement requires a voluntary sale by its holder),[19] liability rules (another party may destroy the entitlement if he is willing to pay an objectively determined value for it), or rules of inalienability (transfer of the entitlement is not permitted, even between a willing seller and a willing buyer).

In our model we can think of the three alternatives as different values of ρ, where $0 \leq \rho \leq 1$. The value $\rho = 0$ characterizes a world with liability-type remedial protection, which minimizes the transaction and strategic cost of reallocating the right, $C_{ij} \, (\rho = 0) = 0$. The value $\rho = 1$ characterizes the inalienability regime with infinite costs for any prospective reallocation $C_{ij} \, (\rho = 1) = \infty$. The intermediate values of ρ represent liability-type regimes, with transaction costs ranging from zero to infinity, according to the degree of strategic bargaining between the parties.[20] In our specific context, the choice of remedy should take into account the peculiar asymmetry of the transaction costs created by a dysfunctional fragmentation of property. Choosing a remedy in such an asymmetric scenario requires balancing a wide range of concerns.

Calabresi and Melamed (1972) showed that for the general case of positive transaction costs, property-type remedies may impede efficient reallocations of rights. Likewise, inalienability rules foreclose value enhancing property arrangements because courts and legislatures are unable to evaluate the subjective value and idiosyncratic preferences of the parties. Therefore, liability rules emerge as the best candidate for the difficult task of balancing individual autonomy against efficiency concerns when there are positive transaction and strategic costs.[21]

In the realm of non-conforming property arrangements, positive transaction costs often generate one-directional stickiness in the transfer of legal entitlements. As discussed above, externalities and holdouts are two major impediments to transfers, which are directly related to each other in the anticommons setting.

The optimal legal remedy will minimize the net social cost of both externality and holdout costs in any particular institutional setting.

Quite interestingly, the asymmetry may justify the selective use of different remedies for the same entitlement or relationship, as this hybrid approach is a potential instrument for correcting the asymmetric frictions encountered in the transfer of such rights. In this setting, legal rules may offer different remedial protection in two legal situations that first appear equivalent because the asymmetric, strategic, and transactional impediments to the transfer of such rights justify the differing treatment of apparently identical legal positions.

This paper submits that courts and legislators, consciously or unconsciously, account for the asymmetric effects of property fragmentation with a selective use of remedies to compensate for the one-directional stickiness of the voluntary exchange. Likewise, legal systems take into account the asymmetric transaction costs caused by right fragmentation and select default rules designed to minimize the total deadweight losses of property fragmentation.

In the following section I will briefly discuss some of the areas of the law where this hypothesis can be applied.

Asymmetric remedies and the principles of unified property

I suggest that legal systems have in different ways developed rules that are consistent with the solution to the asymmetric Coase theorem. Legal systems attempt to identify the optimal choice of rules and structure of remedies that will minimize the total deadweight losses from dysfunctional property fragmentation.

Modern legal systems avail themselves of different dogmatic constructs, but three main approaches generally are employed to balance the effects of these non-conforming property arrangements: (a) the creation of rules promoting reunification mechanisms for neglected or outmoded property rights; (b) granting selective remedial protection for atypical property rights; and (c) jurisprudential creation of a general principle of *favor libertatis*, namely a strong presumption in favor of unified and unrestricted ownership. These legal instruments will be discussed next.

Reunification mechanisms for fragmented property

In recent years, the proliferation of atypical property arrangements (such as private communities and residential subdivisions) has necessitated reunification mechanisms to deal with anticommons problems. Modern property law includes a sort of "gravitational force" which joins property fragments and terminates obscure, neglected, or outmoded property claims. As pointed out by Rose (1999), legal systems pursue this goal in a variety of ways, disposing of unduly burdensome claims against property and limiting the right to oppose property transactions only to the original parties and to third parties who had sufficient notice of the arrangement. Recording systems are a key factor: unrecorded or unregistered claims, for example, are forfeited against innocent third party buyers. Other contractual limitations on the use of property that are not visible or properly recorded also cannot be enforced against subsequent purchasers.[22]

Similarly, rules of liberative and acquisitive prescription (at civil law) and statutes of limitation (at common law) are also frequently used to extinguish outmoded property claims. In some common law jurisdictions, real covenants automatically expire after a statutorily fixed period of time unless renewed (Dwyer and Menell, 1998). In civil law jurisdictions, full property rights are not subject to liberative prescription,[23] but limited property rights often are. For example, the term for the prescription of *nominate* property rights is usually 20 or 30 years.[24] In contrast, one must bring action for injunction or damages if an innominate or atypical property right (such as building restriction or subdivision covenants) is violated in a much shorter period of time.[25] In all these cases, statutes of limitation do not merely bar the action to enforce the atypical property right, but rather extinguish the real right itself, in essence reunifying the fragmented property with respect to third parties.[26] Upon prescription of the rights, the restrictions are treated as if they never existed, and the property is permanently freed of all the burdens that had been violated.[27]

These rules have been applied quite liberally. For example, according to traditional civil law principles, liberative prescription can only accrue against actual violations to which there has been no response for the entire duration of the statute of limitation. This approach is consistent with the conception of *usucapio libertatis*, namely the reinstatement of complete freedom of use after the extinction of pre-existing restrictions on the property. But courts are often much more active, freeing the property from other related limitations.[28] Likewise, courts have construed the prescription of a restriction against a given property parcel as tantamount to abandoning the restriction for the entire community or subdivision,[29] resulting in an exponential increase in the reunification of fragmented property.

From a policy perspective, these doctrines are problematic, since they undermine the force and stability of the original contract to restrict the use of the land. Such doctrines, however, can be explained as attempts to mitigate the effects of asymmetric transaction costs and resulting inefficiencies of fragmented property.[30] In most cases, the availability of these *ex post* reunification mechanisms protects the integrity of the *ex ante* fragmentation of property: because the dangers of entropy in property and anticommons welfare losses are eliminated, the value of the initial decision to fragment the property is maintained.

Asymmetric transaction costs and the selective use of remedies

Selective remedies also minimize the effect of fragmentation and anticommons losses. Quite interestingly, even legal systems that have recognized new forms of atypical property provide them less remedial protection. In contrast to other real rights (e.g. affirmative or negative easements) at common law, atypical real rights (such as real covenants) are enforceable only with damages.[31] Indeed, although it is now recognized that covenants transfer with land, an individual still cannot obtain an injunction to enforce his rights even upon proof of a valid covenant. The right holder can obtain a judicial declaration of his rights, but the defendant can persist in the violation simply by paying damages.

The limited protection given to atypical (or innominate) rights still characterizes the modern-day law of remedies in both common law and civil law jurisdictions. Professors of Property law often cite this fact as one of the many unexplained puzzles of their field,[32] assuming that availability of liability-type remedies for certain categories of real rights is merely coincidental. In a popular textbook on property, Dwyer and Menell (1998, p. 760) observe that "because of one of the many historical accidents that plague property law, real covenants are enforced by a damages remedy only." I suggest that these anomalies are not merely happenstance.

As discussed above, the asymmetrical effects of entropy in property dictate that remedies should be determined based on the expected directional costs, as opposed to the average or total transaction costs in the contract or property relationship. This justifies a system that favors more liberal use of property-type remedies when redressing claims of owners of non-fragmented property and that requires limited liability-type protection in response to claims concerning dysfunctional property. This selective use of remedies is analogous to a gravitational force that can overcome entropy in property. These legal mechanisms promote the reunification of rights and privileges that should naturally be held by a single owner, given their complementarity. This reunification regenerates the natural conformity between the complementary attributes of a right (e.g. between use and exclusion rights), even though, because of the natural laws of entropy, the restoration of the *status quo ante* requires additional expenditures.[33]

Interestingly, most of these default reunification mechanisms do not apply with respect to typical property rights,[34] which, in fact, already are internal consistent, thereby eliminating the need to favor reunification over preserving the *status quo*. Conversely, non-conforming property arrangements (i.e. those that dismember the closely complementary attributes of a property right) are either (a) subject to time limitations, or (b) enjoy the effect of automatic reunification mechanisms discussed in the previous section. In addition, application of selective remedies can minimize the welfare loss occasioned by dysfunctional fragmentation of property.

Only substantial and systematic asymmetries in transaction costs, could justify the use of directional remedies.[35] Examples of such asymmetries include those produced by (a) structural attributes of the relationship; (b) an uneven number of parties; or (c) asymmetric strategic incentives among the contracting parties. Whenever such systematic differences are expected, remedies might be chosen in order to minimize the expected social deadweight loss that could vary within the same relationship in response to a wide range of concerns.

"Favor libertatis" and the natural conception of property

The recognition of new forms of property rights further necessitated the articulation of general principles to minimize the risk of entropy in property. These principles are derived from the concepts of absolute property, advocated by eighteenth-century jurists, and most are simple applications of the ideals of unity in property.

The resulting conception of property as an absolute right suggests that owners enjoy property through a direct relationship with the thing they own, without any need for cooperation by third parties. This characterization of an absolute right distinguishes it from the nature of a relative right (such as personal obligations and credit rights) the fulfillment of which depends on the active cooperation of another party. This classification of rights has given succeeding generations powerful rhetoric in which absolute rights (such as property and right of the person) only create negative obligations enforceable *erga omnes*, effectively equating property with (negative) freedom.[36] During the twentieth century, the equation between the structure of absolute rights and freedom became commonplace in legal, economic, and political theory.

Civil law courts have also subscribed to this general principle, developing an interpretive presumption in favor of a unified property that is often referred to as the *favor libertatis* principle. It suggests that restrictive burdens on property must be interpreted to promote, to the extent possible, the freedom of the burdened property.[37] This presumption is clearly related to the post-French Revolution ideals of unity in property. From a purely interpretive perspective, however, it departs from the general principles governing the interpretation of contracts, which mandate that the contracts should be interpreted to ensure that they can produce some effects, even if such effects limit the property's freedom.

In the absence of a general presumption of *favor libertatis*, common law courts have taken another approach to unity, enshrined in the doctrine of "changed circumstances." This allows courts to eliminate restrictions that have lost their original purpose and value, without having to obtain the unanimous consent of the various right holders (Rose, 1999). A subdivision restriction, for example, might require the use of outmoded architectural details or the use of outdated and inefficient building materials. A contractual abrogation of such subdivision covenant may prove difficult because of the likely holdout problems of the various property-holders' rights.

Traditionally, common law jurisdictions enforced real covenants at law even though changes in the surrounding environment (e.g. gradual transformation of a residential subdivision into a commercial or industrial area) undermined the original purpose and value of the parties' covenant. In recent years, however, the majority of states have adopted a different rule to deal with obsolete real covenants, holding that the doctrine of changed circumstances is a defense to a claim for damages and may be used to terminate a real covenant.[38]

If a sufficient number of covenant restrictions have been violated, courts tend to consider the general subdivision plan as abandoned.[39] At that point, all other covenant restrictions are extinguished and the use of the property is freed for all general purposes (Yiannopoulos, 1983).[40]

Rational owners and the relevance of alternative remedies

The ideal choice of remedy for entropy should consider the effects of a dysfunctional fragmentation of property, balancing a wide range of concerns. As for the general case, policymakers should consider that the choice of alternative remedies has both prospective and retrospective effects.

Prospectively, alternative remedies would lead rational owners to make different decisions under property as opposed to liability rules. Differently from what argued by Epstein (1982), I suggest that, in the absence of an appropriate choice of remedies, the rationality of the property owners will not be sufficient to minimize the cost of entropy in property. Rational parties – it is conceded – will anticipate any devaluation from fragmentation and would take into account the expected present value of forgone opportunities when fragmenting the entitlement. But the (rationally chosen) level of fragmentation will differ under different remedies. In a liability-type regime, owners would choose a level of fragmentation of their property, considering the lower expected reallocation costs induced by the liability remedy. Conversely, under a property-type rule, owners would choose a different (and lower) level of fragmentation, given the higher costs of rebundling property at a later stage. In sum, the choice of different remedies affects the social loss occasioned by the rational choices of property owners, simply because rational owners would make different choices under different remedies.

Retrospectively, the choice of different remedies has an important effect on the control of entropy in property. In the realm of non-conforming property arrangements, entropy generates one-directional stickiness in the transfer of legal entitlements. As discussed earlier, externalities and holdouts are two major impediments to rebundling fragmented property. The optimal legal remedy will be the one that minimizes the net social cost of externalities and holdout costs in any particular institutional setting. In the property context, the presence of one-directional transaction and strategic costs would justify a more selective use of liability-type remedies.[41] The hypothesis that legal systems would grant a less extensive property-type protection in favor of non-conforming property arrangements seems to find some support in the comparative study of real remedies. Likewise, other legal rules may create default reunification mechanisms. Time limits, statutes of limitation, liberative prescription, rules of extinction for non-use, and so on, can all be regarded as legal devices to facilitate the (otherwise costly and difficult) reunification of non-conforming fragments of a property right.

These legal solutions can be analogized to a gravitational force, reunifying rights that, given their strict complementarity, would naturally be held by a single owner. This tendency toward reunification works to rebundle property rights in order to regenerate the natural conformity between use and exclusion rights (and, more generally, between any two complementary fragments of property).

Conclusions

Dysfunctional property fragmentation generates one-directional stickiness in the transfer of legal entitlements.

The recognition of such one-directional friction lays out a promising research agenda for the study of laws and institutions designed to cope with such asymmetry. Along the lines of other well known efficiency hypotheses of the common law, a positive hypothesis can be formulated according to which courts and legislators, consciously or unconsciously, account for the asymmetric effects of property fragmentation in designing default rules and remedies. This tendency may be reflected in the legal system's reluctance to grant extensive property-type protection in favor of non-conforming property arrangements and in the creation of default reunification mechanisms for atypical property right arrangements.

If any normative corollary should be articulated, it should be a note of caution in the current trend of toward diffuse and fragmented "propertization." The formulation of a unitary framework of property is extremely valuable in this respect, pointing to the critical content of the traditionsl dogmas of unified and absolute property.

The reformulation of the Coase theorem for the case of asymmetric transaction costs reveals that the adoption of dual remedies allows for a more liberal use of property-type remedies in some high-transaction-cost relationships, without creating inefficient impediments to the optimal reallocation of rights.

Notes

1 Professor of Law and Director, Law and Economics Program, George Mason University, School of Law. I would like to thank Mike Mollerus, Clay Gillette, Paul Mahoney and Paul Stephan, III for their valuable comments during the early development of this idea.
2 I am using this term to refer to the second law of thermodynamics, according to which every process that can occur spontaneously will go in one direction only and will result in a release of energy that cannot be recaptured, so that the amount of entropy in the universe will continually increase.
3 Heller (1999) cites the fairy tale of Humpty Dumpty to illustrate his point. When Humpty Dumpty is shattered into pieces even all the king's horses and all the king's men can not reassemble him, which stands in contrast to the ease with which he broke into pieces in the first place.
4 As in the physical world, where it takes considerable additional energy to roll a rock back up a hill, after it has rolled down on its own, it takes considerable financial and legal effort to reunite property rights that have been split. Parisi *et al.* (2000) observe that even reversing a simple property transaction can result in monopoly pricing by the buyer-turned-seller; reunifying property that has been split among multiple parties engenders even higher costs given the increased difficulty of coordination among the parties.
5 Non conformity between use and exclusion rights (and more generally, between any two complementary elements of a property right) often give rise to asymmetric transaction and strategic costs.
6 Not all division of property is dysfunctional: the fragmentation of a large estate into lots that can be developed may well be desirable. Difficulties arise when closely complementary property rights, such as the right to use land and exclude others from it, are separated.
7 In a related paper Parisi (2001) suggests that property is subject to a fundamental law of entropy, namely that it is affected by one-directional bias leading toward increasing fragmentation. The paper further suggests that the application of the laws of entropy to property indicates that the one-directional tendency toward fragmentation can be avoided only in the purely abstract world of zero transaction costs.
8 In a related paper, we utilize this conception of unified property to explain the rise and fall of functional conceptions of property in Western legal history (Depoorter *et al.*, 2000).

9 The relevant variable along the commons-anticommons continuum is given by the degree of substitutability, or complementarity, between the various components of the property right. The inefficiencies monotonically increase with the degree of complementarity of the property fragments. In the commons case, the use rights are substitutes with respect to the residual value of the property (e.g. the reduction in the use of any of the joint owners is sufficient to increase the residual value of the property). In the anticommons case, the exclusion rights are perfect complements with respect to the valued use of the property (e.g. the consent of all exclusion right holders is necessary for any use of the joint property).

10 The misalignment of incentives results from positive externalities that are not captured in calculating the interests of the right holders (Parisi *et al.*, 2000). This result has been first illustrated by Buchanan and Yoon (2000), with respect to joint property owners who can independently sell "permits" concerning the use of the commonly owned resource. In order to use the property, third party users need to obtain a permit which is independently priced and sold by each co-owner.

11 We can think of the consent of each veto holder as a strict complement (or a fixed-proportion input) in the joint reunification decision.

12 To illustrate, we can think of the different "pricing" incentives of joint and fragmented owners. The decision of joint owners on whether to sell a common resource to a third party – even if subject to a unanimity rule – would be very different from the decision of fragmented owners selling, and independently pricing, their respective fragments to a third party. The reason for this difference is quite straightforward. Joint owners, have control on the sale of the joint property, but once the sale to a third party takes place, the revenue from the sale is divided in proportion to their respective shares of ownership. Conversely, fragmented owners price independently, controlling both the feasibility of the global sale to a third party and the distribution of surplus among the various fragmented owners. In the absence of sustainable price coordination, the equilibrium pricing of the fragmented owners would be different from that of the joint owners.

13 As pointed out in Parisi *et al.* (2000), if the common resource is subject to multiple anticommons-type exclusion rights, each co-owner will have incentives to withhold resources from other users to an inefficient level. This is implied by the fact that none of the investing parties obtains the full increment of the resulting revenue from an increase in their investment. Therefore all invest less than the efficient level. The problem of underutilization is exacerbated if the right is fragmented into more than two exclusion rights, with more than two agents deciding independently on their activity or price (Schulz, 2000). Buchanan and Yoon (2000) show that an increase in the number of agents with exclusionary rights enhances the problem of underutilization in their price-driven anticommons example. In more general form, Schulz (2000) shows that similar results are obtained in a quantity-driven anticommons setting. The results are consistent with the exacerbation of commons problem with an increase in the number of users. For example, in the symmetrical commons case, the Libecap and Wiggins (1984) study on common pool oil resources documented the positive correlation between the number of involved parties and the preemptive exploitation of the common pool resource.

14 The expected number of *ex post* reallocation for any initial allocation i is given by the product of the (exogenous) probability $p(j)$ (i.e. the probability that j would be the optimal final allocation) and the chosen frequency of allocation i, $\phi(i)$.

15 With linear cost functions, we would expect the most efficient final allocation to be always coinciding with the chosen initial allocation and all other alternative initial allocations to be chosen with probability zero. If there are convexities in the cost function (or other non linearities in the owners' utility functions) we may expect some mixed allocations with values of the control variable in the range $0 < \phi(i) < 1$.

16 In spite of such challenges the gist of the original proposition remains standing. Richard Epstein (1997), an eloquent exponent of the property right school, while advocating the general preferability of property-type remedies, concedes that liability rules dominate as the appropriate remedy for cases of necessity and large-scale holdout problems, subject to appropriate institutional safeguards.

17 Kaplow and Shavell (1996) explain why liability rules are often employed in cases of harmful externalities, while property rules are more commonly utilized to protect ownership and title, preventing non-consensual transfers of possessory interests in things.

18 The point is already present in the analysis of Calabresi and Melamed (1972, p. 1125).

19 Note that with high litigation costs, a liability rule effectively turns into a property rule favoring the injurer (see Kaplow and Shavell, 1996 p. 755). But the same may be said of property-type remedies that are too costly to enforce.

20 Parisi *et al.* (2000) specify the variables that are likely to determine the extent of strategic dissipation, which include, (a) the number of fragmented owners; (b) the degree of complementarity between the property fragments; and (c) the existence of effective price coordination mechanism and/or existence of outside competitive market constraints.

21 This is consistent with the general result of Calabresi and Melamed (1972), who have shown that, under most circumstances, liability-type remedies achieve a combination of efficiency and distributive results which would be difficult to attain under the alternative property-type and inalienability-type solutions.

22 Rose (1999) further observes that this creates incentives to publicize and to record their claims and, most importantly, to use standard-form property packages.

23 Property is obviously subject to acquisitive prescription (i.e. adverse possession).

24 See for example, Article 617 of the French Civil Code, setting a 30 year prescription term for *usufruct*. Likewise, Paragraph 195 of the German BGB establishes a general 30-year prescriptive period applicable to real actions. Conversely, Articles 970 and 1014 of the Italian Civil Code establish a 20-year prescription, for *emphyteusis* and *usufruct* rights, respectively.

25 For example, according to Article 781 of the Louisiana Civil Code (as revised in 1977), "no action for injunction or for damages on account of the violation of a building restriction may be brought after the lapse of two years from the commencement of a noticeable violation." See also the official Comment (a) under Article 781, which states that this provision does not change the law, when instead it has been emphatically noted by Yiannopoulos (1983) that such prescriptive terms depart substantially from the general rules governing the prescription of contractual obligations (with a 10, rather than 2-year prescription).

26 These prescription terms are often surprisingly short. See for example, the case of the Louisiana statute of limitations extinguishing the real rights after two years from the commencement of the violation. Note that, in the same jurisdiction, a personal action for the enforcement of restrictions would be subject to a much longer 10-year term of liberative prescription. See Lousiana (LA) Civil Code Article 3499, as revised in 1983; (formerly Article 3544 of the 1870 code). Also see Yiannopoulos (1983).

27 See Yiannopoulos (1983) discussing LA Civil Code Article 781, as revised in 1977.

28 According to long standing legal principles, the extinction of one type of a restriction due to the lapse of a statute of limitation does not affect the enforceability of other types of restrictions, nor does it extend to other situations (e.g. freeing other lots from the type of restriction that have been violated). Nonetheless, as Yiannopoulos (1983) points out, courts have recently held that when an owner uses his property for commercial purposes contrary to subdivision covenants during a period in excess of two years, the property is freed of all restrictions pertaining to commercial use.

29 According to Article 782 of the LA Civil Code, building restrictions terminate "by abandonment of the whole plan" or by "a general abandonment of a particular restriction." Abandonment, like prescription, does not merely bar the right of action for

the enforcement of restrictions; it extinguishes the real right. See LA Civil Code Article 782, as revised in 1977, extensively discussed in Yiannopoulos (1983).

30 Along similar lines, a survey of American property law by Michael Heller (1999) reveals what he terms a "boundary principle" which limits the right to subdivide private property into wasteful fragments. Property law responds to excessive fragmentation with the use of a variety of rules and doctrines such as the rule against perpetuities, zoning and subdivision restrictions, property taxes and registration fees, etc. See Heller (1999, pp. 1173–1174), citing zoning and subdivision restrictions such as minimum lot sizes, floor areas, and setbacks that prevent people from spatially fragmenting resources excessively. Heller suggests that, by making the creation and maintenance of fragments more costly, such as through annual disclosure expenses, excessive fragmentation into low-value fragments will be deterred and existing fragments will be abandoned so that the state can afterwards rebundle them.

31 In case of a breach of a real covenant, for example, the dominant landowner can only obtain relief through damages.

32 See also Stoebuck (1977).

33 Restoring the original natural arrangement requires legal and transactional efforts (just like rolling the stone back up the hill requires physical efforts with an increased expenditure of energy). In short, after the reunification things may look like they did before, but the journey is not without social costs.

34 Merrill and Smith (2000) pose the interesting question as to why such preoccupations arise only with respect to atypical real rights. The authors' conclusion dismisses Heller's (1999) anticommons explanation of the *numerus clausus* doctrine and suggests that the goal of such rules is the minimization of information costs.

35 The implementation of a paradigm of "directional remedies" obviously requires *ex ante* information concerning the magnitude of directional costs. The choice of remedies undertaken in the previous section, in fact, refers to *ex ante* choices of optimal remedies. Remedies are selected on the basis of the expected directional costs, and would not be applicable in situations where no systematic directional differences can be expected. An *ex post* evaluation of such costs, while potentially improving upon the allocational efficiency, would increase the uncertainty of the available remedial protection for the current owners, reducing the incentives for value-enhancing investments for rational, risk-averse owners.

36 Mattei (2000, p. 123) observes that the "taxonomy requiring the object of ownership to be a tangible material thing can be explained as an expulsion from the domain of property law of those powers not related to a physical relationship with land, as used to be the case with most feudal property rights."

37 As an application of this principle, documents that establish restrictive covenants must be interpreted in favor of, rather than against the freedom of the servient estate (Yiannopoulos, 1983).

38 *Hess v. Country Club Park*, 213 Cal. 613, 2 P.2d 782 (1931); *Restatement of Property* §564. For a more extensive discussion, see Dwyer and Menell (1998) and Stoebuck (1977).

39 In the Louisiana jurisprudence, the abandonment of a particular restriction is construed as an abandonment of a real covenant, affecting all parties to the original covenant. Changes in the vicinity of the subdivision, but not within it, are thus without effect on the validity of the building restrictions in the subdivision (Yiannopoulos, 1983).

40 Article 783 of the LA Civil Code declares that doubt "as to the existence, validity, or extent of building restrictions is resolved in favor of the unrestricted use of the immovable." According to Louisiana courts, since servitudes and covenant restrictions often have effects similar to those of other building restrictions, any covenant that establishes restrictions on property use ought to be interpreted in *favorem libertatis* (Yiannopoulos, 1983). Thus, when there is doubt as to the content or validity of a restriction (e.g. a question on the validity of a subdivision plan or real covenant), the doubt is resolved favoring the unrestricted use of property.

Yiannopoulos also provides several cases and examples explaining that when a particular subdivision restriction has been abandoned, the properties in the same subdivision are freed from that restriction only. Thus, a change in the neighborhood from residential to commercial does not automatically affect other functionally unrelated restrictions (e.g. setback from property lines) but may affect other functionally related limitations.

41 In the field of contracts, a more liberal use of specific performance may be expected with respect to contracts that are aimed at reunifying non-conforming fragments of property, rather than contracts that are aimed at creating such fragmentation. Recontracting is, in fact, substantially cheaper in the latter case, reducing the need to conserve the original agreement.

Bibliography

Alchian, Armen A. (1965), "Some Economics of Property Rights," 30 *Il Politico* (4), 816–829.

Ayres, I. and Eric Talley (1985), "Solomonic Bargaining: Dividing a Legal Entitlement To Facilitate Coasean Trade," 104 *Yale Law Journal*, 1027.

Banner, Stuart (1999), "Two Properties, One Land: Law and Space in 19th-Century New Zealand," *Law and Social Inquiry* (forthcoming-December 1999).

Buchanan, J. and Yong J. Yoon (2000), "Symmetric Tragedies: Commons and Anticommons Property," *Journal of Law and Economics*, forthcoming.

Calabresi, Guido and Melamed A. Douglas (1972), "Property Rules, Liability Rules and Inalienabilty: One View of the Cathedral," 85 *Harvard Law Review*, 1089–1128.

Coase, Ronald H. (1960), "The Problem of Social Cost," 3 *Journal of Law and Economics*, 1–44.

Depoorter, B. and Parisi, F. (2000), "Rethinking the Economic Foundations of Fair Use Doctrines and Authors' Moral Rights," ELER Working Papers.

Depoorter, B., Parisi, F., and Schulz, N. (2000), "Spatial v. Functional Conceptions: A Dual Model of Property," 5 *CASLE Working Paper Series*, 34.

Dwyer, John P. and Peter S. Menell (1998), *Property Law and Policy: A Comparative Institutional Perspective*, New York: Foundation Press.

Eggertsson, Thrainn (1990a), "The Role of Transaction Costs and Property Rights in Economic Analysis," 34 *European Economic Review*, 450–457.

Eggertsson, Thrainn (1990b), "Economic Behavior and Institutions," Cambridge: Cambridge University Press.

Ellickson, Robert C. (1991), *Order Without Law: How Neighbors Settle Disputes*, Cambridge, MA: Harvard University Press.

Ellickson, Robert C. (1993), "Property in Land," 102 *Yale Law Journal*, 1315–1344.

Ellickson, Robert C. and Tarlock, A. Dan (1981), *Land-Use Controls: Cases and Materials*, Little, Brown and Company, Boston and Toronto, 620.

Ellickson, Robert C., Rose, C.M. and Ackerman, B.A. (1995), *Perspectives on Property Law*, Boston, MA: Little, Brown.

Epstein, Richard A. (1982), "Notice and Freedom of Contract in the Law of Servitudes," 55 *Southern California Law Review*, 1353–1368.

Epstein, Richard A. (1997), "A Clear View of the Cathedral: The Dominance of Property Rules," 106 *Yale Law Journal*, 2091–2120.

Gordon, H.S. (1954), "The Economic Theory of a Common-Property Resource: the Fishery," 62 *Journal of Political Economy*, 124–142.

Hanemann, W. Michael (1991), "Willingness to Pay and Willingness to Accept: How Much Can They Differ?," 81 *American Economic Review*, 635–647.

Hardin, G. (1968), "The Tragedy of the Commons," 162 *Science*, 1243–1248.

Heller, M.A. (1998), "The Tragedy of the Anticommons: Property in the Transistion from Marx to Markets," 111 *Harvard Law Review*, 621.

Heller, M.A. (1999), "The Boundaries of Private Property," 108 *Yale Law Review*, 1163–1223.

Heller, M. and Eisenberg, R. (1998), "Can Patents Deter Innovation? The Anticommons in Biomedical Research," 280 *Science*, excerpted as "Upstream Patents = Downstream Bottlenecks" in 41.3 *Law Quadrangle Notes*, 93–97 (Fall/Winter 1998).

Kahneman, Daniel and Tversky, Amos (1979), "Prospect Theory: An Analysis of Decision Under Risk," 47 *Econometrica*, 263–291.

Kaplow, Louis and Steven Shavell (1996), "Property Rules Versus Liability Rules: An Economic Analysis," 109 *Harvard Law Review*, 713.

Krier, James E. and Schwab, Stewart J. (1995), "Property Rules and Liability Rules: The Cathedral from Another Light," 70 *NYU Law Review*, 440.

Libecap, Gary D. (1989), *Contracting for Property Rights*, Cambridge: Cambridge University Press, 132 p.

Libecap, Gary D. and Wiggins Steven N. (1984), "Contractual Respones to the Common Pool," 74 *American Economic Review*, 84.

Mattei, Ugo (2000), *Basic Principles of Property Law*, Westport, CT: Greenwood Press.

Michelman, Frank I. (1968), "Property, Utility and Fairness: Comments on the Ethical Foundations of 'Just Compensation' Law," 80 *Harvard Law Review*, 1165–1258.

Ostrom, Elinor (1977), "Collective Action and the Tragedy of the Commons," in Hardin, Garrett and Baden, John (eds), *Managing the Commons*, San Francisco, W.H. Freeman, 173–181.

Parisi, F. (1995), "Private Property and Social Cost," 2 *European Journal of Law and Economics*, 149–173.

Parisi, F. (2002), "Entropy in Property," *American Journal of Comparative Law,* 50, 595–622.

Parisi, F., Schulz, N., and Depoorter, B. (2000), "Duality in Property: Commons and Anticommons," University of Virginia Law and Economics Working Paper Series #00–08.

Rose, Carol M. (1986), "The Comedy of the Commons: Custom, Commerce, and Inherently Public Property," 53 *University of Chicago Law Review*, 711.

Rose, Carol M. (1994), *Property and Persuasion: Essays on the History, Theory and Rhetoric of Ownership*, Westview Press, Colorado, 317.

Rose, Carol M. (1999), "What Government Can Do for Property (and Vice Versa)," in Nicholas Mercuro and Warren Samuels (eds), *The Fundamental Interrelationship between Government and Property*, Connecticut: JAI Press Inc., 209–222.

Schulz, Norbert (2000), "Thoughts on the Nature of Vetoes When Bargaining on Public Projects," *Würzburg Economic Papers*, 00–17.

Scott, A.D. (1955), "The Fishery: the Objectives of Sole Ownership," 63 *Journal of Polital Economy*, 116–124.

Smith, Henry E. (2000), "Semicommon Property Rights and Scattering in the Open Fields," 29 *J. Legal Stud.*, 131.

Stoebuck, William B. (1977), "Running Covenants: An Analytical Primer," 52 *Washington Law Review* 861, 882–885.

Thomas W. Merrill and Henry E. Smith (2000), "Optimal Standardization in the Law of Property: The Numerus Clausus Principle," 110 *Yale Law Journal*, 1.

Yiannopoulos, A.N. (1983), *Civil Law Property Coursebook: Louisiana Legislation, Jurisprudence, and Doctrine*, 3rd edn, Baton Rouge: Claitor's.

5   On incomplete property

A missing perspective in law and economics?

Antonio Nicita

Introduction

This chapter explores the meaning and extent of incompleteness in property and its contribution to the current debate in the law and economics of property and property rights.

In economic theory the notion of incompleteness has been deeply analysed in the case of contracts (Hart, 1995; Bolton and Dewatripont, 2005; Nicita and Pagano, 2005), while the debate on incompleteness in property is still in its infancy, even if there are several relevant exceptions (Demsetz, 1967; Libecap, 2002).

The aim of this chapter is to outline the fundamental questions raising within the law and economics approach, when incompleteness applies not only to contracts but also to the institutions of property and property rights. The motivation for developing a research in this field lies in the circumstance that the origin of incompleteness in contracts is generally not attributed to specific features of the institution considered ('the contract') but it relies on the intrinsic limits of human nature. An *incomplete contract* is typically defined as an agreement where contractual obligations are observable to contractual parties but not verifiable *ex post* by third parties (a judge or an arbitrator) to whom parties might eventually recur when controversies arise. The emergence of (a degree of) un-verifiability of contractual terms might be generated by several circumstances, such as parties' bounded rationality and uncertainty on future events, high transaction costs in writing and accurately describing any contractual feature (also called 'ink costs'), high transaction costs to go to court and so on. All the above circumstances have to do with human pervasive inability to exactly define, foresee and enforce with certainty any contingency that might affect the economic performance of contractual arrangements.

In the analysis of contractual practices, there is ample room for uncertainty, bounded rationality, ambiguity, non-contractibility of uses, vagueness and incompleteness. Nothing as such can be envisaged in the literature on property rights. The *homo economicus* thus appears to be twofold: on one hand he is pervasively bounded in his capacity to *ex ante* define all the contingencies that may affect the content of bilateral contractual agreement, on the other, society in its entirety is always able to define a 'social contract' in which the institution of property is a fully defined object whose primary characteristics are that of securing full control over resources, thus promoting stability of expectations and incentives' alignment. One may thus observe a tension, if not a contradiction, between the economic analysis of contracts and the economic analysis of property and property rights. Looking at the law and economics theory of incomplete contracts one might ask whether abandoning the ideal-type of perfectly competitive markets also produces some relevant consequences on the way in which all the institutional frames for market (beside 'contracts') are established.

In the following paragraphs it is suggested how the notion of incomplete property affects the traditional meaning of externalities in economic theory and the necessity of clearly distinguishing between *ex ante* transaction costs (due to the externality induced by the degree of incompleteness in property) and *ex post* transaction costs (due to the vast array of market failures which inhibit Pareto-relevant exchanges) in Coase theorem.

Mirroring two nirvanas in law and economics: complete markets and complete property

According to one of the most authoritative definitions of contractual incompleteness (Hart, 1995), to say that some uses are non-contractible means saying that they are unverifiable by a third party, say a Court. However, if Courts are unable to solve controversies over incomplete contracts, it is at least odd to assume that they can easily ascertain the exact content of property. More generally, one might rightfully suspect that the sources of incompleteness in contracts may also extend at least to some of the 'uses' bundled in property.

For some economists the notion of incomplete property is simply an oxymoron: property is perceived as complete, and property rights are just economic goods in the traditional sense. Private property rights are excludable and non-rival economic goods. Thus as long as economic theory is able to define an economic good, it will be easy to define a correspondent property right and an associated market for that good. When the focus is exclusively related to private property rights the mainstream paradigm of *complete markets* in economics is thus usually coupled with that of *complete property rights*.

Some legal scholars would agree with the mainstream paradigm of complete markets.

In the *Black's Law Dictionary*, property is defined as 'the right to possess, use, enjoy a determinate thing (either a tract of land or a chattel)' or as 'the right of ownership' so that 'the institution of private property is protected from undue governmental interference', or finally as 'a bundle of rights'. The Blackstonian tradition, for instance, depicts property as 'the sole and despotic dominion' held in 'total exclusion' of the rights of others (Blackstone, 1766). According to that view the legal system that defines and protects property rights should always complete property rights in the specific sense that the design of 'despotic dominions' should grant owners against (reciprocal) interference. According to this view, if the legal system performs well, there are not islands of uncertainty (undefined ownership or incomplete exclusion) in the ocean of perfectly excludable property rights. Property thus is meant to be pervasive and ubiquitous. Here, the meaning of completeness in property rights is twofold: from one side property is complete in the sense that it includes all the attributes (uses and 'substance') of property which grants sole dominion to the owner; from the other, property is complete in the sense that the system of property rights is designed as a coherent institutional ordering such that the 'quality' of property rights (their definition and enforcement) is the same for every owner (that means that the quality of ownership rights does not depend on the specific features of the assets and/or on owners' economic conditions).

Above, there is a tension among these two 'legal' notions of 'complete' property. While the latter seems assuming that a *right/duty* relationship is defined over every actual and potential use embedded in the property bundle, so that any overlap among uses is an empty set, the former implies that the right/duty relationship is not necessarily defined over all actual and potential uses, but that a system of 'power' is established so as to grant a 'sole dominion' to the owner over actual and potential uses. With respect to this last approach, 'complete property' is defined as 'the entirety of the rights, privileges, powers, and immunities that is legally possible for a person to have with regard to land and, or any other thing, apart from those that all other member of society have in the land or thing' (*Black's Dictionary*). That means that 'complete property' here is interpreted as the set of legal and presumptive rights[1] which create a legal equilibrium (Pagano, 2006) such that property is always protected against externalities, that is, against others' claims over alternative and rival uses of the entitlements bundled in property (Nicita *et al.*, 2005).

The definition of complete property couples with the definition of complete markets. They are two legal and economic nirvanas since both refer to an ideal world in which economic and legal equilibria are stable without any evolutionary change in preferences, technology, economic opportunities and externalities. All the potential uses of property rights (and thus all the potential markets which might be generated by rights exchange) are perfectly defined and known from the beginning to all (actual and potential) economic agents. There are no conflicts and/or externalities: every use is already defined and has a marketable price so that economic resources are always allocated to their most valuable uses (and owners). When it is not defined, presumptive rights (i.e. the Hohfeldian relationship between power and immunity) are deemed as if they were legal defined rights.

When the ideal-type of complete markets and complete property is abandoned, the analysis is pushed into a more realistic world in which externalities abound and where conflicts over the definition and the allocation of property rights are pervasive. In such a world, what property is, that is, the nature and the extent of the uses bundled within, is not clearly defined once for all, rather it is continuously shaped by the nature of the potential externalities which may grow over time.

From a law and economics point of view, that requires both legal and economics scholars to solve the trade-off between *ex ante* and *ex post* definition of the content of property rights, also from the point of view of *ex ante* (incentives to make specific investments on assets exposed to potential free access) as well as *ex post* (ability to give access to some exclusive uses in property to the most valuable user) efficiency. That means in turn facing the challenge of investigating the optimality features of alternative institutional devices in absorbing externalities through an evolutionary system of rights definition and enforcement.

Incomplete property, externality and the meaning of transaction costs

In perfect competitive markets the outcome of economic exchange of property rights is that of a Pareto-relevant equilibrium (Bowles, 2003). Given initial endowments, market equilibrium is reached automatically so that the mere existence of potential gains from trade generates automatically that trade so that 'eternity can be experienced in a second' (Coase, 1988, p. 15). Under that framework, there is no need for legal rules or institutions performing the aim of facilitating economic exchange. As the Coase theorem shows, this is the tautological outcome of perfect competitive markets: when transaction costs are negligible and property rights are well-defined, economic resources will automatically end up in the hands of those agents who value them the most, independently of any initial assignment of property rights on those resources. However, as long as transaction costs grow in dimension, potential Pareto-relevant exchanges could be inhibited bringing to an inefficient outcome. The incredibly vast literature on Coase theorem and transaction costs has mainly focused on the role of *ex post* transaction costs to be sustained in order to carry out a transaction. *Ex post* transaction costs thus refer to a case in which there are potential gains from trading a right or an entitlement whose property is already defined. The focus there is on those costs that inhibit a Pareto-relevant exchange and on their absorption. A different perspective lies in the problem of the *ex ante* transaction costs to be sustained to define property rights. When *ex ante* transaction costs are high, the problem is that two or even more 'potential' owners become reciprocal claimants for rival undefined uses of some entitlement bundled in counterpart's property. There, it is not a matter of carrying out Pareto-relevant exchange, but it is a matter of generating the pre-condition for efficient market exchange, which is that of creating property rights.

These are two related, but quite different problems. While the first (the role of *ex post* transaction costs in market exchange) might be referred to any market failure that inhibits Pareto relevant exchange over well-defined property rights, the latter has to do with the specific problem of *ex ante* defining a socially enforced property right over entitlements perceived as a presumptive right by at least two alternative claimants. Only this last problem (the one associated with *ex ante* transaction costs) should be depicted as the problem of externality, re-interpreted that as a problem of property incompleteness.

This distinction between *ex ante* and *ex post* transaction costs highlights, in my view, a quite neglected relationship between (the nature of) property rights and (the nature of) externalities which has been neglected for long in the literature on Coase theorem.

The Coase theorem (Coase, 1960) has been traditionally interpreted[2] as a theory of the superiority of free market exchange on state regulatory intervention for externalities' absorption. As Coase (1988) has later pointed out, his 1960 article has been widely cited and discussed only with reference to the first part of the analysis (concerning a world with zero transaction costs), 'neglecting other aspects of the analysis'[3] as those remarking 'the fundamental role which transaction costs do, and should, play in the fashioning of the institutions which make up the economic system'. The Coase theorem, which thus covers only a part of a more general argument, could be formulated in the following way: 'if transaction costs were assumed to be zero and the rights of the various parties well defined, the allocation of resources would be the same' independently of the initial allocation of rights. The consequence of this assertion is that

> how the rights will be used depends on who owns the rights and the contractual arrangements into which the owner has entered. If these arrangements are the results of market transactions, they will tend to lead to the rights being used in the way which is the most valued, but only after deducing the costs involved in making these transactions. Transaction costs therefore play a crucial role in determining how the rights will be used.

The mere existence of an externality (which in Coase's terms is simply defined as 'harmful effects') therefore 'does not imply that there is a *prima facie* case for governmental intervention (taxation or regulation)'. Sometimes, 'if with governmental intervention the losses also exceed the gains from eliminating "externality" it is obviously desirable that it should remain'. It could happen that when externalities occur, 'the only reason individuals and private organizations do not eliminate them is that the gain from doing so would be offset by what would be lost (including the cost of making the arrangements necessary to bring about this result)'. It comes out that the Coasean boundary between market decentralized exchange and governmental intervention (and, more generally, the choice among alternative economic institutions) should be essentially referred to the dimension of transaction costs and to the potential distortions attributable to public centralized intervention.

As some authors have noticed (Cooter, 1987; Allen, 1991; Parisi, 1999; Usher, 1999), under the Coasean framework, the notion of transaction costs could be expanded so as to include quite every potential source of market failure in allowing efficient bargaining over an externality, thus including not only all kind of *ex post* transaction costs sustained for the exchange of given rights, but also all the *ex ante* transaction costs to be sustained for the definition of rights and/or for contracting over the initial allocation of rights (Bernhölz, 1997; Anderlini and Felli, 2004). Cheung (1983), for instance, has argued that in the absence of transaction costs 'the assumption of private property rights can be dropped without in the least negating the Coase Theorem'.

Moreover, if one accepts the idea the property rights are well-defined then the only motivation for having a Pareto-relevant externality to persist over time should be found in parties' inability to reach any efficient *ex post* trade. In this respect, the problem of externalities' absorption, in Coase's view, seems to do mainly with the problem of minimization of the *ex post* transaction costs to be carried out in order to proceed towards an efficient market exchange of well-defined property rights.

However, the original Coasean intuition outlined two separate assumptions for the Coase theorem to work: zero transaction costs *and* well-defined property rights. What does it mean that rights should be well-defined? This question involves the following ones: who is entitled to define rights in the first instance? How is she selected? How are rights maintained and enforced over time?

If property rights are not well-defined, then externalities in the form of reciprocal claims over rival uses (Nicita *et al.*, 2005) do inevitably emerge even in a world of zero *ex post* transaction costs. In this case, externalities would be generated by *ex ante* transaction costs to be carried out in order to define complete property rights.

As a consequence, the relationship between externalities and property in the Coase theorem turns to be ambiguous. It seems to depend on the nature of transactions costs. When the costs of defining *ex ante* a system of complete property rights are prohibitive then externalities do emerge as reciprocal claims over rival uses. When property rights are well-defined, but *ex post* transaction costs over the exchange of those rights are prohibitive, then the externality is depicted as the social waste of having a suboptimal Paretian allocation (in this respect the notion of externality would coincide with that of an inefficient market configuration).

While it is reasonable to admit, according to Buchanan and Stubblebine (1962), that the process of absorption of a Pareto relevant externality is always a Pareto improvement, it is controversial to say that any time we have a Pareto relevant exchange we are solving a pre-existent externality. Some confusion between these two distinct situations may mislead the reasoning upon externalities and transaction costs. Some potential Pareto improvements could be inhibited in the market by relevant transaction costs but the resulting status quo is not an externality. If Mr A values the assets owned by Mr B more than B does but transaction costs reduce the expected benefits of Mr A to a point that Mr A gives up, the missed Pareto-relevant exchange could be depicted as an externality? At the same time, if Mr A takes without consent the assets from Mr B, the negative effect for Mr B is not an externality: it is the direct negative effect of a theft. On the other side, if Mr A's use of the river in his land, which trespasses also Mr B's property, is inhibiting a rival use of the river by Mr B and if those rival uses were not clearly defined in either Mr A's or in Mr B's bundle of property rights, then an externality is certainly occurring.

It should not be surprising that the Coase theorem has been mainly studied under the lens of *ex post* transaction costs, with the consequence of neglecting to investigate the role of *ex ante* transaction costs in affecting the definition of property rights. Next section will try to assess the relationship between property and externality.

Reconciling property and externality

Focusing the analysis on the *ex ante* transaction costs to be sustained in order to clearly define property rights (and thus imposing *erga omnes* the correspondent duties not to interfere with owners) suggests that the notion of externality should be interpreted as the opposite of the Blackstonian meaning of property. If an externality emerges as the reciprocal *veto* opposed by two claimants over rival uses then it is clear how externalities do emerge as a direct consequence of incompleteness in property. According to Hohfeld's fundamental jural relations, if a right is well/defined, it is always coupled with a correspondent duty to abstain from interference against owners. Thus, by definition, a well-defined right over an asset x prevents any externality over x. On the other side, if it is not clear whether or not the use y is included in the asset x, then rival claims over that use could emerge. In a world of zero *ex ante* transaction costs, every potential use has a correspondent right, socially recognized and enforced. When, however, the costs of *ex ante* defining all the potential uses embedded in property are prohibitive, many uses will pre-exist to an appropriate and socially enforced definition of a right over them, and thus externalities may emerge. In this respect, the degree of an externality will depend on the degree of incompleteness. In terms of Hohfeld's classification it is possible to say that when rights are not well-defined, also correspondent duties are equally not defined and thus rival presumptive owners will both exercise a conflicting privilege or liberty. For an externality to grow one has to imagine a world of incomplete rights and some joint claim over undefined uses bundled in neighbouring property rights (Nicita *et al.*, 2005). There is an inverse relationship between the degree of completeness of property rights and the emergence of externalities. Of course, for an externality to occur it is not sufficient to have incompleteness in property. It is also necessary to have a reciprocal claim over the rival use which is not covered by a clearly defined property right. This is a re-formulation of Demsetz's (1967) original theory on the emergence and on the evolution of property rights. According to Demsetz, property rights do emerge as an efficient legal response to externalities. What converts a harmful or beneficial effect into an externality is that the cost of bringing the effect to bear on the decisions of one or more of the interacting persons is too high to make it worthwhile (Demsetz, 1967). The creation of a property right over an externality reduces the costs of inducing interacting agents to create a market for beneficial or harmful effects. In Demsetz's view the emergence of new property rights takes place in response of the desires of the interacting persons for adjustments to new benefit–cost possibilities. The main intuition provided by Demsetz is that externalities induce the emergence of property rights and, for a given legal system, new externalities (generated for instance by technological change) induce either new rights or a change (but not necessarily an exchange) in existing rights: property rights develop to internalize externalities when the gains of internalization become larger than the cost of internalization. [...] Internalising such effects requires a process, usually a change in property rights.

The important thing to be stressed here is that the standard law and economics literature on property rights usually treats property and externality as two distinct questions. Property rights are generally intended as complete bundle of defined uses, while externalities are mainly represented as nuisance problems coming from social interaction or interdependence in specific cases. Cooter and Ulen (1988) defines externalities as the (particular) problem of non-separability of individual property rights rather than as the question of incompleteness of property rights. As a consequence they confine the emergence of externality or nuisance problem to specific or sectoral cases or phenomena (as polluting activities) rather than representing them as a pervasive feature of property rights in a world of incomplete rights.

Most authors these days are ready to grant property a dimension of incompleteness, although there is little if nothing on the origin and nature of this 'incompleteness' (see among others, Allen, 2000; Lueck and Miceli, 2005) as also on its consequences. Paradigmatically, it should be noted that in the original work of Demsetz (1967), the incomplete dimension of property is not even considered although he more recently recognized it to be a pervasive feature of property.

This notion of externality as incompleteness in property also affects the normative side of the Coase theorem. The relevance of *ex ante* property rights definition for a Coasean market to work puts emphasis on the institutional nature of the market, and on the constant need, besides the market, of a regulatory authority able to properly define rights whenever an externality does emerge and which grants rights' enforcement against non-holders' interference. While focusing exclusively on *ex post* transaction costs induces law and economics scholars to investigate the institutional frames that do best in *ex post* allocating economic resources, the problem of externalities as incomplete property leads to the analysis of the institutions which minimize *ex ante* transaction costs. This conclusion, which does not depend on the existence and on the dimension of *ex post* transaction costs, throws new lights, in our view, on the definition of state–market boundaries stressing their complementarity. State intervention for externalities' absorption should thus be referred not only to direct intervention on rights' allocation (as in the Pigouvian case), but also on rights' definition and re-definition over time.

The Coase theorem with incomplete property: Sen vs Coase

The analysis of the role played by *ex ante* and *ex post* transaction costs in affecting the efficient allocation of property rights could be developed through a comparison between Sen's paradox and the Coase theorem. In 'the Impossibility of a Paretian Liberal', Sen (1970) argues that 'in a very basic sense liberal values conflict with the Pareto principle. If someone takes the Pareto principle seriously [. . .] then he has to face problems of consistency in cherishing liberal values'. As a consequence, 'if someone does have certain liberal values, then he may have to eschew his adherence to Pareto optimality'. Sen (1970) defines liberal values as personal liberty over certain matters in which each person should be free to decide what should happen, no matter what others think, so that the choice of that person over that matters must be taken to be the better for the society as a whole. Liberal values thus imply, according to Sen (1970), that each person, for at least certain matters, should be protected against others' externality over his choice domain: 'given other things in the society, if you prefer to have pink walls rather than white, then society should permit you to have this, even if a majority of the community would like to see your walls white'.

Thus it is easy to include in the liberal values depicted by Sen also the entitlement bundled in a property right. Ownership, in Sen's respect, attributes to the owner the full liberty to select the uses bundled within without any concern towards society and/or external interference.

Thus, if I prefer to have pink walls rather than white in my house, liberal values imply that society should not affect this decision concerning my own property. However, on the other side, if all my friends hate watching pink colour so as to kindly refuse any invitation to my party, then a social inefficient equilibrium will emerge. Here is the paradox and the inconsistency between liberal values and Paretian exchange.

The Sen's paradox could be trespassed if minimal liberty includes the liberty to renounce to select some of the uses which generate *ex post* negative externalities (Nicita and Savaglio, 2006). If I prefer a pink house without friends to a white happy house full of people, then the social choice induced by my liberty does not generate any negative externality and my minimal liberty is preserved. However, if I prefer having crowded parties in my houses, I can decide to alienate my right to decide the preferred colour of my house when that colour contrasts with social preferences. In other words, when agents' choices produce reciprocal externalities, it is always possible to re-define the original choice domain over which choices are expressed, so as to preserve *ex post* minimal liberties and to reach superior Paretian outcomes. In this case minimal liberty and Pareto principle will be consistent (Gibbard, 1974): when there is no externality the right's holder will reveal his right according to his preference orderings, aligned with social preference orderings; when there is an externality, the right's holder will reveal his preference orderings by alienating his right, according to the Coase theorem prediction. In other words, having well-defined property rights over uses embedded in property creates the condition for having a possibility result for a Paretian Liberal (Nicita and Savaglio, 2006) at least when *ex post* transactions costs are negligible.

On the other side, when society fails to introduce any well-defined allocation of property rights over the relevant resources, conflicting preferences are destined to persist and the impossibility of a Paretian Liberal will extend to a Coasean Liberal as well, leading thus to the impossibility of a Coasean Liberal, an outcome which, insofar, is independent of the level of transaction costs: when the Coase theorem holds, the Sen's paradox fails and viceversa.

All in all, in this setting, the emergence of alienable rights has the purpose to solve any conflict among preferences over a pair of alternatives. The definition of an alienable right assigns to the holder a set of choice that may not be violated by any other agent. Only the right holder may indeed decide to renounce to that set of choices, when the emergence of an externality (others' claim over another option) re-defines his set of choices so as to induce him to alienate that right.

The emergence of the impossibility of a Coasean Liberal shows that the optimal attributes of (perfect competitive) markets, as its allocative efficiency, always require as a pre-condition, a well-defined system of alienable rights, that is, a State which for every possible action or issues defined over all possible contingencies, provides a system of property rights, a system of rules for market exchange and a system of public enforcement when controversies come out.

Defining incomplete property

In a recent work, Nicita *et al.* (2005) remove the assumption of completeness introducing the notion of incomplete property intended as a bundle of both defined and presumptive rights, where the latter are potentially exposed to the emergence of externalities. *Ex ante* defined rights constitute, under this framework, the *core* of ownership rights over uses socially enforced by organized consent at any given time. In other words, the core of a property right comprises only well-defined right/duty jural relationships, in Hohfeld's terminology, which are compatible with *ex ante* transaction costs. All those uses for which no clear right/duty relationship is clearly defined *ex ante* belong to the *periphery* of the property bundle. In their regard, right-holders can only exercise presumptive rights, subject to the emergence of externalities. This perspective highlights the existence of a complex co-evolutionary relationship between property and externalities: while property rights do emerge to solve externalities, access to existing property rights may generate new externalities and so on. Moreover, the incomplete dimension of property may allow to shed new light on some controversial issues in the economic analysis of property.

The incomplete property rights perspective shows that the institution of ownership, conceived of as an incomplete bundle of rights, composed a core and a periphery, serves a double efficiency function: it provides *ex ante* incentives and it allows to economise on the *ex ante* costs of definition of property rights. In introducing the concept of incomplete property, it has been traced a distinction between the core and the periphery of property bundles. The existence of a core of rights over well-defined uses performs the kind of efficiency functions emphasized by proponents of the 'full control' theories of property: it ensures certainty of expectations and therefore provides *ex ante* incentives. At the periphery of the property bundle, there are those uses that are rival in nature and determine the emergence of externalities. This also may be interpreted to serve an efficiency function. Indeed, the fact that the rights over some of the uses bundled in property are defined only *ex post* might be said to have the effect of minimizing *ex ante* transaction costs. Rival claims will normally not arise on each of the undefined uses bundled in property, so that only the *ex post* transaction costs connected to the solution of externalities will be incurred.

The 'strength' of property depends, in this framework, both on the breadth of the core and on the scope of the undefined uses over which a clear right–duty relationship is established *ex post* in favour of the holder of rights over the core. In other words, one might say that the 'strength' of property, and therefore the extent to which property can provide *ex ante* incentives, is inversely related to its degree of incompleteness.

The main consequence of this argument is that there should be no presumption on the optimality of complete property bundles. In talking about incomplete property, I'm not suggesting implicitly that optimal policy would always call for an increase in the degree of *ex ante* definition of property. Quite on the contrary I think that, in presence of both *ex ante* definition costs and *ex post* transaction costs of various kinds, there is no reason to assume that there is a positive relationship between the degree of completeness of the property bundle (and consequently the 'strength' of property) and overall efficiency.

In interpreting property as inherently incomplete, it becomes unclear whether increased strength necessarily translates into increased overall incentives. This would be the case in a world in which there was no friction in the *ex post* reallocation of rights over each of the uses bundled in (complete) property. In such a world, perfect unbundling of rights over uses of a given resource would occur and rights would smoothly flow towards those with maximum incentives to invest. As long as *ex post* transaction costs do exist, however, it might not be assumed that assigning *ex ante* all the available rights over a given resource maximizes overall incentives. Given that allocation of use rights to one party minimizes the incentives of the parties excluded from ownership, the existence of an invariably positive relationship between the degree of completeness of property and overall efficiency in the allocation of ownership might only be presumed if the assumption that the efficient owner will always be selected *ex ante* is made.

The complex governance of transactions with incomplete property: a research agenda

In this chapter, I have suggested how looking at the incomplete dimension of property seems to be a promising research avenue for scholars in the law and economics and in the institutional economics fields. Describing property as a bundle of both a core of defined rights and a periphery of presumptive rights potentially exposed to externalities, Nicita *et al.* (2005), cast new light on how we understand the mechanisms of the governance of transactions. In this section I will not deepen the vast array of implications induced by property incompleteness on the theories of institutional governance of transactions; rather I only intend to outline some possible directions for future research.

A first direction of research regards the role played by property incompleteness in the Coase theorem. The Coase theorem affirms that if transaction costs are assumed to be zero and the rights of various parties well defined, the final efficient allocation of resources would be the same under any initial allocation of property rights. Here, there are two conditions for the theorem to hold: zero transaction costs and well-defined rights. Without further qualifications, the second assumption is somewhat redundant. If rights are well defined that means that *ex ante* transaction costs to define right/duty relationships are zero. From this intuition derives the conclusion of Cooter (1987) that the theorem is a tautology since it simply affirms that when transaction costs are zero we are in a first best world. If rights are well defined there are no externalities, but simply *ex post* market exchange. However, introducing the notion of incomplete property in the Coase theorem allows us to overcome the above tautology and to highlight the complementarity relationship between the process of 'public' definition of rights and duties and the role of the market in promoting efficient allocation of rights. Under an incomplete property framework, the Coase theorem could be reformulated as follows: if an externality occurs over undefined uses, and if *ex post* transaction costs are zero, the (re)definition of rights over rival uses will always lead to *ex post* efficient allocation of newly defined rights. In this respect, if the *ex ante* transaction costs to define rights are zero, and *ex post* transaction costs to exchange rights are negligible, then the sole market mechanism will lead resource to the most efficient use of rights. However, when *ex ante* transaction costs are relevant, the market may perform well only if a system of rights definition is implemented. There are at least two ways of (re)defining property rights. The first is the unification of property's bundles through market exchange. The second is to publicly define new rights, through a process of bundling and unbundling of rival uses from which the externalities emerge. As a consequence, in the latter case, market performance in allowing *ex post* efficient allocation goes hand in hand with society's ability to define property rights (Nicita and Savaglio, 2006).

A second potential venue of research opened by the introduction of property incompleteness in a Coasean framework moves from the comparison between Coase (1937) and Coase (1960). Property incompleteness may suggest that decisions to vertically integrate may derive not only from the analysis of compared transaction costs of *make vs buy*, as in Coase (1937), but also on the dimension and on the direction of *ex post* transaction costs to be carried on in order to properly define a right over a rival use between neighbouring properties. In other words, the owner of the firm can be induced to 'buy' all the assets over which someone else's use may produce an externality, when those rights are undefined. The nature of the firm thus is also affected by the degree of completeness of property, in the sense that integrating rival uses under the same ownership minimizes the potential for externalities. Thus the *optimal dimension of property assets* to be possessed by a sole owner may depend, not only on the *ex post* transaction costs of enforcement as in the Williamsonian framework and in the new Property Right School, but also on the *ex ante* and the *ex post* transaction costs of definition of rights. The perspective of incompleteness in property may here suggest that the Coase theorem maintains its relevance if we apply it to the problem of allocation of presumptive rights that generate externalities rather than to the exchange of core rights. That means that we need to distinguish and compare *ex ante* and *ex post* transaction costs. Moreover, another point that future research may investigate is whether we should expect, besides other correlations, higher property concentration when both the degree of incompleteness and the *ex post* transaction costs of bundling and unbundling rival uses are very high.

The above argument implies that, with incomplete property, transactions could be plagued by the emergence of externalities even in a world of complete contracts. This suggests that the efficient allocation of property rights may also be affected not only by owners' ability to efficiently use their core rights, but also by their ability to cope with externalities when they arise. In Williamson (1985), for instance, the emergence of private orderings characterized by the 'forbearance' role of the manager who maintains the authority over firm's assets, is functional to the overcoming, for a given transaction, of the inefficiencies related to the incompleteness of contracts. However, since externalities may raise the need of publicly (re)defining property, the role of 'forbearence' may extend also to the process of presumptive rights' definition in private orderings among corporate constituents.

The perspective of property incompleteness outlines the institutional complementarities existing between first order and second order jural positions in the Hohfeld–Commons paradigm, as envisaged by Pagano (2006): the degree of property incompleteness in first order jural relationships is affected also by second order jural relationship, that is, by the way in which individuals have access to the power of changing first order jural relations. Since, according to Commons (1924), this power is affected by several concurring institutions – such as the legal system, the degree of market competition, corporate governance, trade unions, consumers associations, lobbies, culture and social norms – the way in which these public and private institutions interfere with each other shapes economic and legal transactions and thus the co-evolution of property and externalities in economic systems.

Acknowledgement

This chapter is part of a research conducted under MIUR and REFGOV projects. I would warmly thank Ugo Pagano, Matteo Rizzolli and Alessandra Rossi for the cross fertilization, coming also from the joint research and writings on this topic. Thanks also general discussions, helpful comments and suggestions on this topic to Ian Ayres, Giuseppe Bellantuono, Eric Brousseau, Bob Ellickson, Bruno Deffains, Gray Libecap, Dan Lueck, Pier Luigi Monateri, Franceso Parisi, Roberto Pardolesi, Giovanni Ramello, Ernesto Savaglio, Simone Sepe, Franceso Silva, Massimiliano Vatiero. Usual disclaimers apply.

Notes

1 Given by the Hohfeld's fundamental jural relations of power and immunity. See also Pagano (2006) and Nicita *et al.* (2005).
2 The Stigler's version, as Coase refers (1988, p. 12).
3 The following quotations refer to Coase (1988, pp. 12–13).

References

Alchian, A.A. (1965) 'Some economics of property rights', *Il Politico*, 30, 816–829.
Alchian, A.A. (1998) 'Property rights' in J. Eatwell, M. Milgate and P. Newman (eds), *The New Palgrave: A Dictionary of Economics*. New York: MacMillan.
Allen, D.W. (1991) 'What are transaction costs?', *Research in Law and Economics*, 14, 1–18.
Allen, D.W. (2000) 'Transaction costs', in B.D.G. Bouckaert, and De Geest Gerrit (ed.), Cheltenham, UK and Northampton, MA: Elgar, 893–926.

Anderlini, L. and L. Felli, (2004), 'Costly Contingent Contracts: A Failure of the Coase Theorem, Legal Orderings and Economic Institutions', in Fabrizio Cafaggi, Antonio Nicita and Ugo Pagano (eds), London: Routledge.

Bernhölz, P. (1997) 'Property Rights, Contracts, Cyclical Social Preferences and the Coase Theorem: A Synthesis', *European Journal of Political Economy*, 13, 419–464.

Blackstone, W. (1766) *Commentaries on the Laws of England*, Oxford: Clarendon Press.

Bolton, P. and M. Dewatripont (2005), *Contract Theory*, Cambridge, MA: MIT Press.

Bowles, S. (2003) *Microeconomics*, Princeton: Princeton University Press.

Cheung Steven, N.S. (1983) 'The Contractual Nature of the Firm', *Journal of Law and Economics*, 26, 1–21.

Coase, R. (1960), 'The problem of social cost', *Journal of Law and Economics*, 3, 1–44.

Coase, R. (1988) *The Firm, the Market and the Law*, Chicago, IL: Chicago University Press.

Commons, J.R. (1924) *Legal Foundations of Capitalism*, Transaction Publishers.

Cooter, R.D. (1987) 'The Coase theorem', in J. Eatwell, M. Milgate and P. Newman (eds), *The New Palgrave: A Dictionary of Economics*, 457–460.

Cooter R. and T. Ulen 1988, *Law and Economics*, Harpers Collins Publishers.

Demsetz, H. (1967) 'Toward a theory of property rights', *American Economic Review*, 57, 347–359.

Gibbard, A. (1974) 'A Pareto-consistent libertarian claim', *Journal of Economic Theory*, 7, 388–410.

Hart, O. (1995) *Firms, Contracts and Financial Structure*, Oxford: Oxford University Press.

Hohfeld, W.N. (1913) 'Some fundamental legal concepts as applied in judicial reasoning', *Yale Law Journal*, 51, 951–966.

Libecap, G. (2002). 'A Transcations-Cost Approach to the Analysis of Property Rights' in E. Brousseau and J.-M. Glachant (eds), *The Economics of Contracts: Theories and Applications*, Cambridge: Cambridge University Press, 140–158.

Libecap, G.D. (2002) 'A transaction-costs approach to the analysis of property rights', in E. Brousseau and J.-M. Glachant (eds), *The Economics of Contracts: Theories and Applications*, Cambridge: Cambridge University Press, 140–148.

Lueck, D. and Miceli, T.J. (2005) 'Property law', in A.M. Polinsky and S. Shavell (eds), *Handbook of Law and Economics*. Amsterdam: Elsevier.

Nicita, A. and Pagano, U. (2005) 'Law and economics in retrospect', in E. Brousseau and J.-M. Glachant (eds), Cambridge, UK: Cambridge University Press.

Nicita, A., Rizzolli, M. and Rossi, M.A. (2005) 'Towards a theory of incomplete property rights', mimeo.

Nicita, A. and Savaglio, E. (2006) *Minimal Liberty and the 'Coasian Liberal': Boundaries and Complementarities between the State and the Market*, London: Routledge, 2006–forthcoming.

Pagano, U. (2006 forthcoming) 'Legal positions and institutional complementarities', in F. Cafaggi, A. Nicita and U. Pagano (eds), *Legal Orderings and Economic Insitutions*, London: Routledge.

Parisi (1999) 'Coase Theorem and Transaction Cost Economics in the Law', in G. Jurgen and Backhaus, (eds), *The Elgar Companion to Law and Economics*, Cheltenham, UK and Northampton, MA: Edward Elgar, 7–39.

Sen, A. (1970) 'The impossibility of a paretian liberal', *Journal of Political Economy*, 78, 152–157.

Usher, D. (1999) The Coase Theorem is Tautological, Incoherent or Wrong', *Economics Letters*, Elsevier, 61, 3–11.

Williamson, O.E. (1985) *The Economic Institutions of Capitalism: Firms, Markets, Relational Contracting*, New York: Free Press.

Part II

An old bottle for new wines?

The extensions of property rights

6 Intellectual property and the efficient allocation of social surplus from innovations

Michele Boldrin and David K. Levine

> The only patent that is valid is one which this Court has not been able to put its hands on.
>
> (Dissent by Jackson J. in Jungerson vs Ostby and Barton Co. 335 US 560, 80 USPQ 32 (1948))

Introduction

The times oh, have they changed, since Justice Jackson wrote his dissenting opinion in 1948. The world, it seems, is heading the opposite direction and it has officially entered the era of *Universal Intellectual Property* (UIP). Anyone doing any "thing" anywhere, who believes it to be "useful" and "novel", can and should try to claim complete and exclusive monopoly power over said thing, its uses, its copies, its more or less related variants. The "thing" may be a manufactured object, a production process, a business method, a string of computer code, a plant seed, an animal species, or just any usable concept such as, for example, "how to swing a swing." There will always be a court, most likely: a US Court of Appeals for the Federal Circuit, willing to classify the thing as a "novel idea susceptible of commercial exploitation." Universal Intellectual Property has acquired the status of a public religion, at the core of which stands the shockingly profound revelation: Anything that can be *monopolized ought to, by whoever lays claim to it first*. From this, economic prosperity will follow, as the high preachers of this new religion do not tire of reminding us.

Around the world, the tide is rising: India has just adjusted its patent laws to comply with TRIPS requirements in the areas of pharmaceutical and biotechnologies in particular, China is slowly but surely doing the same for both copyright and patents, the EU pushes forward with the European Patent harmonization plan, Mexico, Brazil, and other developing countries are hard pressed to follow soon. That the European Parliament, in a rare moment of wisdom and foresight, rejected the proposal to patent software to compensate Mr Gates for the annoyances that a moderately diligent Competition Commissioner had brought upon Microsoft during the last six years, is only a temporary setback. The tide is rising, and nothing seems capable of stopping it; as a succesful pamphlet reminded us a few years ago "Rembrandts [are hiding] in the attic" and the "greatest untapped asset opportunity" is waiting to be tapped by dexterous users of patents and copyright. But, is there a reason to try stopping it? What is wrong with the idea and the practice of Universal Intellectual Property?

To start seeing what is wrong with UIP, we may want to consider the basic metaphor that appears to be inspiring its current zealots. This beloved metaphor goes like this: the process of securing intellectual property over ideas is logically and economically equivalent to the establishment of well-defined property rights on parcels of unowned land. Without well defined and secure property rights, the fertile lands of the Western frontier could not be efficiently cultivated or put to pasture, greatly reducing economic development. Similarly, if ideas are not the exclusive private property of someone, they cannot be developed and brought to fruition. The wide open and uncharted territories of profitable and appropriable ideas are there, just ahead of us – mostly lawyers – the brave colonizers of the Third Millenium. Ideas make up the green and productive fields of the new economy which we will conquer – court-battle after court-battle, lobbying-raid after lobbying-raid – and finally set to profitable use, ridding them, in due course, of Indians, undesirable outlaws, squatters and pirates of all kinds and races.

This is the new UIP movie, now playing at theaters around the globe and therefore certainly also hear you. This article asks: May something be wrong with it? Our answer is quite radical, as we find that almost everything is in fact wrong with this vision. We focus on legal theories of Intellectual Property (IP) that have an economic underpinning, that is: on legal theories arguing that UIP is a desirable state of the world because it somehow maximizes social welfare and allocates it efficiently among potential claimants. As such, we are not concerned with legal theories of IP based on natural rights, axiomatic theories of justice, or other ethical and metaphysical principles. In particular, we cannot rule out the hypothesis that the foundation of UIP lies in its being a revealed truth, making it therefore irrefutable.

Ideas in the public domain

Eldred vs Ashcroft

A historical battle for the advancement of the UIP frontier was fought and won a few years ago in the Congress of the United States, and its result subsequently engraved in stone by the US Supreme Court. In 1998 the US Congress extended the term of copyright by 20 years (through the Copyright Term Extension Act (CTEA), better known as the "Sonny Bono Act"), while simultaneously extending also its breadth and dramatically stiffening the penalties associated to its violation (through the Digital Millenium Copyright Act). The extension of copyright term has been retroactive, applying not only to new works, but also to existing ones. In spite of the obvious and well known economic argument[1] that extending copyright on existing works cannot possibly increase their supply, a number of specious arguments[2] have been advanced as to how retroactive extension somehow serves to "promote the progress of [...] useful arts."[3] Subsequently, the US Supreme Court acquiesced to these principles in its ruling

Eldred et al. vs Ashcroft, No. 01–618, January 15, 2003. The Court majority ruled that (Syllabus, pp. 2–3)

> The court found nothing in the constitutional text or history to suggest that a term of years for a copyright is not a "limited Time" if it may later be extended for another "limited Time." [...] In petitioners' view, a time prescription, once set, becomes forever "fixed" or "inalterable." The word "limited," however, does not convey a meaning so constricted. At the time of the Framing, "limited" meant what it means today: confined within certain bounds, restrained, or circumscribed. Thus understood, a time span appropriately "limited" as applied to future copyrights does not automatically cease to be "limited" when applied to existing copyrights. [...] History reveals an unbroken congressional practice of granting to authors of works with existing copyrights the benefit of term extensions so that all under copyright protection will be governed evenhandedly under the same regime. Moreover, because the Clause empowering Congress to confer copyrights also authorizes patents, the Court's inquiry is signifi-cantly informed by the fact that early Congresses extended the duration of numerous individual patents as well as copyrights. Lower courts saw no "limited Times" impediment to such extensions. Further, although this Court never before has had occasion to decide whether extending existing copyrights complies with the "limited Times" prescription, the Court has found no constitutional barrier to the legislative expansion of existing patents. See, e.g., McClurg, 1 How., at 206. Congress' consistent historical practice reflects a judgment that an author who sold his work a week before should not be placed in a worse situation than the author who sold his work the day after enactment of a copyright extension. The CTEA follows this historical practice by keeping the 1976 Act's duration provisions largely in place and simply adding 20 years to each of them.
>
> The CTEA is a rational exercise of the legislative authority conferred by the Copyright Clause. On this point, the Court defers substantially to Congress. Sony, 464 US, at 429. The CTEA reflects judgments of a kind Congress typically makes, judgments the Court cannot dismiss as outside the Legislature's domain. A key factor in the CTEA's passage was a 1993 European Union (EU) directive instructing EU members to establish a baseline copyright term of life plus 70 years and to deny this longer term to the works of any non-EU country whose laws did not secure the same extended term. By extending the baseline United States copyright term, Congress sought to ensure that American authors would receive the same copyright protection in Europe as their European counterparts. The CTEA may also provide greater incentive for American and other authors to create and disseminate their work in the United States.

Two points are worth noticing here.

1   That the extension of term that the CTEA implements is a "rational exercise" of legislative authority by Congress; which is certainly the case.

2   That the retroactive extension is justified by three reasons:
     (i) as a way of providing equal treatment to all copyright holders;
     (ii) as an "equilibrium" response to the EU move of extending copyright to
          70 years; and
     (iii) because it may provide greater incentive for the creation and dissemination
          of copyrightable work; none of which make any sense.

The copyright term has been repeatedly increased since its initial adoption in
1790 when a term of 14 years was established, with major increases taking place
in 1831, 1909, and 1976; the last extension, in The Copyright Act of 1976, added
20 years to the then existing term. The CTEA retroactive provision, therefore,
further extends the term for exactly those items for which the 1976 Act had
already provided a retroactive extension. In spite of this obvious fact, the Court
states rather incredibly (p. 7)

> Concerning petitioners' assertion that Congress might evade the limitation
> on its authority by stringing together "an unlimited number of 'limited
> times'," the Court of Appeals stated that such legislative misbehavior
> "clearly is not the situation before us."

Let us forget the Court's peculiar interpretation of reality and of what Congress
may or may not be planning to do – after all, we must wait until 2018 for a
further extension to take place and, even in that case, the arithmetic fact that go
is not an unlimited number will be available to our ingenious Justices. Let us try,
instead, to see why the substantive reasons provided under (2) do not make
any sense.

Consider, first, the equal treatment argument. The Court writes (p. 14)

> [S]ince 1790, it has indeed been Congress's policy that the author of yester-
> day's work should not get a lesser reward than the author of tomorrow's work
> just because Congress passed a statute lengthening the term today.

This is quite fine, indeed. One wonders, though, if the same logic should not
be applied whenever Congress passes a piece of legislation that, by affecting, say,
the fiscal code impacts on the economic reward that private agents receive. Any
income tax cut should, then, be retroactive as it clearly makes no sense to tax past
income at a higher rate "just because Congress passed a statute" reducing the tax
rate "today." Quite obviously, the same applies to tax increases, social security
contributions, tariffs, and what not, making for a rather interesting, if volatile,
economic environment; not to speak of the very creative budgeting and national
income accounting procedures this would bring about, very much to the delight
of financial markets that, notoriously, thrive under volatility. Most interestingly,
though, would be the case in which Congress – in an uncharacteristic act of
economic rationality – decided to reduce copyright and patent terms at some
future date. By the same token for which both Congress and the Supreme Court
argued for retroactivity in 1998, we suppose, the copyright term's reduction

should also be retroactive in order to make sure that the *"Congress's policy that the author of yesterday's work should not get a"* larger *"reward than the author of tomorrow's work just because Congress passed a statute"* shortening *"the term today"* be dutifully implemented. Maybe we are not properly trained in the subtleties of legal logic, and maybe there is a hidden paragraph somewhere in the Court's ruling explaining why copyright holders are exceptional economic agents, so that the rule of uniformity applies to them in terms different from those it applies to other economic agents and, in particular, explaining why uniform treatment only applies when terms increase and not when they decrease. We just could not find such paragraph, hence the equal treatment justification for retroactive extension just reads like highly creative economic nonsense.

Move next to the motivation in (2.ii), that is, reacting to the EU's decision to extend copyright term to life plus 70 years. Again, we quote from the majority opinion (p. 15)

> By extending the baseline United States copyright term to life plus 70 years, Congress sought to ensure that American authors would receive the same copyright protection in Europe as their European counterparts. [. . .] ("[M]atching th[e] level of [copyright] protection in the United States [to that in the EU] can ensure stronger protection for US works abroad and avoid competitive disadvantages vis-à-vis foreign rightholders.")

In case you were wondering from where our Supreme Court gets its economic wisdom, footnote 12 of the Opinion reports that "The author of the law review article cited in text, Shira Perlmutter, currently a vice president of AOL Time Warner, was at the time of the CTEA's enactment Associate Register for Policy and International Affairs, United States Copyright Office." Let us leave the political economy of UIP for later, and stick to the logical argument for the time being. Hence, what is the logic here? From the Court's own words it seems purely a redistributive concern: if the US does not raise its copyright term the US author publishing in Europe will receive less money, in that market, than their European counterparts. Again, this is quite fine, in the sense that the US Constitution does not prevent Congress from redistributing income, by various statutory means, from one subgroup of the population to another. In this case, clearly, Congress must have feared that writers, musicians, and assorted movie "stars" who are citizens of the US would have faced poverty and denutrition lacking the *additional* 20 years of copyright revenues from the European markets. So being it, there is no point in quarrelling: redistributing to the poor and indigent movie stars from the rich and powerful consumers is certainly a commendable aim of Congress, if not one explicitly stated by the Founding Fathers in the Bill of Rights. Redistribution being redistribution, though, one wonders why a lump sum transfer has not been chosen by Congress and recommended by the Court: it would have achieved the same egalitarian aim while sparing us the distortionary effect of 20 additional years of monopoly in the markets for copyrighted materials. True, the median voter may have found a new tax to finance Hollywood stars' Colombian cocaine habit somewhat unpatriotic.[4]

The substantive economic point here being that the EU decision to extend the length of copyright term for its citizens is perfectly immaterial to the well being of either US citizens or authors; if anything, it makes them better off as long as the copyright term is not extended also in the United States. Let us see why. Consider first the fundamental economic reason for providing copyright – the details of which are critically examined later. This says that copyright is given to allow creators to collect enough revenue to compensate for their creative effort. Consumers, therefore, benefit indirectly from copyright because, while paying a monopoly price to creators, receive the creation in exchange, while lacking copyright they would receive nothing. The EU move increases such rents for European creators, and leave them unaltered for everyone else as copyright terms for citizens of other countries were not lowered, either in the EU or anywhere else. This implies: (a) EU creators are richer, (b) EU consumers may or may not be better off (supposedly, they get more creations but, certainly instead of supposedly, get also more monopoly distortions), (c) US creators are not poorer as they receive at least the same rents they received before,[5] (d) US consumers are better off as they pay the same price as before for creative work but enjoy the – supposedly – higher number of EU creations. In plain words, by extending its copyright by 20 years, the EU had forced its consumers to face a risky proposition – more distortions for sure, more culture maybe – in order to make its creators richer. It had also done a somewhat equal favor to US creators and consumers by strenghtening their market position. With the CTEA, the US Congress has made sure that also American consumers are forced to face a risky proposition, making them worse off than they were in the interim period; this is the price paid to transfer additional rents to US creators. We therefore reach the same conclusion as before, that is, the CTEA is explained by a desire to transfer income from the US consumers to the US producers of copyrighted materials, and neither it improves economic efficiency nor it is the appropriate equilibrium response to the EU's move. In particular, the "competitive disadvantages" that the AOL vice-president mentions remain completely mysterious. What could they be? If the US had not extended its term, US publishers of books, movies, and music could have put on the US market lots of European creations with an expired (in the United States) copyright, while their European counterparts would have been unable to do so for other 20 years. This seems to us an advantage, not a disadvantage. At the same time, in the EU markets, the EU subsidiaries of the US publishers could have exploited the longer copyright term to earn more monopoly profits at the expense of the European consumers. At worst, should the EU not have allowed the European subsidiaries of American companies to use the additional 20 years of copyright protection, they would have had the same competitive stance they had had until 1998.

Finally, comes the third, and more substantive economic point (p. 16)

> In addition to international concerns, Congress passed the CTEA in light of demographic, economic, and technological changes, Brief for Respondent 25–26, 33, and nn. 23 and 24, and rationally credited projections that longer

terms would encourage copyright holders to invest in the restoration and public distribution of their works, id., at 34–37; see H. R. Rep. No. 105–452, p. 4 (1998) (term extension "provide[s] copyright owners generally with the incentive to restore older works and further disseminate them to the public").

Which "rationally credited projections" the Court refers to we do not know and, frankly, we do not care; there is always someone somewhere with a PhD in economics from some place, who is willing to forecast that elephants will eventually fly if the tax code is appropriately changed as recommended by the lobby that financed his research. As the Court reports no numbers, and nowhere in the literature are serious numbers to be found that support such a forecast, we will move on to the theoretical underpinnings of this motivation. To be honest, these are not very clearly spelled out in the Court's opinion. In particular, the various footnotes one can find between page 16 and page 19 – supposed to substantiate the incentive effect – are rather disappointing. Apparently, the Supreme Court of this land believes that life expectancy for creators has increased of about 20 years since 1976, which is about ten times the actual value. Equally apparently, the same Court, also believes that Quincy Jones, Bob Dylan, Carlos Santana and Don Henley wrote what they wrote and played what they played because of the (p. 17, footnote 15)

> belief that the copyright system's assurance of fair compensation for themselves and their heirs was an incentive to create.

No further argument is given in support of the incentive theory, hence, out of respect for the Supreme Court of the United States, let us move on to debate those academics that, in a somewhat more articulated form, have argued that such an incentive exists, is substantial, and follows from well founded and well reasoned microeconomic theory. As William M. Landes and Richard A. Posner appear to have been the two most prolific and most coherent supporters of this view within the law and economics literature, it is to their recent writings, Landes and Posner [1989, 2003], Posner [2004], that we turn.

Scholarly pursuits

The two most significant arguments are that creations of any kind should not be left in the public domain, because the public domain suffers from congestion and overuse, and that intellectual property rights are necessary to provide appropriate incentives not just to "create" but also to "maintain" existing works. Notice the similarity with the "land ownership is good" argument, and notice also what this argument says; IP are not just good for creating new things, but also for maintaining them. Hence, in the case of copyright at least, this line of reasoning often ends up arguing that an unlimited copyright term may be desirable. Notice that this line of argument rests on the principle that a normative foundation for the law is the maximization of social wealth, that is, the achievement of economic efficiency in the sense of Pareto – irrespective of its redistributive consequences among heterogenous economic agents. We are not questioning this principle here, in fact – and in spite of personal and philosophical misgivings with both its logical foundations and moral implications – we will use it as a yardstick in all that follows.

Let us start from the fundamental metaphor according to which *ideas = pasture*;

> The counterpart to the common pasture in intellectual property is the public domain [. . .] The term refers to the vast body of ideas and expression that are not copyrighted, patented, or otherwise propertized.
>
> (Landes and Posner, 2003, p. 13)

One reason for rights in ordinary property is indeed to prevent congestion and overuse. For example, if a pasture is public, I do not take account of the negative effect my grazing sheep have on the availability of grass for your sheep. Because roads are public, I do not consider that my driving on the road makes it more difficult for you to get to work. Because the ocean is public, I do not consider that catching fish leaves fewer for you. This is the "tragedy of the commons" and in each case it means that the pasture, road, or ocean will be overused.

Contrary to common wisdom, most common – if not wisdom – in legal circles – the public domain for ideas is the logical and practical *opposite* of the common land/pasture/ocean. The public domain of ideas is the necessary (not sufficient, but strictly necessary) precondition for competition in these markets, and social efficiency therein. On this we focus, and this is the content of the present section.

Is the public domain for ideas like a common? Does my using ideas in the public domain have an adverse effect on your ability to use them? Certainly common sense suggests "there can be no overgrazing of intellectual property . . . because intellectual property is not destroyed or even diminished by consumption."[6] That I might make use of an idea does not make you less able to use it. Indeed it seems obvious that welfare is increased when more people become cognizant of a useful idea, whereas overall productive capacity is not increased when more sheep try to eat from the same square foot of pasture or when different rescue teams compete in salvaging first a given sunken ship.

As we have already seen, Congress and the Supreme Court apparently do not agree, and Landes and Posner[7] also claim that "Recognition of an 'overgrazing' problem in copyrightable works has lagged." In fact it has not, because there is no coherent theory or evidence that points to such a problem.

There are three key elements to understanding why the arguments in favor of retroactive copyright are incoherent. Understand first, only copies of ideas matter from an economic standpoint; in fact: only copies of ideas matter from any practical stand point! If all the copies – in books and minds alike – were to vanish, the abstract existence of the idea would be of no use, at least to the practical real man, while it may be of some, undefined, use to the unpractical metaphysical men that seem to populate legal journals. Understand second, the public domain is not a common of unowned ideas or public property. When an idea is in the public domain, someone still *owns* each copy of the idea or work. To make copies you will have to own or purchase a copy of the idea first. Rather than being like a common, the public domain is like the ideal of a competitive market – such as that for wheat – with many owners/producers of essentially the same product competing with each other. Understand finally, although my using an idea does not make you less able to use it, it may well make you less able to sell it. Which means, my owning a copy of the same idea as you does not make the idea less valuable from a social point of view, but certainly reduces the market price of your copy of the idea. Economists call this phenomenon "pecuniary externality," my selling to a customer changes his demand for your product, and find it a valuable feature of competitive economics. Consumers are made better off by the fact that very many copies of a given good exist, as the market price of such good is set by the marginal consumer, that is, the one that values it the least, thereby allowing all those that value it more to acquire a substantial surplus by purchasing their copies of the good at less than their marginal utility.

Consider the case of food. If my restaurant sells Richard a large meal, he is not likely to go across the street to your restaurant and buy another; my selling him a large meal does not prevent you from using your food, but it does prevent you from selling it to Richard. So too with ideas. If I sell Richard a copy of my Bible, I do not prevent you from making copies of your Bible, but I will reduce your profit because Richard will not buy from you. This is a pecuniary externality. By way of contrast, by taking fish from the sea I am not merely taking your customers, I am taking an economically useful good or service. Economists refer to the former as a "pecuniary" externality, and the latter as a "technological" externality. Pecuniary externalities are a good thing – the incentive to steal customers is an essential part of the normal and efficient functioning of the competitive system. Technological externalities are a bad thing, leading to overuse.

Supporters of intellectual property, and of copyright extension in particular, seem to be blind to such distinction. Landes and Posner, who provide the least incoherent exposition of why retroactive extension of copyright might be a good thing, acknowledge that the "assessment of welfare effects of congestion requires distinguishing technological from mere pecuniary externalities." They then go on to say concerning the Mickey Mouse character "If because copyright had expired anyone were free to incorporate the Mickey Mouse character in a book, movie, song, etc., the value of the character might plummet." The value for whom? It cannot be the social value of the Mickey Mouse character that plummets – this increases when more people have access to it. Rather it is the market price of copies of the Mickey Mouse character that plummets. As Landes and Posner admit, "If this came about only . . . as the ordinary consequence of an increase in output, aggregate value would actually increase." They then assert "however, the public might rapidly tire of Mickey Mouse." But this is in fact the ordinary consequence of an increase in output. If I eat a large meal, I am less hungry – the value to me of a meal is diminished, and restaurants will find I am not willing to pay them much money. No externality is involved: as more of a good is consumed, the more tired people become of it. For there to be an externality, it would have to be the case that my consumption of Mickey Mouse made you more tired of it – an improbability, to say the least.

Although Landes and Posner make the verbal distinction between pecuniary and technological externality, they do not appear to understand it. They quote from a book on Disney marketing:

> To avoid overkill, Disney manages its character portfolio with care. It has hundreds of characters on its books, many of them just waiting to be called out of retirement...Disney practices good husbandry of its characters and extends the life of its brands by not overexposing them...They avoid debasing the currency.[8]

This is of course exactly how we would expect a monopolist to behave. If Disney were to be given a monopoly on food, we can be sure they would practice "good husbandry" of food, most likely leaving us all on the edge of starvation. This would be good for Disney, since we would all be willing to pay a high price for food. But the losses to the rest of us would far outweigh the gain to Disney. It is a relief to know that, after all, Mickey Mouse is not such an essential ingredient of the American diet.

In passing, notice here a serious problem with the interpretation of economic efficiency that seems to have become common among legal scholars writing in this field. In the example earlier, taking the monopoly power over food away from Disney is often interpreted as not necessarily efficient. This is because, while consumers are better off, the entity called "Disney" is worse off after competition in the market for food is established. This is not the appropriate place to go through the theorems of modern welfare economics, but it is the appropriate place to mention the faulty argument to the interested reader, just in case.

Landes and Posner also express concern that Mickey Mouse's "image might also be blurred or even tarnished, as some authors portrayed him as a Casanova, others as catmeat, others as an animal rights advocate, still others as the henpecked husband of Minnie." Since in common parlance calling something "Mickey Mouse" is not intended as a compliment, one might wonder how Mickey Mouse's reputation could be more tarnished than it is. Regardless, bear in mind that the only things that matter are copies of the idea of Mickey Mouse. If Mickey Mouse falls into the public domain, someone might well use his or her copy of the idea of Mickey Mouse to produce, say, a pornographic film starring Mickey Mouse. But would this tarnish the copies of the idea of Mickey Mouse in the minds of millions of 6-year-old children? It is hard to see how: ordinarily children of this age are not allowed to see pornographic films. Presumably those people that choose to see the film are those who benefit from this portrayal of Mickey Mouse.

How does their doing so interfere in any way with anyone else's enjoyment of their vision of Mickey Mouse? To put things in perspective, one of us considers if a sign of bad taste to spread Parmigiano-Reggiano cheese on any pasta with a sauce based on sea food. Nevertheless, this does not prevent him from being married to, and having often pleasant dinners, with a spouse that has exactly the opposite preference: as long as there is pasta, Parmigiano-Reggiano is welcome, no matter what the sauce is. In the rare occasions in which only one dish of pasta with a clam sauce is available, this clearly creates a little debate that reduces overall welfare. Which should make it painfully clear why it is socially good to have as many copies as possible of Mickey Mouse, and of pasta dishes alike.

To understand the distinction between a pecuniary and technological externality more clearly, consider the case of music. By and large, my listening to my copy of my music does not interfere with your listening to your copy of your music – there is no externality. But if I play my music very loudly, it may in fact interfere with your enjoyment. One solution to this very real technological externality would be to give a monopoly on the sale of stereo equipment to the Disney Corporation. As a good monopolist, they would limit the supply and raise the price of stereos. As a result, I would not be able to afford such powerful equipment, and would be forced to play my music less loudly, thereby reducing the externality. Mild negative externalities are common in everyday life. One "solution" is the creation of monopolies that will limit supply of the ingredients used to produce externalities. But most of us understand that this "cure" is worse than the disease. Cars are major generators of negative externalities, from air to noise pollution, but nobody has yet advocated solving the problem by creating a world monopoly on cars.

Landes and Posner go on to say

> One purpose of giving the owner of a copyright a monopoly of derivative works is to facilitate the scope and timing of the exploitation of the copyrighted work – to avoid, as it were, the "congestion" that would result if once the work was published anyone could make and sell translations, abridgements, burlesques, sequels, versions in other media from that of the original (for example, a movie version of a book), other variants…The result would be premature saturation of the market, consumer confusion (for example, as to the source of the derivative works,) and impaired demand for the original work because of the poor quality of some of the unauthorized derivative works.

This seems to us to be both at odds with reality and profoundly anti-market and anti-competition. Yes, the competitive market is full of interesting products. We can buy many brands, styles and colors of shirts, jackets, and shoes. Yet apparently consumers are not so profoundly ignorant as to be unable to figure out which brands, styles, colors, and products they wish to purchase; they apparently do not need the Disney Corporation to work this out for them. In the competitive markets of the free world there are lots of good products, lots of excellent products, and even more cheap and low quality products. So what? Seabright [2004] celebrates the diversity produced by competition; Lindsey [2001] warns us against those who do not trust the decentralization of the free market and wish to bring the "dead hand" of central authority to sort out the confusion. Unlike Landes and Posner, we do not see the need for the organizing authority of the monopolist to substitute for the diversity of the marketplace.

In an effort to give substance to their argument, Landes and Posner point to three examples of "works of... elite culture that have been damaged by unlimited reproduction: the Mona Lisa, the opening of Beethoven's Fifth Symphony, and several of Van Gogh's most popular paintings." We would like to know what evidence Landes and Posner have for this assertion. Searching Amazon for "Beethoven" in classical music brings up three items as most popular. The first is a collection of all nine symphonies; the second is a compilation of the fifth and the seventh. So apparently, despite the damage done by unlimited reproduction, the fifth is still well liked by many people – or are we to imagine that they skip the opening because it has been so damaged by unlimited reproduction? Or are Professors Landes and Posner suffering from the snobbish and European tendency to consider works of art "debased" once they become known and appreciated by the "unrefined" masses?

More or less the opposite of the "overgrazing" argument is the "maintenance" argument. Here it is argued that only with a monopoly is there adequate incentive to "maintain" ideas. The extreme example of the "maintenance" argument is the argument that providing a copyright monopoly will actually increase availability, the registrar of copyrights going so far as to say "lack of copyright protection... restrains dissemination of the work."[9] Lemley [2004], who criticizes what he refers to as *ex post* arguments for copyright along lines that parallel our own,[10] puts it succinctly: "It is hard to imagine Senators, lobbyists, and scholars arguing with a straight face that the government should grant one company the perpetual right to control the sale of all paper clips in the country, on the theory that otherwise no one will have an incentive to make and distribute paper clips." Lemley also cites empirical evidence showing, not surprisingly, that public domain works are far more widely available than works from the same time period that are still under copyright.[11]

A bit less ridiculous is the following type of argument: we can imagine that Disney might have less incentive to produce new Mickey Mouse movies if they face competition in the market for Mickey Mouse dolls – some of the good feeling for Mickey Mouse generated by the movie will spillover into increased demand for other producers' Mickey Mouse dolls. This would appear to be, indeed, a case of real externality, albeit positive instead of negative; lacking a way of compensating Disney for the positive effect it is having on the demand for Mickey Mouse dolls, Disney's movie output would be too low. The problem with this analysis is that it is wrong. Mickey Mouse movies and Mickey Mouse dolls are examples of goods that are complements – increasing the quantity of one raises the demand for the other. But many goods are complements: for example, peanut butter and jelly. And quite rightly no one worries that there would not be enough peanut butter produced because part of the effect of producing more peanut butter is that it will raise the demand for jelly. Basically what this argument overlooks is the reciprocal effect: when the competition produces more Mickey Mouse dolls, it will also raise the demand for the Mickey Mouse movie.

This fallacy can been seen again in Landes and Posner's example of "the Disney Corporation [spending] tens of millions of dollars refurbishing the Mickey Mouse character, both by subtle alterations in the character and by situating it in carefully selected entertainment contexts in an effort to increase the appeal of Mickey Mouse to the current generation of young children." This is a classical example of complementary goods – the release of the "improved" Mickey Mouse raises the demand for "unimproved" Mickey Mouse – but again, there is no adverse incentive as the increased supply of "unimproved" Mickey Mouse in turn raises the demand for the improved version.[12]

Landes and Posner also try a more subtle tack. They focus not so much on tie-ins between related goods, but rather on "promotional" efforts. "Consider an old movie on which copyright had expired that a studio wanted to issue in a colorized version… Promoting the colorized version might increase the demand for the black and white version, a close substitute… the studio would have to take into account, in deciding whether to colorize, the increase in demand for the black and white version." Here it seems that promotion of the colorized film, is a complement to both consumption of the colorized film and the black and white version; insofar as it is merely a statement about goods being complements, we have already seen there is no economic issue. But more to the point: in all competitive markets producers lack incentives to promote the industry. Individual wheat producers do not have much incentive to promote the healthy virtues of wheat, fisherman do not have much incentive to promote the healthy virtues of fish and so on.[13] It is hard to see that the problem with old movies, books, and music is different either qualitatively or quantitatively than in these other competitive markets. Yet quite rightly no one argues that we need grant wheat or fish monopolies to solve the "problem" of underpromotion.

It is worth reflecting briefly on promotional activities in competitive industries. Surely information about, say the health benefits of fish, is useful to consumers; equally surely no individual fisherman has much incentive to provide this information. Is this some form of market failure? No – in a private ownership economy consumers will have to pay for useful information rather than having it provided for free by producers. And pay they do – doctors, health advisors, magazine publishers all provide this type of information for a fee. There is no evidence that competitive markets underprovide product information. Rather in the case of monopolist, because the value of the product mostly goes to the monopolist rather than the consumer, the consumer has little incentive to acquire information, while the monopolist has a lot of incentive to see that the consumer has access to it. So we expect a different arrangement for information provision ("promotion") between competitive and non-competitive markets. In the former, the consumer pays and competitive providers generate information. In the latter, firms will subsidize the provision of information.[14]

Ironically, Landes and Posner give their own arguments only a tepid endorsement. Referring to the ill effects of overgrazing, they point out "there are counterexamples: the works of Shakespeare seem unimpaired by the uncontrolled proliferation of performances and derivative works, some of them kitsch, such as Shakespeare T-shirts and the movie Shakespeare in Love." We would point out that comparing someone to Winston Churchill, unlike Mickey Mouse, is a compliment not an insult. They go on to the resounding conclusion that "there is potentially a legitimate concern here, one that economic analysis should not ignore completely." Well, we have taken their advice, as we have not ignored them completely. What is most striking about this halfhearted conclusion is that Landes and Posner begin their book with a list of arguments against copyright and reach a rather stronger conclusion:[15]

> The foregoing nine points constitute the case against an incentive-motivated need for copyright... and especially against the incentive-motivated need for long copyright terms. For even with regard to expressive works especially vulnerable... copyright protection lasting [no] more than a few years [should be adequate] to recover the reasonable cost of creating the work.

This is ironic, as we have seen that the non-incentive based arguments that they themselves give only tepid endorsement too are in fact wrong.

Loosers

The Supreme Court opinion in 01-618 contains only two dissenting opinions, one by Justice Stevens and the other by Justice Breyer. While we agree with most, but not all, of what they say, we will not quote from them, but quote instead from Breyer [1970]. This is, in part, because the dissenting opinions – in particular that of Justice Stevens – focus mostly on the retroactive extension of term, and in part because words of wisdom are worth repeating, even when, and especially when, they are going around unlistened.

Contrary to other legal scholars, Breyer understands economics, as he can figure out that positive consumer surplus is not a bad outcome, at least from a social view point (pp. 285–286)

> It is often said that the author should receive the "value" of his work to society – a value that might be measured in terms of what those who benefit from the book would be willing to pay rather than do without it. But few workers receive salaries that approach the total value of what they produce. [. . .] workers in competitive industries make products that sell at prices well below what many of their buyers would be willing to pay for them. We do not feel that owners, managers, or workers in such industries are for this reason morally entitled to higher wages. Indeed, when a worker without competition – perhaps because he is the only doctor in the area, or the only engineer capable of building a certain bridge – could charge a price close to the total value of his services to the buyer, we normaly encourage competition, which will force him to charge less.

His conclusive policy recommendations in 1970 were already the following, very actual ones (pp. 350–351)

1   The period of copyright protection is at present too long and should not be extended beyond fifty-six years.
2   The law should allow individuals to make single copies of magazine articles and extracts from books without obtaining permission to do so from copyright

owners. The details of this exemption can be determined by the study commission which the Revision Bill would establish.

3   The law should allow individuals and small groups to store copyrighted material in computers and to use it for research purposes without obtaining permission from copyright owners.
4   Computer programs should not receive copyright protection at the present time.

And the very final conclusion

> The generally unsatisfactory nature of the congressional hearings on the Copyright Revision Bill underlines the importance of these conclusions. The hearings reveal little critical analysis of industry claims that protection is needed. They show little awareness of the possible harms of extending protection. Rather, the data amassed at the hearings is unsifted, often irrelevant, fact and opinion, and many critical facts about affected industries, are missing. Of course the hour is late: the revisors have long been hard at work. Yet one cannot escape the conclusion that more empirical work and more thoughtful analysis is needed before the Copyright Law is significantly revised.

More common fallacies

Additional theoretical and empirical work is certainly needed, as Breyer advocated thirty-five years ago, to better understand the impact that IP has on innovation, creation, and overall economic welfare. In the thirty-five years since those words were written, abundant research, indeed a gigantic amount of research, has been produced on the subject of which, though, very little has taken a critical approach. In fact, and until the events of the late 1990s have somewhat helped to reopen the debate, most research has supported the general principle that IP is good for society at large, not bad as we actually claim here and in related work (see, for example, Boldrin and Levine [2005a,b] and references therein.) This is due to one, fundamental, reason: common, legal, and economic wisdom argues that competitive markets are not suitable for trading copies of ideas, as ideas are intrinsically different from other economic commodities. For the most part these arguments are incorrect, and to their common fallacy we now turn.

Instead of arguing if IP protection should be extended or not, if its term should be of 20 years for patents and 75 for copyright, or possibly vice versa, we would like to question the very same idea that IP is necessary and useful for fostering invention. Our basic contention is the following: exception made for a few, and altogether minor, exceptions, IP is not necessary for efficient innovation. The efficient allocation of surplus from innovation can and would be achieved by properly regulated competitive markets, and such distribution of surplus among inventors, imitators, and consumers could provide, on average, the correct incentives for the efficient amount of creation to take place in society. Therefore, as a matter of legislative principles, IP should be abolished and replaced with the opposite system of property rights. A system in which creators have the same rights as other producers, that is: the right to own and sell the fruits of their work, and in which legal monopoly power is not assigned to them over their ideas, unless a substantial case is made that the innovation could not materialize lacking the specific monopoly privilege.

To understand the common fallacy one needs to start from the examining the basic principle, put forward long ago by Kenneth Arrow [1962], according to which ideas and information constitute a very peculiar kind of commodities, unsuitable to be traded in competitive market. This is not true: along most dimensions, ideas are not different form other commodities, and those few dimensions along which ideas are different do not generally affect the functioning of competitive markets. Here are some often-heard arguments, which we have shown to be fallacious.

(I) It is argued that in competitive markets innovators would be unable to appropriate more than an infinitesimal share of the social value of their ideas.

This is a recurrent theme in much business, managerial, and industrial organization literature, where it is apparently believed that economic efficiency requires innovators (or producers more generally, we would believe) to appropriate all the social value of their products. Were this to be the case, any market transaction in which some positive social surplus is realized would be inefficient as producers are "leaving something on the table," to consumers in fact. This, as our earlier quotation shows, was already very clear to Breyer in 1970, still a large literature, written by self-proclaimed economists and management strategy experts, keeps assuming or stating the opposite. But, obviously, socially efficient provision of ideas/goods requires, instead, that all ideas/goods with a positive social surplus (i.e. social value larger or at most equal than social cost) be produced. How such surplus is split between producers, consumers, and other entities (suppliers of intermediate inputs, government, etc.) may, and in general will, affect if all goods with positive social surplus are produced, but there is no general presumption that too few goods will be created unless producers appropriate the whole social surplus. In general, in fact, we would expect producers to bring goods, or ideas, to the market, as long as the private costs of doing so is exceeded by the private gains.

Hence, from a social perspective, one should ask: for all ideas with a positive social surplus, is it the case that competitive pricing allows producers to appropriate enough revenues to compensate for their private opportunity cost? Strangely enough, this question is seldom asked in the theoretical literature on innovations, and never, to the best of our knowledge, in the empirical one. This fallacy, as we have shown, for example, in Boldrin and Levine [1999, 2004a], misses the fact that ideas combine attributes of both consumption and capital goods. They can be used directly for consumption, such as reading a book, or watching a movie, or they can be used as an input in production, by making copies of a book or movie, or by producing other goods, for example, by using the idea for an improved production process. That the original copy of an idea is the capital good (the tree) from which all other copies (the fruits) must originate enables innovators to appropriate the net present value of all future copies through competitive pricing. Corn seeds, for example, can be eaten or used for producing additional corn, so also combine characteristics of consumption and capital goods. Competitive markets for corn generate the appropriate incentive to invest in corn seed. The initial copy (or copies, when simultaneous innovation occurs) of an idea are generally produced through a process which is different from the one used to make subsequent copies, as in the case of original research versus teaching. Most capital goods (original research) are used to produce commodities other than themselves – but the fact that capital goods might be used to reproduce themselves poses no particular problem for competitive markets. In the semi-conductor industry, for example, reduction in chip size makes it possible to construct capital equipment that can be used to produce even smaller chips.

(II) There are suggestions that ideas are subject to "spillover externalities," or what we might call informational leakage. That is, the existence of the idea enables people to learn it and make use of it without the permission of the owners.

Some even argue that ideas can be copied for free. In practice, few ideas are subject to informational leakage, and in all cases are costly to reproduce. In the case of copyrightable creations, where the ideas are embodied in physical objects such as books, informational leakage is not an issue. In the case of scientific advances, reflection shows that it is also not the case. While in some sense scientific ideas are widely available, usable copies of scientific ideas are not so easy to come by. Even Newton's laws, our example in the next section, require a substantial amount of time and effort to understand. For all practical purposes copies are limited to those people who understand the laws and books that explain them. Without paying someone to teach you or buying a book that explains Newton's laws, you are not terribly likely to learn them merely because they are in the public domain. As teachers and professors we earn our living by our ability to communicate ideas to others, and in doing so creating new copies of them. Overwhelming historical evidence shows that diffusion and adoption of innovations is costly and time consuming.

(III) Leaving ideas in the public domain, as it would be the case under a system where IP were ruled illegal, is socially inefficient and leads to a "tragedy of the commons" for creative activity.

We have already argued in previous section. Why this claim is fundamentally incorrect. Once copyright or patent have expired, there are many copies of an idea, each a good substitute for the other, and each owned by someone. If you want to use the idea, make copies, or turn it into something else, you must first acquire a copy of it from one of the current owners. If there are many owners, each competing with each other to sell you the copy of the idea, you may be able to obtain it relatively cheaply, even though you intend to turn it into a highly valued new good. But the fact that you can buy ingredients cheaply is a good consequence of competitive markets, not a bad one. In fact, the evidence suggests that the market for goods in the public domain functions well, with copies widely available and reasonably priced: finding a copy of a book by Dickens, for example, is no great problem.

Thinking out of the UIP box

We have worked out elsewhere – see Boldrin and Levine (1999, 2002, 2004a) – formal, mathematical, and quantitative models of why creative activity can thrive under conditions of competition and does not require, at least in principle but also in practice, the monopoly privileges that current IP legislation attributes to creators and inventors. Here we illustrate verbally the basic intuition underlying our analysis, using a well-known historical example to fix ideas.

Economic, and more generally social, progress is the long run, and altogether surprising, result of the continuous creation of new commodities, of their free exchange among individuals, and of the competition among producers of different goods, be they creators or imitators. Economists have long realized that there would be but a slow and possibly inconsequential improvement in human living standards without sustained innovation. This point was argued, most forcefully, by Joseph Schumpeter in *The Theory of Economic Development* (1911). With constant technology and a constant set of goods, the process of capital accumulation, when based only on the saving of a share of the yearly income flow, would generate but a fraction of the growth in per capita income we have witnessed since the inception of human history. Accumulation of capital under a constant technology, history and common sense conjure to suggest, cannot go very far due to the presence of fixed resources and the diminishing returns they bring about. Innovation is the engine of change and economic development, hence understanding its nature, internal mechanisms, and the social and institutional factors that bring it about or impede it, is, we believe, the single most important problem faced by the social sciences. It is our contention that understanding innovation is tantamount to understanding competition, that the latter is a necessary condition for the former and that, under very general circumstances, it is also sufficient. If innovation is the flow that enriches us all, then competition is the spring from which it erupts.

Innovation, for us, is the creation of the first copy of a good/process/idea that did not exist before. As the word "idea" is used here to denote all innovations, its usage should be briefly clarified. In our terminology, Isaac Netwon's innovation did not consist just in "thinking" the gravitational laws, but in the process of embodying them in his mind first, and in formulas and written expositions later. When, in 1687, he completed the manuscript of his *Philosophiae naturalis principia mathematica* and had it published, "Newton's innovation" was completed. All subsequent copies of the *Principia* were reproductions of that first copy of his idea, and they were produced with a technology different from the one he had to use to obtain his first manuscript. Notice, that with "copy" here we refer here to either a physical copy of the actual book or the (equally physical, if less visible) copy of the gravitational laws embodied in the brain of another scientist or layman, that is, a piece of socially valuable human capital. Indeed, and this is something crucial, the social value of Newton's innovation is more properly measured by the number of copies of his laws existing in the second form (actual human capital) than in the first (copies of the book.) All such copies stemmed from Newton's original copy and the social value of the latter would have been much smaller, or even negligible, without them. Newton's reward, either in terms of intellectual prestige or in terms of actual wealth and social status, became so high because very many copies (of either type) of the *Principia* were eventually reproduced. In our terminology, the first copy of the gravitational laws is the "prototype" and it embodies, for the first time, Newton's idea; the *innovation technology* is the one Newton adopted to figure out the gravitational laws and write the *Principia*. The *imitation technology* is the one used by subsequent publishers of the book and by whoever learned and understood the content of the *Principia*. Notice, which is relevant, that the *Principia* were published before the Statute of Anne introduced some (weak by current standard) degree of IP legislation in the United Kingdom.

Notice that the final products of the two technologies are, functionally speaking, equivalent: a copy of the *Principia* is a copy of the *Principia*, and a human that understands the principles and laws of gravitation is, at least from this narrow point of view, equivalent to any other human who understands the same principles and laws. This point will become relevant later on, when discussing the *public domain* for ideas. Notice also that both technologies use a variety of inputs to obtain their final product, that some of these inputs are previous innovations (e.g. Kepler's Laws) and that such inputs can be acquired on competitive markets under No Intellectual Property (NIP), but would have to be obtained from monopolists by acquiring many licenses under IP. There are two exceptions, to what we just said. First, the innovation technology uses a particularly scarce input, Newton's geniality in this case, which greatly limits the number of initial prototypes that can be obtained. Had we been concerned with a less dramatic invention, simultaneous creation by a number of different and independent innovators would have been likely, as it is often the case in practice. Still, the total amount of "creative ability" available at any point in time to make prototypes of a new ideas is quite limited. In the jargon of economics, there is always *limited creative capacity* of prototypes at any given point in time. In the particular case of scientific inventions or of artistic creation, this limitation of creative capacity may persist for a long time: new scientific discoveries are very difficult to understand, that is why we have PhD programs and post-docs, and live performances of, say, new music hard to imitate, which is why live concerts are often sold out and very expensive. The imitation technology also uses a special kind of input, and that is a pre-existing copy of the *Principia* (in case we are considering a publisher making copies of the book) or, generally, someone who has already understood its content (in case we are considering a student learning gravitational laws). Either way, also this particular input(s) is in limited supply; strictly speaking, this is true at any point in time and even now, but it is especially true in periods close to the time in which the first prototype of the *Principia* appeared. In summary, the imitation technology also faces a *limited productive capacity*, the size of which is basically determined by the number of copies of the idea "Newton's Gravitational Laws" embodied in humans/books at any point in time.

A little reflection shows that this set of properties is not specific to the particular case of the *Principia*, but applies quite widely (we would say: universally) to other innovations. The differences are quantitative, never qualitative: new valuable ideas are always embodied in either people or things; innovative capacity is always limited; imitation/reproduction always requires copies of the idea and hence stems from the original prototype even if in some rare cases imitation may not require large investments; reproductive capacity is also quite limited for a substantial number of periods after the innovation takes place; new ideas almost always require old ideas to be created, and creation is more and more a complex and cumulative incremental process; finally, consumers are always impatient and would rather have the stuff today than tomorrow. Our theoretical analysis builds upon such properties, and an additional one: it took quite a while for Newton to come up with the gravitational laws (falling apples notwithstanding) and, for what we know, even longer to fully articulate them in the manuscript of the *Principia*. Further, the *Principia* was not a minor, infinitesimal departure from or improvement upon previous knowledge, but a substantial one indeed. This property is also general, at least qualitatively! Producing the prototype, via the invention technology, requires quite often a large investment, which we want to think of as an *indivisibility*. While it is not true that a sizeable indivisibility is involved with the production of prototypes of every idea, it is true that this is often the case, and that this feature of creative activity should be taken in proper account when discussing the allocation of economic surplus from creative activity.

Finally, a few words to further clarify our approach to the problem. We ask what is socially optimal, and how incentives should be provided (i.e. which market structure can provide the appropriate incentives) for the *socially optimal amount of creative activity to take place*. The problem of providing incentives for innovation should not be confused with the protection of rents of intermediaries, or rents of established artists, or creators more generally. The issue here is not what makes creators richer or as rich as possible, but how to allocate to them enough of the surplus from creative activity so that they have the incentive to carry it out efficiently, from a social view point. This requires focusing on the concept of *opportunity cost*, that is, to ask: when a potential innovator considers the choice between engaging in creative activity or doing something else, his opportunity cost is determined by how much income he would receive from doing something else. Efficiency requires that, should the innovator opt for creation, he should receive from the latter at least as much as he would receive from the alternative activity, that is: his opportunity cost. When the market structures allows the innovator to receive more than his opportunity cost, this additional rent serves no socially useful purpose. *Per se*, this additional rent may just be a pure transfer, which does not affect economic efficiency; nevertheless, more often than not, and in particular when monopoly power is involved, this additional rent accrues to the innovator because he has the incentive to provide less innovations, or less copies of his innovations, than socially efficient. In this case the additional rent is not just a neutral transfer from consumers to innovators (which may be unfair, but irrelevant for efficiency) but a socially costly and inefficient tax on consumers, less copies of ideas are available to the people than it is desirable and technologically feasible. Our critique of current IP laws focuses mainly on this second aspect.

Technological innovations continuously change the opportunity cost and reservation values of the various agents involved in creation. So, for example, the invention of the printing press made the craftsmanship accumulated over century of artisans and monks unnecessary for copying or for production of new books. This was a blessing, for writers of books and their readers, but also a curse for those artisans who suddenly lost their long established title to a substantial share of the social value of every book, new or old that it be. Given current technologies, and the continuous improvement in the innovation and reproduction technologies, it would be crucial to measure what the opportunity costs of creators and innovators actually are. Unfortunately, this is an endeavor to which applied economists, especially in the area of industrial organization, have dedicated minimal attention and we are not aware of any study estimating the minimum future expected income needed to attract potential innovators into creative activity.

Conclusion

While the functioning of competition in the market for goods has been the subject of study for a long time, and our knowledge of the subject appears to have progressed substantially since the times of Adam Smith, it is often felt that the same is not true of the market for ideas. Indeed, there is a widespread view that ideas are dramatically and intrinsically different from goods and that the "economics of knowledge" needs to be grounded on different premises and adopt different modeling strategies than the rest of economics. In our work we reconsidered this issue and concluded that, while the economic theory of ideas does require modifications in some of the more common assumptions with which markets for regular commodities are handled, such differences are much less dramatic than one would have expected *prima facie*, and that a great deal of common economic wisdom applies equally well to the economics of knowledge. This allows us to critically reconsider a number of theoretical issues sitting at the intersection between the theory of innovation and technological change and growth and trade theory, to conclude that much common wisdom, including the legal wisdom bestowed upon us by the Supreme Court of the United States, is either empirically groundless or logically faulty, and that some old, and possibly uncommon, wisdom, should be brought back to bear on the study of technological change, growth, and trade.

Central to understanding the market for ideas and the incentives for the adoption of new ideas is discovering how ideas might be different from other goods. The starting point of the economic analysis of innovation is to recognize that the economically relevant unit is a copy of an idea. That is, typically, many copies of an idea exist in physical form, such as a book, a computer file or a piece of equipment, or in the form of knowledge embodied in people who know and understand the idea. When embodied in humans, copies of ideas are labeled with a variety of different names, which often obscure their common nature: skills, knowledge, human capital, norms, and so on. Careful inspection shows, though, that each and everyone of these apparently different entities is, at the end, nothing but the embodied copy of an idea, and that the latter was either discovered first by the person in whom it is currently embodied, or acquired (possibly via observation and imitation) from other humans, in whom it had been previously and similarly embodied. Economically valuable copies of ideas do not fall from the heavens, like manna, but are the product of intentional and costly human efforts. Only these copies matter, first, in the sense that if they were all to be erased, the idea would no longer have any economic value, and, second, in the sense that the copies are relatively good substitutes for each other: whether a copy of an idea is the original copy or the hundredth copy, it is equally economically useful. From the perspective of the functioning of markets, then, property rights in copies of ideas is assured by the ordinary laws against theft – what is ordinarily referred to as "intellectual property" protects not the ownership of copies of ideas, but rather a monopoly over how other people make use of their copies of an idea.

Notes

1 See, among others, http://cyber.law.harvard.edu/openlaw/eldredvashcroft/supct/amici/economists.pdf
2 For example, Miller commentary, reproduced also as Congressional Testimony and available at http://www.public.asu.edu/~dkarjala/legmats/hatch95.html, which also contains a careful critique of Miller's arguments by Dennis S. Karjala.
3 From the US Constitution.
4 In case you find our tone somewhat disrespectful of the Supreme Court, we very much regret it. Nevertheless, the part we cite is literally the only argument the said Court provides to give substance to the idea that it is good national policy for the Congress of the United States to legislate according to the wishes of the EU Commission in Bruxelles. Certainly, we could have taken another approach and argued, on post 9/11 Patriotic Act grounds, that US legislation should express the will of the US citizens and not that of some, probably anti-American, technocrat in Bruxelles. This is, in fact, what we do next.
5 Our usage of "at least" and "not poorer" is intentional. Indeed, to the extent that demand for creative work is downward sloping and creative works are partial substitutes for each other, the US creators are actually richer. This is because monopolist prices are higher than competitive ones, hence, if the prices of EU creations increase once the copyright term increases there, US creators can keep their products as competitive as they were before in the EU markets, and still slightly raise their prices.
6 From Karjala [1998] and cited in Landes and Posner [2003].
7 Landes and Posner's discussion of overgrazing and maintenance can be found on pp. 222–234 of [2003].
8 Britt [1990] pp. 22 and 26.
9 Quoted in Lemley [2004].
10 We should point out that Lemley's argument that if monopoly rights are provided there is no reason to provide them to the creator is wrong. Regardless of who starts with the monopoly rights, as long as they can be sold without prohibitive transactions costs, they will wind up in the hands of whoever can manage them the most efficiently. In practice most copyrights are in fact transferred to corporations and publishers. If monopoly rights are to be provided, the advantage of providing them to the creator (other than the obvious difficulty of figuring who else to give them to), is that it does create an additional incentive for creation, however miniscule it might be.
11 See also Karjala [2004] and our own analysis in Boldrin and Levine (2005b, chap. 4).
12 Note that the classical fixed cost argument for intellectual property is absent here – certainly Disney could spend a few million more or less "refurbishing the Mickey Mouse character."
13 That is why promotional campaign for milk, cereals, and fish are usually carried out by some industry-wide association, and not by individual firms.

14 Of course the monopolist, unlike the competitive providers, will have no incentive to provide accurate information. We rarely see Disney advertising that, however true it might be, their new Mickey Mouse movie is a real dog, and we should go and see the old Mickey Mouse movie instead.
15 Landes and Posner [2003] p. 50.

References

Arrow, Kenneth [1962]: "Economic Welfare and the Allocation of Resources for Invention," in *The Rate and Direction of Inventive Activity: Economic and Social Factors*, A Report of the National Bureau of Economic Research, 609–625. Princeton: Princeton University Press.

Boldrin, M. and D.K. Levine [1999]: "Perfectly Competitive Innovation," available at www.dlevine.com and www.econ.umn.edu/~mboldrin

Boldrin, M. and D.K. Levine [2002]: "The Case Against Intellectual Property," *American Economic Review Papers and Proceedings*, 92, 209–212.

Boldrin, M. and D.K. Levine [2004a]: "IER Lawrence Klein Lecture: The Case Against Intellectual Monopoly," *International Economic Review*, 45, 327–350.

Boldrin, M. and D.K. Levine [2004c]: "IP and Market Size," available at www.dlevine.com and www.econ.umn.edu/~mboldrin

Boldrin, M. and D.K. Levine, [2005a]: "The Economics of Ideas and Intellectual Property," *Proceedings of the National Academy of Sciences*, 102, 1252–1256.

Boldrin, M. and D.K. Levine [2005b]: *Against Intellectual Monopoly*, www.dklevine.com/general/intellectual/against.htm

Breyer, S. [1970]: "The Uneasy Case for Copyright. A Study of Copyright in Books, Photocopies, and Computer Programs," *Harvard Law Review* 84, 281–351.

Britt, B. [1990]: "International Marketing: Disney's Global Goals," *Marketing*, May 17, 22–26.

Karjala, D.S. [1998]: Statement of Copyright and Intellectual Law Professors in Opposition to H.R. 604, H.R. 2589 and S. 505, The Copyright Term Extension Act, Submitted to the Joint Committees of the Judiciary.

Karjala, D.S. [2004]: "Opposing Copyright Extension," URL: www.public.asu.edu/~dkarjala/legmats/hatch95.html

Landes, W.M. and R.A. Posner [1989]: "An Economic Analyisis of Copyright Law," *The Journal of Legal Studies* 18, 325–363.

Landes, W.M. and R.A. Posner [2003]: *The Economic Structure of Intellectual Property Law*, Cambridge, MA: Harvard University Press.

Lemley, M.A. [2004]: "Ex Ante versus Ex Post Justifications for Intellectual Property," mimeo, UC Berkeley, CA.

Lindsey, B. [2001]: *Against the Dead Hand: The Uncertain Struggle for Global Capitalism*, John Wiley & Sons, New York.

Posner, R.A. [2004] "Eldred and Fair Use," *The Economists' Voice*, September, http://www.bepress.com/ev/vol1/iss1/art3

Seabright, P. [2004]: *The Company of Strangers: A Natural History of Economic Life*, Princeton: Princeton University Press.

7 The uninvited guest
Patents on Wall Street

Robert P. Merges[1]

Academic research could help to understand whether patenting will encourage or discourage innovation, change the nature of financial innovation, encourage more innovation by smaller players, or change the competitive/cooperative interactions among financial service firms. In part, this yet-to-be completed work will simply build upon the extensive body of work in the industrial organization field on patenting. However, trying to understand what – if anything – is different about the financial services industry, and the implications for protection of intellection property and the nature of competition, is likely to be a fertile area for future work.

(Peter Tufano, 2002, p. 37)

How did we get here?

Up until a few years ago, State Street Bank was just another big bank in Boston. But in 1998, the Federal Circuit Court of Appeals used a patent case filed by the bank to transform the law concerning what is patentable. From now on, the bank's name will be irrevocably linked to a landmark case. Like Linda Brown of "Brown vs. Board of Education" fame, or Ernesto Miranda, who lent his name to the famous Miranda Warning ("You have the right to remain silent...￼"), State Street Bank will be forever linked with a major inflection point in US law.

For many in the financial services industries – banking, investment banking, stock brokerage firms, and the like – "*State Street Bank*: the case" was a bolt from the blue. How could patents apply to something as amorphous as the design of a new mutual fund system? Light bulbs, telegraphs, integrated circuits, foolish gadgets like self-tipping hats, maybe; but *financial products*?[2] As my young son might put it, "what's up with that?" And more to the point, regardless of where these new patents came from, how would they affect the financial world? Would they help or hurt the financial services industries in the long run? And had anyone thought this all through before making State Street Bank a household name outside Wall Street and Boston?

In this chapter I tackle some of these issues. My primary goal is to review what we know about innovation in the financial services industries, and try to discuss intelligently the effect patents will have. But first, as a service to readers drawn from these industries who might still wonder how these questions got on the agenda, I will try to explain how the patent system got to *State Street Bank* in the first place.

There are two strands to the story: (a) the subversive effects of computer software; and (b) the growing fascination with intellectual property generally. I consider each in turn.

The long and winding road to software patentability

From the point of view of patent law, the infusion of computer technology has completely changed how the legal system conceptualizes financial services. From a patent lawyer's point of view, many aspects of the financial services industries look like elaborate computer software applications. Despite the differences in climate and dress, Wall Street may as well be Palo Alto, Berkeley, or Redmond, Washington. After all, one can hear the patent lawyer saying, "it's all just software now."

Given this mindset, the patentability of financial services is simply a subset of a larger issue: the patentability of software. This was one of the most troublesome and longstanding issues in patent law for many, many years. Since the early days of the mainframe computer business, when IBM and others tried to get patents on software just as they always had for adding machines and then computer hardware, the patent system tried to grapple with a fundamental conundrum. How could written code – symbols on paper, basically – be a form of technology? Was the patent system of Thomas Jefferson, the MacCormick reaper, Orville Wright, and Thomas Edison the proper home for a series of instructions written down to tell a machine what to do?

The tale of how the patent system stopped worrying, and learned to love computer software is a long one. I will only hit the highlights here. After the Supreme Court expressed grave doubts about the whole enterprise in the early 1970s, software went underground in the patent system. It re-emerged, in the form of patents claiming essentially various pieces of machinery that were assisted by computers running programs (i.e. software). Thus the famous 1980 case of *Diamond v. Diehr*,[3] which upheld the validity of a patent on a rubber curing machine – a machine that happened to be assisted by a computer running software.

From 1980 until the mid-1990s, patent lawyers pushed the envelope defined by the *Diehr* case. Software was buried in patent claims. Wherever possible, attention was directed to conventional industrial processes that were accomplished using a computer, which computer just happened to run software. As these inventions were characterized, software was never an end in itself. Yet patent lawyers were forced to resort to ever more creative feats of characterization, because software was in fact increasingly separate and distinct from the hardware it ran on. Eventually, the elaborate game of "hide the software in the claims" culminated in a series of claim types. I will explain one of several – the "general purpose computer" claim.

In these claims, the invention is described as a "general purpose computer," that is, one capable of running many different programs. The claims go on to state that this computer is "configured" a certain way – configured by software as the computer runs it, that is. Thus to a patent lawyer, when I shut down my Word for Windows application and open Microsoft Excel, I am not just moving in and out of different computer programs, I am creating a new computer! When I open Excel, I am *reconfiguring the hardware*, rather than running a new program.

Although no judge ever actually articulated it, everyone seemed to understand that these characterization games had gotten out of hand. Legal practice did not reflect underlying technological reality. And the computer software industry had simply gotten too big by the 1990s for the patent system to ignore it. Throughout the 1990s there were a series of decisions concerning software that subtly signaled the beginning of the end of many of the old games. Software *qua* software was no longer strictly forbidden. By the mid-1990s, software in useable commercial forms could be effectively patented.

Despite the sense of change, no single case had clearly stated the end of the old regime. Then along came *State Street Bank*. This case represented a perfect opportunity to clear up any lingering doubts about the patentable status of software. And the Federal Circuit took advantage, with its sweeping opinion now so well known to the financial community.

From the perspective of the history sketched here, then, *State Street Bank* did not come out of the blue. Far from it. It was the culmination of a very long digestive process. After initially choking on software, and then letting only a little bit slip through, in disguise, the patent system finally gave in. Financial services software just happened to be on the menu when the Federal Circuit got serious about software.

The "shifting baseline": or, the propertization of just about everything

I have tried so far in this section to put business methods in the context of the evolution of software patent law. But an even broader change has been taking place, one that is also important for an understanding of how *State Street Bank* came to pass.

Not too long ago, intellectual property scholars could speak confidently of "the competitive baseline" – the idea that property rights were a deviation from commercial norms embodied in our legal system. Patents, copyrights, and trademarks were the *exception*; open access to rivals' products was the rule. All this has changed in recent years. As I argued in a recent review article, the principle of philosopher John Locke – labor yields property – has displaced the competitive baseline:

> The shift that has occurred has taken place at the deepest substratum of the field, down where the foundational principles bump and grind against each other. One massive construct, the principle of the competitive baseline, has started to give way. Under this notion, IP rights were envisioned as a rare exception. The general rule – the law's deep default – was open and free competition. This was always opposed by a counter-principal, the idea that

labor equals property. On this view, property rights are a matter of desert: in true Lockean fashion, property arises when you mix your effort with the found assets of the natural world. When seen from the perspective of laboring creators, the proper baseline is to protect all manifestations of creativity that take more than a trivial amount of effort. This was a powerful principle, to be sure, but until recently not usually powerful enough. The great tectonic shift of recent years has reversed this, however. Now it often seems as though the labor-equals-property principle dominates. Increasingly, courts and legislators seem to believe that if one type of labor deserves a property right, then others do as well. And so all manner of intangibles meet with protection – even when, in the past, the competitive baseline would have militated against it.

(Merges, 2001, pp. 2239–2240)

The rise and fall of fashionable ideas is certainly nothing new to the world of finance. One paper on financial innovations is even entitled "Boom and Bust Patterns in the Adoption of Financial Innovations" (Persons and Warther, 1997). My point here is simply that these are boom times for the *concept* of intellectual property. Businesspeople, the media, policymakers, and academics all seem fascinated by it. It is thus no wonder that, when confronted with a claim to property rights over some novel subject matter, a judge living in this environment is less likely to ask "why?" and more likely to say "why not?". This is a simple fact of our world, and no doubt has some influence in cases such as *State Street Bank*.

So where are we now? Table 7.1 gives us some idea. It presents totals for patents in class 705 of the US Patent Classification system which is titled, "Data Processing: Financial, Business Practice, Management, or Cost/Price Determination," for the years 1994 until 2001.[4]

As with so many things, the numbers tell the tale. Financial innovations are very much patentable subject matter now. Now that patents are here, the question is, are they really necessary? To answer that, we need to know something about how financial firms protected their investments in innovations before the advent of patents.

Table 7.1 Total number of patents issued for the years 1994–2001 in class 705 of US Patent Classification system

Year	Patents
1994	165
1995	94
1996	167
1997	198
1998	469
1999	833
2000	1006
2001	837

The "appropriability environment" of traditional financial services industries

The financial services industries appear to be highly innovative. In the area of traded securities alone, it is estimated that in the period 1980–2001, the securities industry generated between 1,200 and 1,800 new types of securities (Tufano, 2002, p. 7). Innovation in securities occurs to fill gaps in available instruments. New securities are constantly being devised to shift risks in ways not otherwise possible, and to provide payoffs for outcomes that current securities do not cover (what financial economists call "market completeness"). Outside securities *per se*, there is no shortage of innovations in the world of finance. New contracts, new transactional technologies such as ATMs, and even entire new exchanges have all been common in the past 25 years.

Scholars of innovation are well aware that intellectual property rights are not the only mechanism firms employ to recoup product development investments. The general term for this issue in the literature is "appropriability" (Teece, 1986). The empirical evidence establishes that patents are considered *essential* to appropriability in only a few industries – most notably, pharmaceuticals and some branches of the chemical industry (Cohen *et al.*, 2000). In other industries, the standard non-patent appropriability mechanisms include:

- lead-time or "first mover" advantages;
- co-specific assets, uniquely adapted for use with the innovation;
- trade secrecy/tacit knowledge.

In financial services, lead-time, co-specific assets, and trade secrecy/tacit knowledge seem to be important. I consider each in turn.

Cost-saving lead time

In a series of highly illuminating studies, Peter Tufano documented the financial innovation process. Tufano's original paper (1989) studied 58 financial innovations introduced between 1974 and 1986. The innovations were in mortgage-backed securities, asset-backed securities, non-equity-linked debt, equity-linked debt, preferred stock, and equities. These innovations were created "almost exclusively" by the largest investment banks, with six banks in particular accounting for over 75 per cent of "pioneering deals" (Tufano, 1989, p. 219). Large banks were more dominant in innovative deals than in deals overall – making financial innovation very much a game for "big players."

Tufano's finding regarding the dominance of large firms in the "innovation game" is echoed by Frame & White (2002, p. 13, fn. 16):

> For example, casual empiricism leads us to notice that relatively large financial services providers have been important innovators. Merrill Lynch was the developer of the "cash management account"; Salomon Brothers was the

leader in developing stripped Treasury securities; the larger commercial banks led in developing and offering "sweep" accounts, ATMs, and Internet transactions for customers. But it would be useful to have a more formal "census" of innovations and their originators and the characteristics of those innovators.

Tufano studied the appropriability strategies of financial innovators. He found that innovation was indeed costly; he estimates that

> Developing a new financial product requires an investment of $50,000 to $5 million. This investment includes (a) payments for legal, accounting, regulatory, and tax advice; (b) time spent educating issuers, investors, and traders, (c) investments in computer systems for pricing and trading, and (d) capital and personnel commitments to support market-making. In addition, investment banks that innovate typically pay $1 million annually to staff product development groups with two to six bankers.
>
> (Tufano, 1989, p. 213)

Tufano finds that investment banks recoup these investments through reduced costs in the market for innovative financial products. The pioneer of a new product has lower costs than its imitative rivals, allowing it to capture a larger market share than imitators. This in turn permits higher profits in the related secondary market for the pioneering product – that is, there are economies of scope. Essentially, even after imitators observe the pioneering product and copy it, the pioneer retains a long-term cost advantage. At the market price set by imitating rivals, the pioneer enjoys "inframarginal costs," and hence supracompetitive profits. Innovators actually charge less than imitators, particularly at first. In addition, a reputation for innovation helps banks in other ways. For example, Tufano describes a class of specialized, client-specific innovations that are rarely imitated (Tufano, 1989: In the market to produce these, a reputation for innovation is of course helpful.)

This cost-advantage mechanism for appropriating innovation costs is not unknown in other sectors. It seems to explain a good deal of readily-copied process innovations in certain industries, for example. The important feature of this appropriability mechanism for our purposes is that it does not rely on property rights to be effective. It does not even rely on informal methods of retaining exclusivity: everyone in the industry understands that "most new products can be reverse-engineered easily and cheaply" (Tufano, 1989, p. 230). Indeed, rapid diffusion of information about an innovation is actually a marketing advantage for pioneering firms.

Tacit knowledge and reputational advantage

A major area of financial innovation in the past thirty years is securitization, the transmutation of difficult-to-value assets into easily tradable securities.

Securitization expert Professor Tamar Frankel has asked why the originators of new securitization practices have not generally sought property rights for them. She begins by noting the difficulty of adapting exiting intellectual property categories to the protection of unique securitization ideas. Next, she considers some of the more subtle appropriability mechanisms – tacit knowledge and reputational advantage. Tacit knowledge can be thought of as know-how: the highly detailed, often context-specific knowledge actually required to do a complex job (Polanyi, 1967). It is hard to specify (as more than one "artificial intelligence" expert can testify), even harder to write down (or "codify"), and even harder still to transfer from one person to another (Cowan *et al.*, 2000). Tacit knowledge is usually therefore defined in contrast to more easily codifiable information.

Frankel argues that tacit knowledge of how to create a novel securitized asset provides a subtle appropriability mechanism to financial innovators:

> [P]aradoxically, "giving away" an innovation provides many monetary benefits. To begin with, these giveaways may not be complete. Unlike disclosure in applications for patents, disclosures of innovations in advertising, presentations or professional publications are not as complete and detailed. Certain experiences, drawbacks and danger points are likely to be omitted. Some say that following cookbooks of famous chefs rarely seems to produce dishes that taste as the chefs' dishes do. That is not necessarily done by intentionally avoiding an important ingredient from the recipe (although some cooks would be tempted to do so). In a complex area with different actors, it is difficult to transfer fully information in such publications so that the reader can replicate the activity without hands on guidance. Just as the water, cooking utensils, and ingredients may not be identical to those used by the author-chefs, so will the quality of the financial assets, the type of clients, and the legal environment of the transactor differ from those of the innovators. These differences may produce difficulties for the novices.
>
> (Frankel, 1998, p. 271)

Frankel also provides evidence of reputational advantages accruing to the creators of securities innovations. In this field, lawyers who help transmute illiquid assets into tradeable securities comprise a small, specialized corner of the legal profession. According to Frankel, "innovators reap the rewards of prestige from enhancing their reputation. For some people, these rewards may be the main driver" (Frankel, 1998, p. 272). This is also consistent with findings by Tufano, who recounts the bankers' view that innovation is the best way to advertise expertise (Tufano, 1989, p. 235).

While one case does not make a trend, a recent trade secret case indicates that appropriability mechanisms other than lead time may occasionally be important. In 1995, Morgan Stanley submitted a proposal to the State of California in response to an unusual request. The State was looking for innovative approaches to securitizing the risks associated with earthquake losses, an insurance market that the State had recently entered in response to perceived market failure in the private insurance business. Investors Guaranty Fund., Inc. ("IGF") is a small firm that apparently specializes in coming up with securitization concepts, and helping large investment banks to implement them. Investors Guaranty Fund claimed that Morgan Stanley's submission to the State was based on IGF's "total integrated system" for securitization of insurance risks. Investors Guaranty, Fund had, it argued, successfully employed this system in other securitization projects in conjunction with other banks.

The trade secret suit was dismissed.[5] The court stated that the IGF system was based on public domain concepts, and was not in fact proprietary to IGF. The court also ruled that the system did not confer a competitive advantage on Morgan Stanley, as the State terminated the securitization experiment and implemented a more conventional reinsurance scheme instead.

Industry appropriability and the prior user defense to patent infringement

There is good evidence that the financial services industry sought to protect established appropriability practices in the wake of *State Street Bank*. Financial services firms lobbied for and obtained a limited defense to infringement which is now part of the US patent statute. Under this "prior user right," firms that have developed and implemented secret internal methods of doing business may not be precluded from using them by later inventors who obtain a patent. A special provision was required to secure this result, as generally US law disfavors a secret prior user compared to a later user who files a patent application.

Prior user rights are common in other countries, particularly in Europe. They provide a measure of protection for firms that develop innovations but do not wish to patent them. They insulate earlier developers from the very expansive reach of property rights granted to later inventors. Many commentators, drawing on the empirical evidence concerning the centrality of trade secret protection as an appropriability mechanism in some industries (Cohen *et al.*, 2000), have argued in favor of a general prior user right under US law. But the actual law enacted in the wake of *State Street Bank* is much more limited: it protects only prior inventors of "a method of doing or conducting business" from infringement liability.[6]

Lawyer/lobbyists for the financial services industry very likely drafted this provision – a common occurrence in intellectual property legislation, as elsewhere.[7] In addition, industry representatives also appear to have drafted comments to be entered into the Congressional Record under the names of lawmakers from New York and New Jersey – Wall Street territory. These comments provide helpful insight into the perceived threat posed by the *State Street Bank* decision. Thus the Senate version of the Congressional Record includes this entry from Senator Charles Schumer (Democrat (D), New York (NY)):

> The first inventor defense will provide the financial services industry with important, needed protections in the face of the uncertainty presented by the Federal Circuit's decision in the *State Street* case . . . [T]his decision has

raised questions about what types of business methods may now be eligible for patent protection. In the financial services sector, this has prompted serious legal and practical concerns. It has created doubt regarding whether or not particular business methods used by this industry – including processes, practices, and systems – might now suddenly become subject to new claims under the patent law. In terms of every day business practice, these types of activities were considered to be protected as trade secrets and were not viewed as patentable material.

> (145 Cong. Rec. S14,836 (daily ed. November 18, 1999),
> at S.14,994 (statement of Sen. Schumer))

The identical statement was entered under the name of Representative Jerrold Nadler (D.-NY).[8] And a similar comment was entered by Senator Robert Torricelli (D.-NJ)., who states that

> Without this defense, financial services companies face unfair patent-infringement suits over the use of techniques and ideas (methods) they developed and have used for years.
> (145 Cong. Rec. S14,836 (daily ed. November 18, 1999),
> at S14,995 (statement of Sen. Torricelli))

As Senator Schumer is quoted as saying, financial product innovations have traditionally been "protected as trade secrets." Based on what we know, lead time and reputation might be added to the list. The point of the legislation is to defend these traditional mechanisms against the onslaught of patents. Because of certain technical features of the defense, however, it is not clear that the defense alone will protect financial services firms from the patents of "outsiders." This explains why large Wall Street firms are at the same time beginning to acquire some patents of their own.[9]

Property rights enforcement and information sharing in "traditional" areas of innovation

One crucial point of importance at this stage of the discussion is to note that not all property rights are enforced. This is often lost on critics of property rights, who positively thrive on presenting and embellishing a gruesome "parade of horribles." With proliferating property rights, we are told, businesspeople could no longer do many things they are accustomed to. Every patent owner could prevent everyone else from using their patented technology. And because they *could*, we are told, they *would*. Does this claim hold up based on what we know about other fields where intellectual property has arrived suddenly on the scene?

In a word, number one example comes from academic science. Here open exchange of research findings was long thought to serve as a model of information dissemination in the absence of property rights. Many observers thought the sudden advent of patents on the fruits of basic scientific research – particularly in the life sciences – was sure to kill the scientific enterprise, or at least inflict a mortal wound. But it did not. The reason was that although scientists (and particularly the research universities that employ them) aggressively acquire property rights, they almost never assert them against other scientists engaged in academic research. A scientist who draws on the work of peers in doing his or her own research follows a well-understood norm in the field: patents are asserted only against commercial entities. Fellow scientists operating within the same research community are off limits. In effect, there is an inner circle within which property rights are mutually "waived." They are only deployed against private firms operating in the outside circle of the corporate biotechnology industry. Even though many academic scientists work across both circles on a regular basis, they recognize that property rights are appropriate only in the outer circle. Patents are "checked at the door" when a researcher enters the domain of pure research. This is why, long after the advent of the property rights revolution in science, pure academic research – and the open, property rights-free exchange of information it depends on – continues to thrive.

A variation on this theme involves cooperative cross-licensing. In some industries, most notably semiconductors, firms aggressively acquire patents. But they are not typically asserted against commercial rivals in litigation. Instead, firms cross-license large patent portfolios. Sometimes two evenly matched firms cross-license with no royalty payments. For technologically unequal trading pairs, lump sum payments or ongoing royalties change hands. In either event, patents serve as "bargaining chips" in an elaborate industry scheme of information transfer. Patents mediate, rather than obstruct, the flow of information.

Would patents lead to continued exchange in the financial services industries? It is hard to say. There is some indication that little has changed in the wake of the *State Street Bank* decision. Perhaps the large firms continue to share information amongst themselves, banking patents only as a hedge against outsiders' attempts to use patents to hold up existing firms. As mentioned earlier, lobbying for a "prior user right" exception to infringement hints that financial firms' main goal in the post-patent era is to make the world safe for their existing practices. So perhaps the free exchange of information about new innovations will continue for the most part.

Past responses to the "patent plague"

Wall Street's reaction to the threat of patents runs contrary to the simplistic theory of incentives inherent in the patent system. But there are other cases where an industry has greeted the introduction of patents as more of a threat than an incentive. It may be instructive to review several of these episodes, with the goal of determining how serious the patent threat turned out to be, and how effective industry responses were.

Nineteenth-century railroads

Our first brief study may seem to come from far afield – temporally and conceptually. But in many ways, the coming of patents to the railroad industry in the nineteenth century looks very like the post-*State Street Bank* world on Wall Street. So far, financial firms have undergone the same shock and surprise as the railroads when they first came to grips with the disruptive effects of patents on established routines of innovation. And Wall Street has responded the same way, though much more quickly – with an aggressive counterthrust to the legal system's incursion into familiar turf. As with the railroads, financial firms have lobbied for legislation to overturn the most damaging aspects of the new patent regime. Indeed, judging by results, Wall Street's response has been more effective so far; the railroads never did succeed in getting favorable legislation passed. By contrast, the railroads slogged things out in the legal trenches for many years before beating back the most threatening aspects of the legal onslaught. Despite the differences, there is much to gain in a quick overview of the patent episode in railroad history.

To begin, there was a great deal of similarity in the way innovation progressed in nineteenth-century railroading and late twentieth-century Wall Street. Innovation in both industries was "an inside job": it was dominated by large, vertically integrated firms (Usselman, 2002). Nineteenth-century railroads not only laid track and scheduled shipments. They also performed service on and made routine improvements to locomotives, switching technology, rails, and all other aspects of railroad technology. Moreover, innovations diffused rapidly to rivals, and this was an accepted part of the business. Far from preventing this flow of information, the chief technology players at the major railroads saw themselves as part of a larger, cross-firm enterprise. They shared a common culture that included an implicit norm regarding new techniques: I share with you, you share with me (Usselman, 2002, p. 65). There was pride in an innovation that others could use, perhaps even some increment to firm or individual reputation.

The "appropriability regime" was dominated by complexity and capital constraints. Locomotive technology, for example, was simply too complex for many firms to get into the industry. There were few rivals around that could gain much from learning about an innovation. New technology alone was rarely seen as conveying a competitive advantage. Reaping the rewards from it required access to the wide array of co-specific assets comprising a full-service rail line. Property rights played a very small role in such a setting.

All this began to change by the 1870s. This era saw a host of "outside inventors" descending on the railroads. They promoted a long series of improvements and enhancements, some centering on safety devices invented in response to highly publicized rail disasters. But many came from mechanics and tinkerers of all varieties, swept up in the fascination with rail and steam that (then and now) seems to hold many in its thrall. The number of patents awarded for various aspects of railway technology grew steadily throughout the nineteenth century (Schmookler, 1967).

A modest number of "outside inventions" were adopted by the railroads during this period. But the patent system really burst into prominence when courts began awarding huge damage awards to the holders of patents who had sued the railroads.[10] In the wake of several much-discussed infringement suits, patent matters rose to the highest levels of discussion within the railroad companies. Although the corporate response took some time to coalesce, by the 1880s the industry was fully mobilized. Two large industry organizations supervised and carefully monitored the progress of important infringement suits, including several at the Supreme Court. Meanwhile, a legislative response took shape. Railroad executives lobbied hard in Congressional hearings against the extension of patents that had been costly to the industry. Lobbying also centered on a bill to overturn a particularly costly doctrine that had arisen in the courts. The "doctrine of savings" used a firm's estimated cost savings due to the use of a patented device as the basis of damage calculations. In the hands of a sympathetic judge or jury, it could lead to very expensive judgments. The industry labored to pass a bill to overturn the doctrine – and very nearly succeeded. But when the Supreme Court in 1878 adopted a more favorable interpretation of the "savings doctrine," the industry finally backed off.[11]

Apart from an increase in lobbying expenditures, did the introduction of patents affect the railroad industry? In particular, did the introduction of patents in any way slow down the course of railroad industry development?

The answer is clearly no. Jacob Schmookler documented railroad industry investment, additions to railroad track mileage, and stock prices for the period 1837 until 1950. All three measures showed robust increases throughout the nineteenth century (Schmookler, 1967, p. 116). Of special note is the fact that particularly sharp *increases* in these measures were recorded at the same time patents were arriving as a major force on the railroad scene (roughly, between 1860 and 1890). Whatever the effects of patents on the railroad industry, they did not bring it to a halt. Of course, growth might have been even more robust in the absence of patents. But realistically, they did not appear to slow the development of this industry in any significant way.

US software industry

The US software industry voiced very similar concerns when software patents became a reality in the 1980s. Cries were heard throughout the community of computer programmers that patents would kill the goose that had laid the golden egg of software creativity in the United States (Merges, 1997, chapter 2). A particular concern was that software patents would give an advantage to large firms, in particular IBM; there was fear over the clash of a "patent culture" – with its attendant high overhead costs – and the freewheeling and productive culture of programmers who were said to write code not strictly for profit, but for technical sophistication and elegance.

A funny thing happened on the way to the demise of the software industry. It never happened. Standard-setting organizations ameliorated some of the problematic effects of having multiple components of complex software products and protocols owned by separate firms. Several early "test cases" found the courts being quite reasonable about scope and validity issues with respect to computer software. And most telling of all, programmers forming startups found that venture capitalists placed a premium on companies with a robust patent portfolio. So leading-edge firms such as Inktomi moved quickly to establish effective patent portfolios. One reading of the history here is that software entrepreneurs found that patents were decidedly *not* just "for the big guys." In any event, the industry continues to move ahead, despite – and in some cases even perhaps because of – the advent of patent protection.

On the other hand, software patents have not changed many of the basic features of the industry, including the importance of "network effects" to many of its products (Saloner and Shepard, 1995). Perhaps there is a deeper path dependency in industrial development than we are aware. An industry, once started on a patent-free basis, establishes an innovation path that later proves relatively impervious to the imposition of patents. Perhaps patents overall simply do not affect the "big variables" of economic life – industry structure, the basic pace of innovation, and so on – in such an industry to any great extent. While these are somewhat humbling thoughts for a scholar who places the patent system at the center of the economic universe, the historical case studies certainly support such a view. Apart from their role in fostering "outside entry," and perhaps a marginal but significant role in making old industries safe for small, entrepreneurial firms, patents do not seem to have shifted the basic parameters of innovation in either railroading or software. If this pattern holds true, we may predict that patents will not significantly impact the overall structure or innovativeness of the financial services industry. To sound a Chandlerian theme: While patents may play a key role in individual firms' *strategies*, they may not have much impact on industry *structure*.

Property rights and the market for "financial technology"

Research on the emergence of "markets for technology" may have something to teach here as well. According to this literature, for a number of reasons active interfirm markets for technology are increasingly popular. The major factors are: (a) increasing creativity in "mining" intellectual assets for profit; (b) reduced fear of selling ideas to major competitors; and (c) improving and expanding know-how about how to propertize and value intellectual assets (Arora *et al.*, 2001; Davis and Harrison, 2001).

Viewed from the perspective of this literature, one interesting question is what effect patents will have on formalizing the exchange of information about financial services innovations. In the past, this information diffused out from innovators to other firms in the relatively "closed circle" of experts in each area.[12] Now, with the advent of patents, these innovations can be (to use the language of economists who study information transfer) "codified." Patents play a role here in helping identify discrete units of information for transfer. They also facilitate valuation, by clearly demarcating the boundaries of a discrete idea, and by feeding into a system of legal and technical experts who specialize in valuation.[13]

Patents can therefore push information exchange from an informal basis to a more formal one. Whether this is beneficial depends on the number of transactions that result under each of the two regimes. Currently, information about financial services innovations diffuses rapidly – through informal contacts among the principal designers of innovations, trade press articles, simple observation of what competitors are doing, and so on. These information exchanges are easy to miss, as they involve essentially zero transaction costs. Every time a businessperson learns something about a competitor's new practice in some area, after all, information has been transmitted. One reason it is easy to miss overlook the economic significance of these learning events is that the information is acquired free of charge.

What happens when information such as this is propertized – when an intellectual property right (IPR) attaches to it? Total transactional volume may well be affected. But how?

If a sizeable proportion of the information is suddenly covered by a property right, the flow of information may well decrease at first. What had been essentially free is suddenly more costly; information acquirers move up their demand curves. Over time, however, a number of offsetting gains might compensate for or justify this additional cost. It is a bedrock assumption of the intellectual property system that certain information will not be produced without the special incentive of a property right. Thus the addition of property rights to the equation will – in theory at least – call forth new and greater creative efforts, resulting in a larger number of innovations. True, some transactions that would have been free will now cost more. But the conventional wisdom from inside the IP system would predict a net increase in innovations. To put it bluntly, there is a possibility that while free transfer of ideas to competitors will end, a robust market in the formal exchange of new financial innovation ideas will lead to more exchanges of more valuable information.

Spinoffs

A related possibility involves spinoffs. Because much of the know-how associated with financial innovations currently resides in large firms, the people to staff new entrant firms will likely come largely from the established players. We are all familiar with many cases of startup companies emerging from the ranks of established players. The dynamic nexus of restless entrepreneurs, venture capitalists, and corporate lawyers is an important component of the institutional infrastructure of Silicon Valley and other innovation-rich regions. Established firms, confronted with this reality, have responded in recent years by saying in effect, "If you can't beat them, join them." The result is a greater number of spinoffs.

Spinoffs could become an important part of the scene in financial services, for a number of reasons. In financial services, broad expertise is required to innovate, at least in some areas. So innovation begins in many cases in large firms. In the language of appropriability, access to the co-specific assets of a large, integrated firm is essential for successful innovation.

But once an innovation is made, there may be reasons why a separate firm makes a better "home" for it. First is the simple fact that huge, integrated firms may not reward the development of the innovation as directly or effectively as a small, highly focused firm. This "incentive intensity" effect is a well-known advantage of small startups. It explains why startups often push more aggressively to expand applications of their basic technology into markets far afield from the business of the parent (see the eSpeed story, just below). Second, in some cases rival firms are far more likely to do business with a small separate entity than with a division of a large integrated rival. When a sophisticated technology-intensive input is being supplied, the buyer may have to reveal sensitive information about its product design or operations. A company may be reluctant to share this information with a direct competitor. This logic seems to be at work at times in the chemical industry, where sophisticated process technologies owing their origins to large, integrated chemical firms are sometimes spun off into independent startups (Arora and Merges, 2004).

Patents appear to play an important role in spinoffs in some industries such as specialty chemicals (Arora and Merges, 2004). Without patents , the risk that the technology will be copied by the spinoff firm's customers is too high. While trade secrecy is a common appropriability mechanism for established chemical firms, spinoffs by definition lack the co-specific assets necessary for a trade secret-oriented strategy to be effective. The only answer is to have strong patent protection.

Is this model possible in financial services? Much depends on the extent to which independent firms can find a market for new financial product and service ideas. If the transaction costs are too high for deals involving these "goods," independent firms will not be viable – regardless of presence or absence of property rights. Markets for pure, disembodied ideas are after all fairly rare. Another consideration is whether independent firms can devise and develop enough of these ideas to remain viable. Perhaps it requires access to many operational details and many different professionals to devise new financial products and services. The dearth of "financial idea startups" to date certainly suggests as much. If "financial idea startups" face the problem of a dry product development pipeline, they will not be viable.

Perhaps the Cantor Fitzgerald spinoff eSpeed is an indication of things to come.[14] eSpeed develops and sells pricing and trading software for various securities markets. It started in the bond market of course, where Cantor Fitzgerald was and is a major player (despite the best efforts of terrorists). Building on Cantor's original $200 million investment in new trading technology, eSpeed is branching out into other markets: energy, bandwidth, futures, telephone minutes, and so on (see www.Cantor.com). It appears that eSpeed is serious about research and development; according to a recent 10-K filing,

> We devote substantial efforts to the development and improvement of our electronic marketplaces. We will work with our clients to identify their

specific needs and make modifications to our software, network distribution systems and technologies which are responsive to those needs. We are pursuing a four-pronged approach to our research and development efforts: (1) internal development; (2) strategic partnering; (3) acquisitions; and (4) licensing. We have approximately 150 persons involved in our internal research and development efforts.... We are continuing to develop new marketplaces and products using our internally developed application software having open architecture and standards. In addition, we have forged strategic alliances with organizations such as Sungard/ASC and QV Trading through which we will work to develop sophisticated, front-end trading applications and products. We expect to license products from and to companies...

(eSpeed 1999 Form 10-K, avail.
www.sec.gov/archives/edgar, at 42)

At the same time, eSpeed is also a fairly intellectual property-intensive firm; according to a 10-K filing,

We expect to rely primarily on patent, copyright, trade secret and trademark laws to protect our proprietary technology and business methods. Our license with Cantor includes four issued United States patents as well as rights under domestic and foreign patent applications, including foreign applications currently filed by Cantor.

(eSpeed 1999 Form 10-K, avail.
www.sec.gov/archives/edgar, at 8–9)

And, to the extent the trade press can be believed, the firm has aggressively pursued markets far distant from Cantor's home base of bond trading.[15] Indeed, its efforts to enforce some of its patents have brought some criticism already.

Startups, or, Silicon Valley comes to Wall Street

Peter Tufano asks whether financial services patents will "encourage more innovation by smaller players" (Tufano, 2002, p. 37). This section explores the possibility that the answer might be "yes," that apart from spinoffs, true startups may become a more common sight in financial services.

To a large extent, a long-time observer of the patent system cannot help notice that the best justification – and sometimes, to be truthful, the *only* one – for the system appears to be to promote the financing of dynamic new entrants. The connection between patents and venture capital financing is a well-accepted part of Silicon Valley practice, though economists are just now taking at a stab at explaining why (Hellmann and Puri, 2000; Gans and Stern, 2002).

Scholars operating in the tradition of Joseph Schumpeter have made connections between entry by startup firms, patent protection, and industry structure and competition. Just as Merges and Nelson (1990) argue that multiple, rivalrous sources of innovation often promote faster economic growth, Boot and Thakor (1997) model how different institutional structures might lead to different levels of innovation. They predict less innovation in a financial system of "universal banking," especially where it involved significant market concentration. On the other hand, where commercial and investment banking are functionally separated, they predict more innovation. As with Merges and Nelson, the basic idea is that competition yields increased innovation.

It is too early for a systematic test of these concepts. But some intriguing possibilities for the future are suggested by firms exploring the startup/patent orientation in financial services.[16]

One such firm is Financial Engines, Inc. This is a Silicon Valley startup, with its headquarters in Palo Alto and backing from a number of prominent venture capital funds.[17] Financial Engines makes a business of providing sophisticated, automated online investment advice for various investors, typically employees of large companies that subscribe to its services. It services dozens of clients which employ thousands of employees. Notable for our purposes is the fact that Financial Engines has a patent-intensive strategy. As of fall, 2002, the firm held five US patents.[18] It also partners with other firms, by licensing its financial advice software systems as components in larger investment services packages.[19]

Another firm with a similar profile is FolioFN, which permits institutional and individual investors to put together customized investment portfolios included fractional shares of various investment instruments. This brings the benefits of diversification to a broader market, and deepens the degree of diversification possible with a given investment amount. The FolioFN approach is based on a series of patents, including US Patent 6,338,047, "Method and System for Investing in a Group of Investments that are Based on the Aggregated, Individual Preference of Plural Investors," issued to Wallman *et al.*, January 8, 2002. As with Financial Engines, the FolioFN business model requires partnering with other firms to broaden the business, particularly individual and institutional investment advisors.

Patents, contracts, and the viability of startups

Both startups described in this section plan to rely on partnering. Recent research teaches that patents may play a role in facilitating technology- or information-intensive transactions such as these (Hall and Ham-Ziedonis, 2001; Arora and Merges, 2004). If this research is accurate, it suggests that patents may influence not only the overall rate of innovation, but also the sources of innovation, and through this, perhaps even industry structure. The basic idea in this literature is that property rights can make small entrants viable at the margin in settings where entrants without property rights rarely survive. Hall and Ham-Ziedonis (2001), for example, study the emergence of small "design boutiques" in the US semiconductor industry. This industry is characterized by very large, vertically integrated manufacturing firms. The small entrants gain access to necessary manufacturing assets by licensing their designs – which is possible only in the presence of strong patents, given the strong probability that manufacturing firms could easily copy expensive designs. In the language of appropriability, patents facilitate contractual access to co-specific assets. The general phenomenon is modeled by Arora and Merges, who also describe a case study drawn from the biotechnology industry. There a supplier of sophisticated inputs used in the manufacturing of biotechnology products survives and thrives dealing with customers whose expertise and know-how would make it easy to copy its "crown jewel" technology. Again, broad patent protection is the key.

It is impossible to say at this point whether financial services patents will permit the emergence of similar success stories. But it is intriguing that experimentation along these lines may be beginning already. Together with the eSpeed case study, these startups show that patents in the financial services industry have the potential to increase the diversity of organizational forms available to innovating firms in this industry.

Conclusion: patents and the ecology of Wall Street

It is not possible to calibrate the impact of patents on financial services with any degree of precision. There will be upheavals – patent lawsuits that roil the industry; announced patent grants that trouble industry leaders and threaten established firms and practices; and an overall concern that patents have changed old practices in unwelcome ways.

But beyond this, in the long haul, I will venture a prediction: patents will not cause any real and lasting problems. I offer this assessment based not on hard empirical predictions, but on two detailed historical case studies, one from the nineteenth century (the railroad industry), one from recent times (the software industry). I chose them because in both industries, the adjustments to patents followed the same general pattern. And in both, early concerns that patents would fundamentally undermine innovation were proven quite wrong.

Wall Street did not need patents. It certainly did not ask for them. Innovation was flourishing without them. And when they came, these strange "incentives" were greeted with skepticism, akin to the Reagan-era joke, "We're from the government. We're here to help."

But now they are here. What will happen? The early fear was that they would upset the natural ecosystem that had evolved without them. Like a civilization cut off from the outside world, Wall Street would suddenly be infected with a novel pathogen. There would be sickness where there had been health and balance.

There may be a patent-related epidemic in Wall Street's future. But I doubt it. The industry-backed prior user rights exemption was an early inoculation. And the industry "immune system" is less likely to be surprised now: firms are more aware that they need to be vigilant in watching what issues from the Patent Office, and in acquiring some defensive patents of their own. There will probably be some high-profile patent infringement lawsuits, but a wholesale blindside of the industry appears less and less likely.

At the same time, some unintended benefits may flow in the wake of patents. Perhaps a few new entrants will be viable that would not have been. Perhaps patents will call forth some extra efforts at innovating in some sectors. Stranger things have happened.

Even if not much good comes of it, Wall Street ought to pause before criticizing the advent of patents. Perhaps in an ideal world, policymakers would have studied the financial services industry carefully for a decade before extending patent protection to financial innovations. Hearings would have been held, factfinding missions conducted. No surprises would have been sprung on an unsuspecting industry by an outsider court with no Wall Street bona fides. The whole exercise would have been much more rational, premeditated, and predictable.

But, as the *State Street Bank* decision demonstrates, that's not how it works in our system. Because our judges are totally independent, they did not have to worry about upsetting Wall Street. And the separation of powers principle enshrined in our constitution means that the Federal Circuit court did not need Congress' permission, or the President's blessing, to throw a monkey wrench into the operations of a major US industry. The court followed the logic of its own area of expertise, and in so doing upset received practices and conventional wisdom. Meanwhile, Congress did not have to clear it with the court when it passed the prior user rights exemption. This sort of institutional dialectic of challenge and response, this series of random outside shocks, is often unsettling at first. Yet it gives our economic and political system vitality, energy, and even – am I really writing this in an academic paper on financial services patents? – a sense of adventure. Ecologists and students of evolution often talk of the beneficial effects of random shocks in the natural world. Perhaps Wall Street ought to pause before criticizing this one. Something good may come of it. In the meantime, old practices will have to be examined. Implicit routines will have to be made more explicit; received wisdom questioned. This may not be all bad. After all, nature teaches that regular events like this are good – that the uninvited guest is sometimes the most interesting one of all.

Notes

1 The chapter has been previously published on the Federal Reserve Bank of Atlanta Economic Review (2003).
2 As many readers will be aware, the *State Street Bank* decision actually goes well beyond financial services. The case authorizes patenting of any "method of doing business," or more precisely, removes "business methods" from the list of things that are not patentable. In this chapter I limit my discussion of *State Street Bank* to its impact in the industry in which it arose – financial services. For more general observations, particularly on the knotty issues of patent quality control the case raises, see Merges (1999).
3 450 US 175 (1980).
4 Class 705 is conventionally associated with business method patents, even though some relevant patents are found in other classes. The patent at issue in *State Street Bank & Trust Co. v Signature Fin. Group, Inc.*, 149 F.3d 1368, 47 USPQ2d 1596 (Fed. Cir. 1998), *cert. denied*, 119 S. Ct. 851 (1999), the case that changed the law in this area, is in this class. *See* US Patent 5,193,056, "Data Processing System for Hub and Spoke Financial Services Configuration," filed 11/3/91 and issued 9/3/93. Note the issue date – an indication that financial services innovations were finding their way

into the patent system even before the practice was explicitly blessed by the Federal Circuit in 1998.

5 Investors Guaranty Fund, Ltd. vs Morgan Stanley & Co., Inc., 50 USPQ2d 1523 (SDNY, 1998).

6 35 USC §273(a)(3) (2002). For more detail, see Robert P. Merges and John F. Duffy, *Patent Law and Policy*, LexisNexis, (3d edn 2002), 172–173.

7 For a limited defense, see Merges (2000) (reviewing literature on alternatives to rent-seeking and capture theories of lobbying). It should also be noted that the sponsor of the bill that included what is now §273 of the Patent Act stated that this provision was not intended solely for the benefit of the financial services industry: "The earlier-inventor defense is important to many small and large businesses, including financial services, software companies, and manufacturing firms – any business that relies on innovative business processes and methods." Congressional Record – Extension of Remarks In the House of Representatives Thursday, August 5, 1999 AMERICAN INVENTORS PROTECTION ACT OF 1999, 145 Cong. Rec. E1788-02, at E1789 (Statement of Rep. Howard Coble, D.-NC).

8 Congressional Record – House of Representatives Thursday, November 18, 1999 CONFERENCE REPORT ON H.R. 3194, CONSOLIDATED APPROPRIATIONS AND DISTRICT OF COLUMBIA APPROPRIATIONS ACT, 2000 145 Cong. Rec. H12798-01, at H12805.

9 For example, in December 2002, CitiCorp had 28 patents, Merrill Lynch 26.

10 See, for example, Chicago & NW Railway Co. vs Sayles, 97 US 554 555–556 (1878) (summarizing district court proceedings from 1865 through 1875); *In re Caewood Patent*, 94 US 695 (1876) (concerning patent for "swedge block" used to repair and straighten worn railway rails).

11 Chicago & NW Railway Co. vs Sayles, 97 US 554 (1878) (reversing lower court opinions and reining in "doctrine of savings").

12 One piece of evidence from a theft of trade secret case involving techniques for securitization suggests that some explicit information transfers have taken place, under the rubric of trade secret licensing. See Investors Guaranty Fund, Ltd. vs Morgan Stanley & Co., Inc., 50 USPQ2d 1523 (SDNY 1998):

> Plaintiff contends that five... banks – First Boston, Goldman Sachs, Donaldson Lufkin & Jenrette, Salomon Brothers, and JP Morgan – had received information from IGF about its system under "confidentiality, proprietary, trade secrets acceptance conditions."

The case was dismissed anyway, on the ground that the plaintiff had not adequately backed up its assertions in this respect.

13 Embodying technical information in a formal property right such as patent can significantly lower the cost of exchanging it with another firm (Arora and Merges, 2002).

14 eSpeed commenced operations on March 10, 1999 as a division of Cantor Fitzgerald Securities. In December 1999, eSpeed was spun off from Cantor Fitzgerald in an Initial Public Offering. http://www.treasuryconnect.com/top_nav/invest_faq.htm#6

15 "eSpeed is Hungry for B2B Markets," Red Herring, January 14, 2000.

16 By some accounts, startup activity in this area appears to be on the increase. See Heaton (2000) (Stating, in discussion of a particular startup, that "[m]any other financial patents are held by similarly situated start-ups and entrepreneurs").

17 See www.financialengines.com.

18 See, for example, US Patent 6,125,355, "Pricing Module for Financial Advisory System," issued Bekaert *et al.* (patent providing a single pricing module that models both fixed-income securities and equity securities into the future in an arbitrage-free model); US Patent No. 6,292,787, issued to Scott *et al.*, September 18, 2001, "Enhancing Utility and Diversifying Model Risk in a Portfolio Optimization Framework."

136   *Robert Merges*

19 See, for example, Tom Lauricella, "State Street, Citigroup Venture To Give Advice on 401(k) Plans," Wall St. J. 6/10/2002:

> For the first time, investors in some 401(k) retirement plans soon will be able to get advice to buy or sell specific investments through the financial-services company administering their accounts. Citistreet, a joint venture of Citigroup Inc. and State Street Corp. that is one of the largest retirement-plan providers, announced the service Monday. Advice provided to investors in the Citistreet plans will be based on analysis and recommendations from Financial Engines Inc., an independent investment-advisory firm.

References

Arora, Ashish and Merges, Robert P. 2004. "Specialized Supply Firms, Property Rights, and Firm Boundaries." *Industrial and Corporate Change*, 13: 451–475.

Arora, Ashish, Andrea Fosfuri and Alfonso Gambardella. 2001. *Markets for Technology: The Economics of Innovation and Corporate Strategy*. Boston, MA: MIT Press.

Boot, A. and Thakor, A. 1997. "Banking Scope and Financial Innovation." *Review of Financial Studies*, 10: 1099–1131.

Cohen, Wesley M., Nelson, Richard R., and Walsh, John P. 2000. "Protecting Their Intellectual Assets: Appropriability Conditions and Why U.S. Manufacturing Firms Patent (or Not)." Nat'l Bureau of Econ. Res. Working Paper 7552.

Cowan, Robin, Paul David and Foray, D. 2000. "The Explicit Economics of Knowledge Codification and Tacitness." *Industrial and Corporate Change*, 9: 211–253.

Davis, Julie L. and Harrison, Suzanne S. 2001. *Edison in the Boardroom: How Leading Companies Realize Value from their Intellectual Assets*, New York: Wiley.

Frame, W. Scott and White, Lawrence J. 2002. "Empirical Studies of Financial Innovation: Lots of Talk, Little Action?," Prepared for the conference on "Innovation in Financial Services and Payments" Federal Reserve Bank of Philadelphia, May 16–17, 2002.

Frankel, Tamar. 1998. "Cross-Border Securitization: Without Law, But Not Lawless." *Duke J. Comp. & Int'l L.*, 8: 255.

Gans, Joshua S., Hsu, David S., and Stenn, Scott. 2002. "When Does Start up Innovation Spun the Gale of Creative Destruction." *Rand J. Econ*, 33: 571–586.

Hall, Bronwyn and Ham-Ziedonis, Rosemarie. 2001. "The Determinants of Patenting in the U.S. Semiconductor Industry, 1980–1994." *Rand J. Econ*, 32: 101–128.

Heaton, J.B. 2000. "Patent Law and Financial Engineering." *Derivatives Quarterly*, 7: 7.

Hellmann, Thomas and Puri, Manju. 2000. "The Interaction between Product Market and Financing Strategy: The Role of Venture Capital." *Review of Financial Studies*, 13: 959–984.

Merges, Robert P. 1997. *Patent Law and Policy*. Charlottesville, VA: Michie Co.

Merges, Robert P. 1999. "As many as Six Impossible Patents Before Breakfast: Property Rights for Business Concepts and Patent System Reform." *Berkeley Tech. L.J.*, 16: 577.

Merges, Robert P. 2000. "Intellectual Property Rights and the New Institutional Economics." *Vand. L. Rev.*, 53: 1857.

Merges, Robert P. 2001. "One Hundred Years of Solicitude: Intellectual Propetry Law 1900–2000." *Cal. L. Rev.*, 88: 2187.

Merges, Robert P. and Nelson, Richard R. 1990. "On the Complex Economics of Patent Scope." *Columbia Law Review*, 90: 839–916.

Merges, Robert P. and Duff, John F. 2002. *Patent Law and Policy: Cases and Materials*, Lexis-Mexis Publishing.

Persons, John C. and Walther, Vincent. 1997. "Boom and Bust Patterns in the Adoption of Financial Innovations." *Rev. Fin. Stud.*, 10: 939.

Polanyi, Michael. 1967. *The Tacit Dimension*, New York: Doubleday.

Saloner, Garth and Shepard, A. 1995. "Adoption of Technologies with Network Effects: An Empirical Examination of the Adoption of Automated Teller Machines." *Rand Journal of Economics*, 26: 479–501.

Schmookler, Jacob. 1967. *Invention and Economic Growth*, Cambridge, MA: Harvard University Press.

Teece, David. 1986. "Profiting from Technological Innovation: Implications for Integration, Collaboration, Licensing and Public Policy." *Research Policy*, 15: 285–305.

Tufano, Peter. 1989. Financial Innovation and First Mover Advantages, 25 *J. Fin. Econ.* 213.

Tufano, Peter. 2002. URL: http://www.people.hbs.edu/ptufano/fininnov_tufano_ june 2002.pdf/

Usselman, Steven W. 2002. *Regulating Railroad Innovation*, Cambridge: Cambridge Unviersity Press.

8 Property rights in human tissue

Julia D. Mahoney and Pamela Clark

For as long as it has been possible to extract benefits from components of the human body, there have been property rights in human biological materials. Although the idea of property rights in solid organs, blood, gametes, and other human tissue triggers unease and even revulsion in many quarters, it is impossible to imagine a world devoid of such rights. Absent property rights in human tissue, current systems of organ transplantation, fertility treatment, anatomical education, and biomedical research would cease to function, with devastating consequences for life and health (Mahoney, 2000).

To state that property rights in human tissue are inevitable does not, of course, provide much guidance as to what sorts of property rights the law should recognize, much less who should have them and on what terms. Determining the proper contours of these property rights requires a number of complex judgments, including ones about how to create incentives for the development and dissemination of life and health saving technologies, the roles of altruism and self-interest in the collection of human tissue, and the autonomy interests of tissue sources.

Not surprisingly, property rights in human tissue have generated fierce controversies, none of which shows any sign of abating soon. These controversies fall into three groups. First, there are disputes over private property rights in human genetic material. While it is acknowledged that such property rights can fuel scientific advances and economic growth, there are worries that a proliferation of or overly broad rights may prove counterproductive. Of particular concern are gene sequence patents (Jensen and Murray, 2005). The second set of controversies revolves around the compensation of tissue sources. Some sources of human biological materials, most notably sperm and ova "donors," often receive compensation while others, including many blood donors and all solid organ donors, are denied payment and instead strongly encouraged to donate (Mahoney, 2000). Practices mandating or urging donations by tissue sources are generally justified on the grounds that payments could compromise the safety of the tissue supply, inflict societal harm by discouraging altruism, or increase the costs of medical services. Finally, there are controversies over the control that sources may exercise over the uses of their tissue. Giving tissue sources powers to restrict uses of excised tissue or allowing them to destroy tissue can have the deleterious effect of preventing human biological materials from being put to productive use.

Nevertheless, many endorse such practices on the grounds that they promote personal autonomy and self-determination. This chapter examines each of these areas of controversy in turn.

Property rights and the distribution of human biological materials

For most of history, human components were of little value to anyone other than their original possessor. To be sure, since ancient times the demand for wigs has fueled a brisk traffic in human hair (Scott, 1981, p. 180) and the inclusion of anatomy studies in medical education in the nineteenth century created a demand for dissectible corpses (Laqueur, 1983). In the twentieth century, however, technological innovations and changing societal attitudes brought about a profound shift in the value (both economic and noneconomic) of the human body. Breakthroughs in the understanding of blood groups and the development of anti-coagulation techniques in the first two decades of the century rendered blood transfusions safer and more effective, leading to an explosion in the demand for blood (Starr, 1998, pp. 40–45). After the Second World War, the acceptance of artificial insemination as a fertility treatment created a need for a steady supply of sperm. In the 1970s, the introduction of powerful immunosuppressive drugs ushered in a new era in solid organ transplantation, transforming a therapy that offered only modest medical benefits into one that routinely added years and even decades to the lives of recipients (Mahoney, 2000). These and other developments meant that by the close of the century there was strong demand for a wide array of human biological materials (Harris, 1996, p. 75). Blood, sperm, ova, corneas, kidneys, livers, hearts, skin, and bone – to list only the most salient examples – are now highly useful to humans other than their original sources. The usefulness of these materials means that they are both valuable, in the sense that individuals and institutions are willing to pay for them, and invaluable, in the sense that the benefits they confer can be termed "priceless."

Yet for all the rejoicing over the medical advances that have made it possible for the tissues of one individual to save or improve the life of another, there is disquiet at the idea that human biological materials can be termed "property." Indeed, even to speak of human components in the language of property strikes many as objectionable. Equating body parts with other routinely transferred goods and services, or so it is averred, may promote an image of humans as fungible, commodifiable objects (Gold, 1996, pp. 164–168). This hesitation to employ property concepts to analyze the collection and distribution of human tissue serves to obscure how networks in these materials function (Mahoney, 2000). The truth is that whatever discomfort the idea of property rights in the human body may stir, there is no useful variety of human tissue in which property rights are completely unknown. What is more, despite impassioned rhetoric to the effect that the human body and its components ought not to be reduced to the status of property, there are no serious proposals to eliminate all property rights in human tissue.

To understand fully the ubiquity of property rights in this area, it is essential to bear in mind that the term "property rights" refers to a wide range of rights regarding resources. Rights to exclude, possess, use, sell, donate, pledge as security, or destroy are all varieties of property rights (Honore, 1987: pp. 165–176; Thomson, 1990, pp. 205–226). And although these rights are often bundled together, it is not uncommon for an individual or institution to have only certain property rights with respect to a resource. Thus the owner of a historic building has the right to sell it but is often severely constricted in his ability to remodel the property. In a similar vein, the holder of a life estate in a piece of land has the right to possess it but lacks the power to devise the property.

When it comes to human biological materials, limited property rights are common. For example, individuals have the power to donate their kidneys, but not to sell them. Hospitals that are allotted solid organs pursuant to applicable regulations have the right to transplant those organs into designated recipients and to collect fees for their services, but not to auction the organs to the highest bidder or to destroy them. Fertility clinics have rights to possess frozen embryos, but often lack rights to implant the embryos into anyone of their choosing, or to use them for research. One entity may have rights to possess a piece of DNA extracted from an individual, while a different entity claims patent rights derived from that DNA (Kieff, 2003). The frequent absence of "full" property rights does not mean that property rights do not exist. Rather, it means that authority over particular human biological materials is sometimes divided between, or even among, more than one rights holder, or that the use and disposition of the materials is subject to government regulation.

Despite the variety of property rights arrangements, there are some constants. For almost every piece of useful human tissue harvested from its source, there is an individual or institution that asserts rights to exclude others from and extract value (either through use or transfer) from that tissue. A moment's reflection reveals that it would be surprising if this were not the case. Any time a scarce resource has substantial use or exchange value, some entity, whether an individual, private firm, nonprofit enterprise, or government instrumentality, will take steps to exert control over it if such control is cost-effective and technologically feasible. There are enormous potential social benefits to according formal recognition to property rights – particularly rights to exclude, use and transfer – in these scarce resources (Demsetz, 1998). Enforcing such rights helps ensure that the lifesaving and health promoting capabilities of human tissue are realized.

Too many property rights? Concerns about the "anticommons" in human genetic material

That property rights in human tissue are for all practical purposes inescapable does not, of course, mean that any and all such property rights will yield societal benefits. As with property rights in general, more is not necessarily better. In recent years, the potential pitfalls of excessive property rights have attracted a great deal of attention. Of particular interest has been the suggestion that a surfeit of rights to exclude might lead to what is termed an "anticommons." Just as the assignment of usage rights to more than one entity can lead to the familiar "tragedy of the commons," in which the value of a resource is dissipated through overuse, multiple rights to exclude can create a symmetrical anticommons tragedy. The difference between the two lies in the fact that tragedies of the anticommons result in the underusage rather than overusage of resources (Buchanan and Yoon, 2000).

No one disputes that anticommons problems can occur. The best known example is that of sequential toll stations on a navigable waterway, where the determination of each sovereign to exact money from passing traffic discourages productive use of the resource (Epstein and Kuhlik, 2004). In the early twenty-first century, however, worries about the anticommons are likely to involve not physical but metaphorical blockages of the streams of commerce and knowledge dissemination. In an influential 1998 article in *Science*, Michael A. Heller and Rebecca S. Eisenberg argued that the "privatization of biomedical research" might be creating "a tragedy of the anticommons through a proliferation of fragmented and overlapping intellectual property rights" (Heller and Eisenberg, 1998, p. 701). Unless privatization is "more carefully deployed," they warned, the most important public goal of biomedical research – namely, the development of life saving and health improving products – could be endangered, as "each upstream patent allows its owner to set up another tollbooth . . . adding to the cost and slowing the pace of downstream biomedical innovation" (Heller and Eisenberg, 1998, pp. 701, 699). While it is true that in theory intellectual property rights can be reallocated through contract and other private arrangements, Heller and Eisenberg cautioned against "uncritical reliance on markets and norms" to ward off potential tragedies of the anticommons (Heller and Eisenberg, 1998, p. 701). High transaction costs in the biomedical arena, the heterogeneous interests of the individuals and institutions that hold these rights and even the cognitive biases to which researchers and others are prone, argued Heller and Eisenberg, could inhibit socially beneficial reconfigurations of rights.

The Heller and Eisenberg article sparked a lively and continuing debate over the effects of intellectual property rights on biomedical advances, with patents on human gene sequences eliciting particularly close scrutiny (Jensen and Murray, 2005; Paradise *et al.*, 2005). There is no question that property rights in human genetic material are extensive: A recent study found that United States patent rights are claimed in almost 20 percent of human genes, with a significant fraction of genes having more than one intellectual property rights holder (Jensen and Murray, 2005). This figure, which the researchers who carried out the study termed "surprisingly high," has exacerbated the already intense debate over whether a multiplicity of gene patents will smother innovation (Westphal, 2005). It is important to note, however, that however plausible the assertion that the recent explosion of intellectual property rights in human genes could stifle the very advances they are supposed to promote, to date the evidence for the existence of a significant anticommons problem in the biomedical sector is sparse (Epstein and Kuhlik, 2004). As patent law expert Edmund Kitch notes, while it is true that "there has been an unusually aggressive use of patenting by some actors in biomedical research, particularly in human genomics," detractors of intellectual property rights have failed to point to a significant number of instances where private property rights have retarded the progress of knowledge and innovation (Kitch, 2003, p. 272). Indeed, a recent article reporting findings from a survey of over 400 biomedical researchers working in the academic, government, and non-profit sectors concluded that at least right now, "access to patents on knowledge inputs rarely imposes a significant burden on academic biomedical research" (Walsh *et al.*, 2005, p. 2002).

In the absence of convincing documentation that progress is being inhibited, there is a strong case to be made for not undertaking radical reforms of legal rules and institutions (Epstein, 2003). After all, unless and until the failures of the current system are identified and analyzed, it will be hard even to begin to craft workable solutions (Kitch, 2003). Moreover, as noted intellectual property law scholar Robert Merges documents, with respect to the biotechnology sector there is reason for optimism that coordinated private action often serves to prevent or ameliorate the negative effects of potential anticommons tragedies. Not only do firms successfully contract around intellectual property rights with regularity, but major pharmaceutical concerns and others have in certain instances agreed to contribute genetic information to the public domain in order to ensure speedy dissemination of the information and preclude others from obtaining intellectual property rights that could in turn be invoked to block innovation (Merges, 2004). As Merges concludes, the fact that biotechnological innovation appears not to have suffered despite the potential anticommons dynamic, together with the demonstrated capacity of industry players to cooperate, is reason to "go slow" in restricting the availability of intellectual property rights in this area (Merges, 2004, p. 190).

The public domain and the limits of privatization

The prospect that there are too many private property rights in human genetic information is not the only concern voiced by those who question the wisdom of the current system. Whether and to what extent the human genome ought to be the target of privatization at all has generated a rich and contentious literature. Some oppose the legal recognition of any property rights in the human genome on moral grounds, arguing that humanity is not a proper subject for private ownership. The problem with this line of argument is that in practice there is no support for the total elimination of property rights in human-related resources, notwithstanding the outrage often expressed at the notion of property in anything having to do with humans. Those who assert that the human genome is unsuitable for private ownership need to explain why private property rights in human genetic materials differ qualitatively from rights in transplantable organs, blood products, and the like, which are both widespread and universally accepted.

A more serious objection holds that leaving the human genome in the public domain is the best strategy for furthering social welfare. Whether this is true is an empirical question that is impossible to answer definitively. Unlike useful physical human tissue, such as gametes and excised cells used in scientific research, genetic information is not an inherently scarce resource. While it is all but impossible to imagine a world in which useful physical tissue is placed in the public domain – with no property rights for specific individuals or institutions defined or enforced – but productive use is nonetheless made of such tissue, it is far from inconceivable that the social costs of defining and enforcing property rights in human genetic information could exceed the social benefits.

The difficulty is that while all acknowledge the value of public domains in the realm of intellectual property and that "depropertizing" intellectual property rights may in some contexts be the soundest public policy (Landes and Posner, 2003, p. 14), it is hard to determine the optimal mix of private and "commons" property. Right now, we have a mixed system, in which significant amounts of human genetic information are freely available, but private property rights in genetic information are extensive. It is true that anxieties are expressed that available patent rights in this area may be too broad (Paradise *et al.*, 2005), with the result that subsequent research that builds on earlier discoveries might be frustrated (Scotchmer, 1991). But as with the alarms raised over the anticommons, there is a dearth of evidence that patent overbreadth is inhibiting progress.

Compensating the sources of human tissue

Of all the controversies over property rights in human biological materials, the issue of compensation of tissue sources has generated the most heated rhetoric. At stake in this debate, it is important to note, is not whether the sources of valuable human tissue ought to have property rights. Rather, the debate is over what those rights will be. Should providers of blood components, transplantable organs, gametes, and other useful tissue have the right either to donate or sell these materials, or only the right to donate?

The system that has evolved in the United States is complicated. Providers of gametes (i.e. sperm and ova) are usually paid, even though such compensation is rarely available in other developed nations (Charo, 2004). Donors of whole blood generally are volunteers, but providers of plasma often receive payment. The National Organ Transplant Act, a federal statute enacted in 1984, prohibits the purchase of specified human organs to be used in transplantation, with the consequence that donors of organs (or, in the case of cadaveric sources, their estates or next of kin) are denied compensation. Tissues used in medical research are acquired through both "witting and unwitting" donation (Charo, 2004, p. 111). Some tissue providers give consent after receiving detailed information about the projects they will be contributing to, while others are not informed that their excised tissue will be appropriated for research purposes (Moore vs Regents of the University of California).

In cases where human sources are required or strongly encouraged by social practice to donate rather than sell their tissue, the chief justifications offered are that payments could jeopardize the safety of tissue recipients or that appealing to self-interest rather than altruism inflicts societal harms. Less frequently, the discouragement or prohibition of payment is defended on the grounds that compensation will increase the costs of medical services. Upon examination, however, none of these justifications is convincing.

Safety concerns

Human biological materials obtained from uncompensated sources are often assumed to pose fewer safety hazards than materials obtained from remunerated ones. This belief is most often asserted with respect to blood products and transplantable organs. The notion that donated human biological materials are necessarily safer took firm hold in the 1960s, following reports that the United States' blood supply, derived in substantial part from paid sources, posed greater health risks to recipients of blood products than did that of Great Britain, which relied on uncompensated donations (Titmuss, 1971). This conviction was reinforced by data collected over several years that indicated that blood obtained from paid donors was at least three times as likely to transmit hepatitis as blood acquired from unpaid donors (Walsh *et al.*, 1970; Alter, *et al.* 1972; National Transfusion Hepatitis Study, 1972; Aach, 1980). The infection of over 8,000 hemophiliacs by HIV infected coagulation factor concentrates manufactured from paid blood sources prior to the advent of heat-treated concentrates in 1984 was taken as further evidence that volunteers are a far safer source of human biological materials than paid donors (Starr, 1998, pp. 271, 337). In addition, several more recent studies have also pointed to the conclusion that paid blood sources have a higher rate of infection with blood borne diseases and that blood providers who respond to cash incentives are more likely to have engaged in risky behavior (Dawson, 1992; Fiedler, 1992; Eastlund, 1998; van der Poel *et al.*, 2002).

But the safety argument is not as straightforward as it first appears. There is strong evidence that the safety of human biological materials is in large part a function of the underlying populations from which the materials are collected (Kessel, 1974). The importance of the identity of tissue sources is illustrated by the experience of the Mayo Clinic, which in the 1970s routinely compensated middle class blood sources drawn from Rochester, Minnesota, and had a disease transmission rate far lower than most volunteer programs (Taswell, 1987). Interestingly, this program converted from a small paid donor population to a larger all-volunteer donor base, and thus had an opportunity to compare rates of disease test positivity between their paid and their volunteer donors. The program found that one of its disease tests, hepatitis B surface antigen, while very low in both groups, was six times higher in the volunteer blood donors. The single HIV positive donor was also a volunteer. Moreover, paid donors donated more often and more reliably than volunteers did. More recent data have also provided reason to conclude that carefully selected paid donors are not less safe than unpaid donors (Strauss, 1994).

Besides the identity of the sources, the safety of human tissue is significantly affected by the screening protocols that institutions put in place to ensure quality.

For example, at the outset of the HIV crisis in the early 1980s, plasma centers – organizations that had long followed the practice of collecting large volumes of blood components from carefully selected, compensated sources – implemented policies of asking lifestyle questions at least six months before the volunteer-dependent blood centers did so. Blood centers reliant on a volunteer donor base were reluctant to ask such questions due to concern that inquiries about risky behaviors might alienate donors. As a result, transfusions with HIV tainted blood infected thousands of recipients (Starr, 1998, p. 271).

Whether safe pools of compensated sources could in fact be established for all varieties of human biological materials is an empirical question. In the area of blood services, success might be achieved through the identification of reliable groups of donors from areas with a low incidence of disease, along with the establishment of appropriate screening procedures. Moreover, nascent technologies have the potential to provide an equivalent measure of safety. For example, pathogen inactivation technologies that neutralize DNA containing organisms, including bacteria and viruses, are now undergoing clinical trials for both platelets and plasma. In the case of transplantable organs, compensation could result in *improved* safety if financial incentives increased the organ supply to a sufficient extent to allow programs to be more selective with respect to which organs to transplant (Barnett *et al.*, 1992). Fears have been articulated, however, that providing compensation could decrease the safety of the organ supply if the availability of payment led to more organs being obtained from lower income groups, which tend to have higher incidences of certain diseases. In addition, offering compensation to living donors could cause safety problems as well as alleviate them, given that all organ donors undergo major surgery at the time of organ collection. Surgery always carries a risk of bleeding, infection and other mishap, and even with the most expert care some fatalities and serious injuries are bound to occur. Should the availability of compensation increase the number of organs harvested from living sources, whatever gains in safety are achieved might be offset by the mortality and morbidity associated with obtaining the organs.

The virtues of altruism

The notion that donations of human tissue are preferable to sales enjoys broad acceptance, particularly among bioethicists. Consequently, compensation of tissue sources is often regarded as, at best, a necessary evil – that is, a strategy to be employed only if exhortations to engage in altruistic transfers fail to yield adequate supplies (Childress, 1997, p. 289).

The assumed moral superiority of relying on altruistic motivations to obtain human tissue, however, presents a puzzle, for it is not clear why the usual method of persuading individuals to part with valuable materials – namely, appealing to self-interest by offering compensation – should be suspect or unacceptable in this context. It cannot be that life and health saving goods ought to be donated rather than sold, for although food, medicine, and other "invaluable" materials are sometimes given away, uncompensated transfers are the exception rather than the rule.

Nor is the claim that human biological materials are unfit for commerce a plausible explanation, given that bargained for exchanges are part of the distribution chain for all types of useful human tissue. Demanding that tissue sources be generous does not remove human biological materials from the commercial realm, but only serves to delay sales to a later stage. This point merits emphasis, for denying compensation to tissue sources is sometimes conflated with preventing the operation of markets in human tissue (Mahoney, 2000).

Another possible explanation for the widespread reluctance to permit tissue sources (or their survivors) to receive money is that such transactions come perilously close to putting a price on all or part of the individuals involved. Yet there are a number of situations in which people do precisely that, with no concomitant denunciations that such valuations are necessarily bad. Life and disability insurances are now routine, even though such products in effect "put a price" on what all agree is invaluable.

Some have defended reliance on noncompensation on the grounds that the availability of payment will encourage tissue sources to assume health risks. It is important to note, though, that there is little relationship between the availability of compensation and the level of risk that tissue collection entails. Payments are forbidden or discouraged in contexts where dangers to tissue sources are minor or nonexistent, including blood donation and the harvesting of transplantable organs from the brain dead. At the same time, compensation is frequently available in situations where actual physical dangers exist, such as ova retrieval. Moreover, the conviction that it is inappropriate to pay people to take on risks but acceptable to urge them to assume those same risks out of altruism has no parallel in other settings where risky human behavior generates societal benefits. The ordinary practice in construction, logging, manufacturing, and other occupational settings where workers are subject to threats to life and health is to compensate workers for the risks they face, not to convince them that they ought to expose themselves to death or injury out of a desire to promote the welfare of others or society at large.

Yet another argument holds that legal rules and social norms that encourage gifts of usable tissue increase social cohesion by forging connections between donors and strangers (Andrews and Nelkin, 1998, p. 55). Under this reasoning, sales of tissue by human sources lead to a more atomistic and selfish society, while donations have the capacity to strengthen communities and promote awareness of mutual interdependence (Singer, 1973). These assumptions, however, display a lack of appreciation of the complexity of altruism. As Albert Hirschman observes:

> Love, benevolence and civic spirit neither are scarce factors in fixed supply nor do they act like skills and abilities that improve and expand more or less indefinitely with practice. Rather, they exhibit a complex, composite behavior: they atrophy when not adequately practiced and appealed to by the ruling socioeconomic regime, yet will once again make themselves scarce when preached and relied on to excess. To make matters worse, the precise location of these two danger zones... is by no means known, nor are these zones ever stable.
>
> (Hirschman, 1986, p. 157)

Hirschman's analysis underscores the difficulties inherent in designing institutions that rely on the inculcation and maintenance of altruism. Although the idea of depending on the forces of generosity to generate a steady supply of life and health saving human tissue may exert an undeniable emotional appeal, the harsh reality is that appeals to self interest yield more predictable results.

What is more, advocates of uncompensated transfers rarely stop to consider the nature and magnitude of the burdens of altruism, or the likely distributional consequences of the selfless behavior they endorse. The costs of altruism can include lost time, physical discomfort and even danger, and foregone opportunities to collect compensation. Altruism can also have the perverse effect of eroding the self-regard and stunting the personal growth of the donor. As political philosopher Jean Hampton notes in her essay "Selflessness and the Loss of Self," those who "commend altruism assume that someone who cares for another even at the expense of her own welfare is an impressive and highly moral figure." This assumption, Hampton argues, fails to take adequate account of the damage that the selfless individual can inflict on herself by putting the needs of others first and thus failing to develop fully her own interests and capabilities (Hampton, 1993, p. 136). Hampton concludes:

> Moral people do not put themselves to one side; they include themselves in the calculation and give themselves weight in the determination of the right action to take...[W]e should not allow ourselves to be pressured – by society, by our religion, or by some philosopher's conception of our "moral duties" – to become the servant of others...The art of living well is to know how to balance competing moral obligations – some of which are to yourself.
> (Hampton, 1993, pp. 164–65)

As for the distributional effects of altruism, it is striking how often uncompensated transfers of human biological materials benefit entities that aggressively pursue their financial self-interest. Indigenous peoples donate blood samples to large pharmaceutical firms that intend to use the donated tissue to develop costly therapies (Marshall, 1997). Many lower and middle class individuals in the United States who agree to serve as cadaveric organ donors would have a hard time obtaining a place on a transplant waiting list in the event of organ failure, due to the common practice among transplant centers of requiring prospective recipients to demonstrate the capacity to pay both for the operation itself and for a long-term supply of immunosuppressive drugs. The most famous US court case concerning property rights in human biological materials, Moore vs Regents of the University of California, involved a cancer patient treated at the University of California at Los Angeles Medical Center who learned that one of his physicians, along with others involved in his medical care, claimed ownership rights in a valuable cell line derived from white blood cells removed in the course of his therapy. Curiously, the troubling spectacle of tissue sources being expected to confer benefits on entities that plan to extract maximum financial returns from the materials they obtain has attracted little criticism.

The impact on the cost of medical services

Forbidding or discouraging the compensation of tissue sources is sometimes defended on the instrumental grounds that not paying sources keeps down health care costs. According to this view, remuneration to human sources constitutes an additional expense, one that is in part or in full passed on to the ultimate consumers of human biological materials and the products derived from them (Evans, 1993; Munzer, 1994). As a result – or so the argument goes – payments to sources will have the likely outcome of decreasing access to life and health saving services.

The trouble with this line of thinking is that there is good cause to conclude that in many instances the effect of payments to tissue sources will be, if anything, the opposite. This is true for two reasons. First, payments to human sources will often increase the available supply of the desired tissue, which in turn can be expected to cause the price of the tissue in question to fall (Blair and Kaserman, 1991). This point is especially germane to discussions of the costs of organ transplantation. As a number of economists have observed, a primary cause of the expense of organ transplantation is that the critical shortage of suitable organs allows transplant programs to charge high prices. If payments to organ donors (or, in the case of cadaveric donors, their estates or surviving relatives) spur a sufficient increase in the supply of available organs, competition among transplant programs will intensify, with the likely result that transplantation costs will decrease.

Second, payments to tissue sources will frequently constitute a cheaper means of collecting tissue than exhortations to engage in altruism. Relying on altruistic donors does not, it bears emphasis, mean that no procurement costs are incurred (Thorne, 1998). Right now, significant sums are expended on public service campaigns aimed at inculcating altruism in potential organ and blood donors. Blood services organizations devote sizeable parts of their budget to donor recruitment, and many find it increasingly more expensive and difficult to recruit volunteer donors. As eligibility requirements have tightened in the face of concerns about HIV, bovine spongiform encephalopathy, Hepatitis C, and other threats to blood safety, the pool of acceptable blood donors has shrunk. To maintain an adequate blood supply, these donors must be replaced, but the cost of recruiting these new, often more reluctant donors can be high.

The experience of the Mayo Clinic is instructive (Taswell, 1987). Not only were paid donors in a number of respects safer than volunteer donors, but the cost of collection per unit for paid donor blood was approximately one-half that for all volunteer blood. The increased costs were attributed in substantial part to the greater costs of recruitment required for volunteer donors, including the necessity for new donor centers and additional personnel to accommodate the needs of volunteer donors. Volunteer donors also had higher no-show rates and donated less frequently, which contributed to reduced efficiency in collections.

Tissue sources, autonomy, and control

For the most part, legal regimes are designed to facilitate the productive use of resources. With respect to human tissue, though, rules and social norms can have the effect of frustrating productive use. One way this occurs is discussed in the previous section of this chapter: By prohibiting or discouraging the compensation of tissue sources, law, and social practice can discourage transfers of valuable tissue that would otherwise take place.

The productive use of human biological materials can also be inhibited by rules and norms that afford tissue sources some measure of control over their excised components, as well as over the disposition of their bodies upon death. Such rules and norms, of course, can be defended on the grounds that the source's autonomy interests mandate that she retain authority over her tissue, both during life and after (Underkuffler, 2003, p. 105). As always when important values are in tension, however, difficult questions arise regarding the weights to be assigned to competing considerations.

The permissibility of research on stored tissue

As a general rule, those who abandon their property surrender all power to control or influence what use is made of it. But in the case of pieces of human tissue left in hospitals, physician's offices, and laboratories, matters are not so simple. Although for over a century it has been common practice among researchers and clinicians to appropriate materials excised in the course of medical diagnosis and treatment without the consent or even the knowledge of the tissue source, in recent years concerns have grown about the potential harms of this practice (Charo, 2004). A number of bioethicists, public officials, and members of the public have articulated the view that individuals have strong autonomy interests in knowing or determining how their tissue is employed, as well as in not having their materials diverted for the economic gain of others. At the same time, though, serious worries are expressed that the recognition of property rights for tissue sources could retard or halt important biomedical research projects (Moore vs Regents of the University of California; Greenberg vs Miami Children's Hospital; Hakimian and Korn, 2004).

At present, there is little law directly on point regarding the collection and disposition of tissue for research activities (Charo, 2004), although over the past decade the freedom of researchers to make use of tissue stores has been somewhat narrowed by government regulation (Hakimian and Korn, 2004). If current trends in biomedical innovation continue, however, questions regarding the ownership of tissue collections will almost certainly gain in urgency (Hakimian and Korn, 2004).

The right to destroy

Of all the rights that humans have regarding their biological materials, the right to destroy appears, at least at first glance, among the least controversial. After all, as a general rule, property owners have no obligations to transfer resources to those who need or could make better use of them. Instead, rights holders can allow resources to stagnate or degrade, or even take steps to obliterate them. Nations with common law traditions have for centuries recognized a robust right to destroy. But the durability of this right may very well reflect less a measured societal judgment that those who control resources should enjoy the power to destroy them than a pragmatic determination that it is unnecessary to devote substantial efforts to preventing owners from engaging is such conduct. One can argue that the right to destroy is unlikely to make a difference in the behavior of owners, given that those with interests in valuable resources normally have strong incentives to care for and preserve them (McCaffery, 2001).

In recent years, however, serious proposals have been advanced that the right to destroy should be modified, particularly with respect to artifacts of cultural significance that may lack substantial financial value (Sax, 1999; Strahilevitz, 2005). And while the bulk of proposals to abrogate or limit the right to destroy involve historical and literary papers, artworks, and buildings of architectural distinction, it has been suggested that the ability of humans to provide for the destruction of useful body components – either their own or those of deceased relatives – should be abrogated, at least with respect to some forms of tissue (Strahilevitz, 2005). Of special concern is the fact that a large number, perhaps even – at least in the United States – the majority, of transplantable organs are not made available for transplant, and are instead destroyed by cremation or permitted to decay after burial. Eliminating the right to destroy in this context could save thousands of lives each year. With respect to other sorts of human tissue, the benefits to life and health would be less dramatic but nonetheless considerable (Strahilevitz, 2005). Of course, it is crucial to note that if compensation for tissue sources and their survivors were available in more contexts, rights to destroy would in all probability be exercised less frequently, for limiting or extinguishing the ability of tissue sources (or their survivors) to exchange resources for value also serves to reduce or eliminate incentives to preserve them.

Although there is no realistic prospect that the rights of tissue sources to destroy their bodily materials will be fully abrogated anytime soon, it is conceivable that the nascent debate over whether the recognition of a strong right to destroy makes sense in the face of modern biomedical technologies could blossom into a more widespread controversy. At the very least, it is conceivable that the growing sentiment that certain forms of cultural property deserve protection from destruction will lay the foundation for reconsideration of the right to destroy other unique and invaluable resouces.

Conclusion

Property rights in human tissue have played – and continue to play – an essential role in the development and distribution of life saving and health enhancing technologies. Notwithstanding the fact that to many the human body seems too private and personal to be an appropriate basis for property, no one agitates for reversing the clock of biomedical progress and returning to a world where property rights in human biological materials tissue are rare. The issue of the acceptability of property rights in human tissue, in short, has been resolved in favor of recognizing and enforcing such rights.

That does not mean that questions regarding what the precise contours of these rights ought to be are easy ones. The challenge for the twenty-first century is to design systems of property rights that encourage innovation and facilitate access to the benefits of biomedical technologies, while providing adequate protection for the interests of tissue sources. In crafting these regimes, legislators, courts, regulators, and other decision makers will be called upon to make many difficult choices, including ones regarding the scope of the public domain in human genetic information, whether and how to expand opportunities for tissue sources or their survivors to receive compensation, and the extent to which the traditional right to destroy property merits modification.

References

Aach, R.D. and Kahn R.A. (1980) "Post-Transfusion Hepatitis: Current Perspectives," *Annals of Internal Medicine* 92: 539–546.

Alter, H.J., Holland P.V., and Purcell, R.H. (1972) "Post-Transfusion Hepatitis After Exclusion of Commercial and Hepatitis-B Antigen-Positive Donors," *Annals of Internal Medicine* 77: 691–699.

Andrews, L. and Nelkin, D. (1998) "Whose Body Is It Anyway?: Disputes Over Body Tissue in a Biotechnology Age," *The Lancet* 53: 51–57.

Barnett, A.H., Blair, R.D., and Kaserman, D.L. (1992) "Improving Organ Donation: Compensation Versus Markets," *Inquiry* 29: 372–378.

Blair, R.D. and Kaserman, D.L. (1991) "The Economics and Ethics of Alternative Cadaveric Organ Procurement Policies," *Yale Journal on Regulation* 8: 403–452.

Buchanan, J. and Yoon, Y.J. (2000) "Symmetric Tragedies: Commons and Anticommons," *Journal of Law and Economics* 43: 1–12.

Charo, R.A. (2004) "Legal Characterization of Human Tissue," in S.J. Youngner, M.W. Anderson, and R. Schapiro (eds), *Transplanting Human Tissue*, Oxford: Oxford University Press.

Childress, J. (1997) *Practical Reasoning in Bioethics*, Bloomington: Indiana University Press.

Dawson G.J., Lesniewski, R.R., Stewart, J.L., Boardway, K.M., Gutierrez, R.A., Pendy, L., Johnson, R.E., Alcalde, X., Rote, K.V., Devare, S.G., and Dawson, G. (1991) "Detection of Antibodies to Hepatitis C Virus in U.S. Blood Donors," *Journal of Clinical Microbiology* 29: 551–556.

Demsetz, H. (1998) "Property Rights," in P. Newman (ed.), *The New Palgrave Dictionary of Economics and the Law*, New York: Stockton Press.

Eastlund, T. (1998) "Monetary Blood Donation Incentives and the Risk of Transfusion-Transmitted Infection," *Transfusion* 38: 874–882.

Epstein, R.A. (2003) "Steady the Course: Property Rights in Genetic Material," in F.S. Kieff (ed.), *Perspectives on Properties of the Human Genome Project*, 153–194, London: Elsevier Academic Press.

Epstein, R.A. and Kuhlik, B. (2004) "Is There a Biomedical Anticommons?," *Regulation* 27: 54–58.

Evans, R. (1993) "Organ Procurement Expenditures and the Role of Financial Incentives," *Journal of the American Medical Association* 269: 3113–3118.

Fiedler, H. (1992) "HIV Seropositivity in Paid Blood Donors," *Lancet* 339: 551.

Gold, E.R. (1996) *Body Parts: Property Rights and the Ownership of Human Biological Materials*, Washington, DC: Georgetown University Press.

Greenberg vs Miami Children's Hospital (2004), 264 F. Supp. 2d 1064.

Hakimian, R. and Korn, D. (2004) "Ownership and Use of Tissue Specimens for Research," *Journal of the American Medical Association* 292: 2500–2505.

Hampton, J. (1993) "Selflessness and the Loss of Self," in E.F. Paul, F.D. Miller, Jr, and J. Paul (eds) *Altruism*, 135–165, Cambridge: Cambridge University Press.

Harris, J.W. (1996) "Who Owns My Body?," *Oxford Journal of Legal Studies* 16: 55–84.

Heller, M.A. and Eisenberg, R.S. (1998). "Can Patents Deter Innovation? The Anticommons in Biomedical Research," *Science* 280: 698–701.

Hirschman, A.O. (1986) *Rival Views of Market Society*, New York: Viking.

Honore, A.M. (1987) *Making Law Bind*, Oxford: Oxford University Press.

Jensen, K. and Murray, F. (2005) "Intellectual Property Landscape of the Human Genome," *Science* 310: 239–240.

Kessel, R. (1974) "Transfused Blood, Serum Hepatitis and the Coase Theorem," *Journal of Law and Economics* 17: 265–289.

Kieff, F.S. (2003) "Perusing Property Rights in DNA," in F.S. Kieff (ed.) *Perspectives on Properties of the Human Genome Project*, 125–151, London: Elsevier Academic Press.

Kitch, E.W. (2003) "Comment on the Tragedy of the Anticommons in Biomedical Research," in F.S. Kieff (ed.) *Perspectives on Properties of the Human Genome Project*, 271–273, London: Elsevier Academic Press.

Landes, W.A. and Posner, R.A. (2003) *The Economic Structure of Intellectual Property Law*, Cambridge: Harvard University Press.

Laqueur, T. (1983) "Bodies, Death and Pauper Funerals," *Representations* 1: 109–131.

McCaffery, E.J. (2001) "Must We Have the Right to Waste?," in S.R. Munzer (ed.) *New Essays in the Legal and Political Theory of Property*, 76–105, Cambridge: Cambridge University Press.

Mahoney, J.D. (2000) "The Market for Human Tissue," *Virginia Law Review* 86: 163–223.

Marshall, E. (1997) "Gene Prospecting in Remote Populations," *Science* 278: 565.

Merges, R.P. (2004) "A New Dynamism in the Public Domain," *University of Chicago Law Review* 71: 183–203.

Munzer, S.R. (1994) "An Uneasy Case Against Property Rights in Human Body Parts," in E.F. Paul (ed.) *Property Rights*, 259–286, Cambridge: Cambridge University Press.

National Transfusion Hepatitis Study (1972) "Risk of Post-Transfusion Hepatitis in the United States: A Prospective Cooperative Study," *Journal of the American Medical Association* 220: 692–701.

Paradise, J., Andrews, L., and Holbrook, T. (2005) "Patents on Human Genes: An Analysis of Scope and Claims," *Science* 307: 1566–1567.

Sax, J.L. (1999) *Playing Darts With a Rembrandt: Public and Private Rights in Cultural Treasures*, Ann Arbor: University of Michigan Press.

Scotchmer, S. (1991) "Standing on the Shoulders of Giants: Cumulative Research and the Patent Law," *Journal of Economic Perspectives* 5(1): 29–41.

Scott, R. (1981) *The Body as Property*, New York: Viking Press.

Singer, P. (1973) "Altruism and Commerce: A Defense of Titmuss Against Arrow," *Philosophy and Public Affairs* 2: 312–320.

Starr, D. (1998). *Blood: An Epic Story of Medicine and Commerce*, New York: Alfred A. Knopf.

Strahilevitz, L.J. (2005) "The Right to Destroy," *Yale Law Journal* 114: 781–854.

Strauss, R.G. (1994) "Concurrent Comparison of the Safety of Paid Cytapheresis and Volunteer Whole Blood Donors," *Transfusion* 34: 116–121.

Taswell, H.F. (1987) "Directed, Paid and Self-donors, Part III," in G. Clark (ed.) *Competition in Blood Services*, 18–38, Arlington: American Association of Blood Banks.

Thomson, J.J. (1990) *The Realm of Rights*, Cambridge: Harvard University Press.

Thorne, E.D. (1998) "When Private Parts Are Made Public Goods: The Economics of Market-Inalienability," *Yale Journal on Regulation* 15: 149–175.

Titmuss, R. (1971) *The Gift Relationship: From Human Blood to Social Policy*, New York: Pantheon Books.

Underkuffler, L. (2003) *The Idea of Property*, Oxford: Oxford University Press.

van der Poel, C.L., Seifried, E., and Schaasberg, W.P. (2002) "Paying for Blood Donations: Still a Risk?," *Vox Sanguinis* 83: 285–293.

Walsh J.H., Purcell, R.H., Morrow, A.G., Chanock, R.M., and Schmidt, P.J. (1970) "Posttransfusion Hepatitis After Open Heart Operations: Incidence After the Administration of Blood from Commercial and Volunteer Donor Populations," *Journal of the American Medical Association* 211: 261–265.

Walsh, J.P., Cho, C., and Cohen, W.M. (2005) "View from the Bench: Patents and Material Transfers," *Science* 309: 2002–2003.

Westphal, S.P. (2005) "Human Gene Patents 'Surprisingly High', A New Study Shows," *Wall Street Journal* (October 14, 2005).

Moore vs Regents of the University of California (1990), 793 P. 2d 479 National Organ Transplant Act, 42 U.S.C. Sections 273–274(f) (2000).

Part III

Shadows and lights

Critical issues, conflicting cases
and alternative paradigms

9   The ongoing copyright as an essential facility saga

Paul L.C. Torremans

Introduction

The IMS Health saga, and to a lesser extent the Commission's decision in the Microsoft case, highlighted once more the difficult relationship between copyright and competition law.[1] These difficulties are particularly apparent when abuse of dominant position and the essential facilities doctrine take centre stage. In this paper I will examine this difficult relationship by taking a theoretical and conceptual approach to start with and this will then be followed by a detailed analysis of the relevant case-law.

Intellectual property and copyright vs competition law

Intellectual property and copyright

The starting points

Two leading studies on the economic analysis of copyright come to the conclusion that the continued existence of copyright makes economic sense. The starting point seems to indicate therefore that the debate should not develop along the lines of intellectual property and copyright or competition law, but should rather focus on the role played by both sets of rules in a free market economy. From a preliminary point of view, one way or the other the two sets of rules seem obliged to work together. We will need to develop a deeper understanding of each of them in order to analyse if and how such co-operation is possible in practice (Lemarchand *et al.*, 2003, p. 17).

The two studies referred to above highlight the conundrum we are trying to solve and the solution of which should underpin any detailed ruling in cases such as IMS Health as follows. In their study on *Law and Economics* Cooter and Ulen summarise it as '[p]ut succinctly, the dilemma is that without a legal monopoly too little of the information will be produced, but with the legal monopoly too little of the information will be used' (Cooter and Ulen, 1988, p. 145). Landes and Posner, in their seminal study 'An Economic Analysis of Copyright Law' emphasise the matter in even clearer terms when they state that 'Copyright protection – the right of the copyright's owner to prevent others from making copies – trades off the costs of limiting access to a work against the benefits of providing incentives to create the work in the first place. Striking the correct balance between access and incentives is the central problem in copyright law.' (Landes and Posner, 1989, p. 326)

Historically copyright is concerned with the protection of literary and artistic works. Examples such as books, paintings and sculptures come to mind. It is important to note in this respect that copyright never set out to protect, let alone grant any exclusivity in relation to ideas. Ideas were to remain in the public domain and therefore freely available for use by anyone. What was protected was the way in which the individual author used these ideas creatively and the resulting expression of his creativity. Only that expression, the individual non-copied expression by the author of a certain idea was protected. A lot of emphasis was therefore put on the link between the author and his work (Torremans, 2001, p. 176).

Justifying copyright

This approach can in part be justified by means of the labour theory, as originally formulated by John Locke (Locke, 1970). In essence the labour theory is the combination of two concepts. According to the first concept everyone has a property right in the labour of his own body and brain and the second concept builds on that by adding that the application of human labour to an unowned object gives whoever applies that labour to it a property right in the previously unowned object. If one applies this to copyright (Nozick, 1974, p. 181), one can see why the starting point of any copyright law is that the author gets the copyright in the book, painting or sculpture. However, the labour theory may not go a lot further than the issue of the allocation of the (copy)right. It does not necessarily explain why an immaterial right needs to be created and why such an immaterial right is necessarily an object for the purposes of the labour theory. The latter is indeed only obviously applicable to real material objects and property. There is therefore a need for an additional element that justifies the existence of copyright and that explains in other words why an immaterial rights in the author's individual expression of an idea needs to be created (Spector, 1989, p. 273).

That other element is purely economic in nature (Torremans, 2001, pp. 14–21). In an efficient free market structure competition takes place at at least three levels and at each level an optimum level of competition needs to be achieved. A balance may therefore have to be struck, as one hundred per cent or perfect competition at one level may effectively rule out competition at the next level. At the bottom of the scale is the consumption level, which interacts with the production level. Perfect competition at the consumption level, that is, the absence of any barriers or restrictions to consumption such as price and scarcity of goods, would create a situation where everyone was free to take anything they fancied free of charge to use or consume it. In such a situation it is arguable that there would be little or no competition at the production level, as there is no reward or anything else to be gained from the production of goods or services that can be consumed, that is, taken away from the producer without anything being given in exchange. It is in these circumstances, a much more logical approach to focus on the consumption side and let others produce the goods or services, even if the whole market system could grind to a halt if everyone adopted this approach. These problems are overcome by the introduction of property rights in the goods or services that are produced. The producer's first *de facto* possession of the goods or services receives legal recognition by means of a property right, which in turn allows him or her to charge for the transfer of the goods or the supply of the services. As such, property rights are used to stimulate competition at the production level, even if this necessarily involves a reduction of competition at the consumption level, as nobody has the unrestricted means to pay for all goods or services. It is important though to keep in mind that the property right in the goods (or services) is not entirely an artificial legal creation. It is rather a form of legal recognition and legal consequences that are given to the *de facto* possession of the goods (or services). Hence the presumption in most legal systems that possession gives rise to title (Lehmann, 1989, p. 12).

The third level is the innovation and creation level and this level interacts in turn with the production level. As was argued earlier, in the copyright sphere we are dealing with works that are the expression of ideas. Starting from these ideas, one has to recognise that they are by their nature public goods and can therefore freely be accessed and used by anyone. The way in which these ideas enter the public domain is through their expression by an individual author, as such expression is required for the transmission of the idea. From an economic point of view it is also important to keep in mind that such access is non-exhaustive in nature. The consumption of the expression does not necessarily make the expression and its material support unsuitable or unavailable for further consumption. It is also the case that in the light of modern (digital) technological advances, the costs of reproduction and distribution of the expression of the idea have become marginal and that such reproduction and distribution is easily achievable and can be done in a minimum amount of time. There is therefore plenty of room for free-riders.[2] Additionally, one should distinguish carefully between the expression of the idea on the one hand and its material support on the other hand. The latter, for example, the ink and paper in the case of a literary work published in bookform, is a material object or good and can be subject to a property right and the protection it provides for the person in possession of the object or good, but the former is as such not included in the scope of that protection. The situation with which we are presented is therefore entirely in favour of competition at the production level. Copying the expression of the idea is easy and cheap and it seems to be free. At the innovation and creation level there is very little in terms of incentive to create. The creator may not be able to recoup the cost of production, as the cost of copying is lower and there is no tool to reap any substantial benefit from such creative activity. In economic terms there is therefore no efficient market of the authors' expression of ideas (Ramello, 2003, p. 118).[3] In a society that sees progress and change as a goal and that believes that creative activity can contribute to the achievement of that goal through the means of the free market such a situation is undesirable, as it will inhibit the achievement of that goal. Copyright is the tool that is created to remedy this imbalance and to give authors a right in their expression of ideas, hence securing appropriate profits deriving from the act of creation for them.[4] Copyright will lead to the creation of an immaterial property right in the expression of an idea by the author, a right which the author can use to secure appropriate profit from his or her act of creation on the market (Maskus, 2000, pp. 28–32). This will enhance creation by providing an incentive and therefore competition on the innovation and creation level will be stimulated, whilst any such right will inevitably to some extent limit competition at the production level as competitors (and former free-riders with them) are no longer free to copy the copyright work. Yet again a restriction on competition (at the production level) is put in place in furtherance of competition (at the innovation and creation level) (Lehmann, 1989, p. 12).

Copyright fulfils here the pro-competitive regulating role filled by the property right when it comes to the consumption and the production level. An important distinction needs however to be drawn between property rights on the one hand and intellectual property rights and copyright on the other hand. Property rights are a legal recognition of a situation, that is, the physical possession of and control over the goods, whereas copyright is not based on a *de facto* situation at all. It is rather an artifice, an artificially created right, put in place by the legislator to regulate competition at the innovation and creation level and to provide the much needed incentive to create. This difference gives copyright a different standing. It was created specifically as a tool to enhance competition by the legislator. Needless to add that the exact content of copyright law must reflect the attempt to provide an adequate level of competition both at the innovation and creation and at the production level. Whilst copyright is a good tool in theory, it cannot be taken for granted that the legislator on each occasion and for each set of facts got it exactly right when determining the content of copyright law in an attempt to strike the right balance between the different levels at which competition takes place.

Recent developments

Up to now we have looked at 'traditional' copyright in literary and artistic works such as books, paintings and sculptures. It is however necessary to add that copyright has developed in two ways in recent years which may have influenced the position (Mackaay, 1991, pp. 1–30). On the one hand copyright has been expanded to protect the results of technological evolutions. Sound recording, films, and also computer software and databases have been brought within the scope of copyright protection. On the other hand we have seen an increasing emphasis on the economic interests of those who exploit copyright works, such as producers and publishers. It may lead too far to discuss all implications of this evolution, but it is important to note that as a result copyright is increasingly used to protect information goods and the investment needed for the creation of these goods. This is clearly visible in the area of databases for example where we have even seen the creation in the EU of a *sui generis* database right to supplement copyright in order to achieve this aim.[5] It is clear that the level of originality involved in the creation of such information goods is lower and that the link with the author and his creativity that makes the work his own individual creation is weaker in these circumstances. This must also weaken the justification for strong copyright protection for these information works as these elements were described above as the basis for the economic justification of copyright (Lucas and Lucas, 2001, p. 37; Lemarchand *et al.*, 2003, p. 18). Another important element is the fact that by their nature information goods have a poor substitutability (Ramello, 2003, p. 118). This applies to some extent to all copyright works, for example, we are interested in a novel because of the way in which the author has expressed the idea, and therefore the novel cannot be easily substituted by another novel in which another author expresses the same idea in his or her different own way, but this factor is more strongly present in relation to information goods. A database of dentists in Scotland cannot easily be substituted by another database of dentists in Scotland, since we really are after the data, that is, we want a complete list of all such dentists, for example. This may well have an impact from a competition law perspective and we will therefore have to return to this point at a later stage. It is therefore now appropriate to have a closer look at the relevant principles of competition law from a theoretical perspective.

Competition law

Competition law has as its stated aim to maximise social welfare by avoiding or correcting specific market failures. Consumer welfare should as a result be enhanced and innovation should be encouraged (OECD, 1989; Anderman, 1998, pp. 5–7). Competition law attempts to achieve this aim through the elimination of competition restricting practices and forms of behaviour, as these lead to inefficient outcomes (Anderman, 1998, pp. 5–6). This kind of activity may well fall into the legal field, but it is clear that the legal rules on competition need to be based on and supported by economic theory if they are to work well and achieve the aims that have been set out.

The agreement between lawyers and economists in this area clearly covers the point that competition law is an instrument to combat monopolistic behaviour which has as an effect to exclude a segment of consumers from the market, relative to the competitive context. But when it comes to the practical application of these principles to the facts of a specific case, economic theory is not exactly capable of providing the legal community and the courts with specific tests to detect and correct such anti-competitive behaviour (Neumann, 2001). This is all the more so in relation to the new information economy. Economic theory is indeed still to a large extent focused on static efficiency and the dynamics of the manufacturing industries. The information economy has quite different dynamic processes, resulting in part from the importance of the rapid technological change to which it is subjected. Since copyright operates increasingly in such an information economy when it is used to protect information goods, it is clear to see that the application of competition law in such cases may not be clear-cut and lead to difficulties.

These difficulties are further compounded by the fact that in the markets for information goods there is a different mode of competition from that found in the market for producers of tangible goods. Whilst price competition is a major element in respect of the latter one, it is far less important in respect of the market for information goods. On the market for information goods one finds non-price competition as a dominant factor. The sunk cost component seems effectively to play the dual role of consolidating on the one hand and of increasing demand and/or creating barriers to entry for potential competitors on the other hand. As a result one sees leapfrogging by competitors in the innovation race when it comes to the market for new tangible products, whilst on the market for information products one sees the emergence of pockets of monopoly power, the creation of which is facilitated by the presence of copyright, and which are used to secure or to reinforce monopolistic positions (Shapiro, 2000). In these latter markets one finds indeed a pattern of progressive concentration, both at national and international level. Information goods are increasingly created and exploited by ever larger groups on a market with a shrinking number of significant competitors (Silva and Ramello, 2000, pp. 415–422).

It is therefore clear that competition law's role is a broad one. There is as such no reason to exclude competition law from playing its role in the information goods market or in the copyright or intellectual property market as a whole. However, on each occasion competition law and its operation in a specific market needs to be underpinned by sound economic principle (Anderman, 1998, p. 5). As has been shown above, there may therefore be specific elements that need to be taken into account when the competition authorities apply competition law in the area of intellectual property and copyright.

Copyright vs Competition Law

As copyright confers an exclusive right there is almost by definition also a possibility that such an exclusive right will be used in one way or another to restrict competition. There may therefore be a conflict between competition law on the one hand and copyright law on the other hand in a given situation (Furse, 2002, pp. 205, 214).

In order to understand the nature of such a potential conflict better, one needs to see how both regulatory systems, that is, copyright and competition law, operate. Copyright operates at a structural level. It puts in place a rewards and incentives structure that applies to all relevant cases and that aims to enhance competition at creation and innovation level by granting an exclusive right in the copyright work that restricts to some extend competition at the production level. In doing so copyright defines (intellectual) property rights. Competition law on the other hand operates in an entirely different way. It operates at the behavioural level and it does so almost on a case by case basis. It is therefore not the case that there is a conflict between two sets of rules that operate in the same way and at the same level (Ramello, 2003, p. 118). Copyright and competition law share the same objective, but they have way of achieving it and they operate at a different level (Lemarchand *et al.*, 2003, pp. 17–19).

Competition law does not operate at the structural level and as such it does not interfere with the structure created by copyright to enhance creation and innovation at competition at that stage. What is true though is that it may wish to interfere at a later stage with some of the behaviour that flows from the grant of copyright. In more down to earth terms, copyright may be used or exercised in an improper way and such behaviour is then regulated and addressed by means of competition law. The factor which complicates matters is that it is to a fair extent the incentives and exclusive rights created at the structural level by copyright that facilitate or at least make possible the emergence of inefficient behaviour that might infringe competition law rules. What can be derived at this early stage is that a system that is designed to regulate behaviour should not operate in a way to undue the structural system put in place by a system such as copyright. The legislator has made a policy decision to put a structure such as copyright in place to enhance and reward creativity and innovation and that decision should be respected. In other words, competition law should restrict itself to its proper role which is to address anti-competitive behaviour, such as any use of copyright that is not pro-competitive as was envisaged when the structural system was set up (Torremans, 2001, pp. 302–309; Whish, 2001, p. 676). This conclusion should not surprise anyone, as it should be kept in mind that it is competition law itself that allows for the grant of exclusive rights if on the one hand they are necessary and unavoidable to obtain the benefits which the rightholder brings about for the consumer and if on the other hand they do not lead to a complete elimination of competition (Lemarchand *et al.*, 2003, p. 19).

An analysis of the case law

Turning to the relevant case law we find that in relation to abuse of dominant position the central issue involved is whether an undertaking in a dominant position can be forced to grant a 'licence' of an intellectual property right it holds and if a refusal to do so implies an abuse of its dominant position. In recent years this issue arose on several occasions in the areas of design and copyright. We discuss these design and copyright cases here together as they strongly draw upon each other.

Volvo and Renault

The issue arose for the first time in two cases which were concerned with designs for spare parts for cars, the *Maxicar vs Renault* case[6] and the *Volvo vs Veng* case.[7] Maxicar and Veng were involved in car repairs and maintenance and wanted to obtain a licence to produce spare parts themselves. When unsuccessful in obtaining these licences they argued that Volvo and Renault occupied a dominant position in the relevant market and that by refusing to grant licences they abused their dominant position. They wanted to see Volvo and Renault obliged to grant the licences and submitted that the Court should interpret Article 82 accordingly. The Court of Justice started its analysis by ruling out the possibility that the existence of the fact that an intellectual property right was obtained could be an abuse of a dominant position. The Court held that the existence and the issue of obtaining an intellectual property right is a matter for the national rules of the member states, which rules determine the nature and extent of the protection.[8] In the *Maxicar vs Renault* case the Court stated that

> the mere fact of obtaining protective rights . . . does not constitute an abuse of a dominant position within the meaning of Article [82].[9]

The obligation for a dominant undertaking to grant a licence (Korah, 1988, p. 381) was ruled out in the *Volvo vs Veng* case:

> the right of the proprietor of a protected design to prevent third parties from manufacturing and selling or importing, without its consent, products incorporating the design constitutes the very subject-matter of his exclusive right. It follows that an obligation imposed upon the proprietor of a protected design to grant to third parties, even in return for a reasonable royalty, a licence for the supply of products incorporating the design would lead to the proprietor thereof being deprived of the substance of his exclusive right, and that a refusal to grant such a licence cannot in itself constitute an abuse of a dominant position.[10]

The situation may however be different if the owner of the right refuses to supply spare parts, fixes prices at an unfair level[11] or discontinues production. Provided that such conduct is liable to affect trade between member states, such exercise of the intellectual property right is prohibited by Article 82 and in this situation the grant of a 'compulsory' licence becomes possible.[12] But it is clear from the cases that more than the existence of the right creating a dominant position and the simple refusal to grant a licence is required, if an abuse is to be proved. The starting point must be that the power to decide whether or not to grant licences is an essential component of the right with which Article 82 does not interfere. The *Volvo vs Veng* case dealt with designs, but the Court's ruling in the *Maxicar vs Renault* case does not permit any different conclusion when patents are concerned.[13]

Magill

In the *Magill* cases[14] the problem arose when Magill wished to publish the listings of programmes of BBC, ITV and RTE in a single weekly publication. The three companies refused to supply those listings and invoked their copyright in the listings to do so. It should be noted that they published their own guides, which thus enjoyed a form of monopoly, and supplied, free of charge, the weekly listings to foreign publications. They also supplied daily listings to the press. The Commission[15] ruled that the three companies abused their dominant position in exercising their copyright in such a way and required that advance information was supplied to Magill. The decision on this point was upheld by the Court of First Instance.[16]

The judgment of the Court of First Instance reads:

> Conduct of that type (the exercise of the copyright in the way described above)...clearly goes beyond what is necessary to fulfil the essential function of the copyright as permitted in Community law.

After failing to find an objective and specific justification for this conduct the Court of First Instance continued:

> ... the aim and effect of the applicant's exclusive reproduction of its programme listings was to exclude any potential competition...in order to maintain the monopoly enjoyed...by the applicant on that market. From the point of view of outside undertakings interested in publishing a television magazine, the applicant's refusal to authorise, on request and on a non-discriminatory basis, any third party to publish its programme listings is therefore comparable...to an arbitrary refusal by a car manufacturer to supply spare parts...to an independent repairer...[17]

The Court of First Instance applied the *Volvo vs Veng* doctrine to copyright. This situation falls under the exception in the doctrine where the grant of a 'compulsory' licence is possible because the intellectual property right is exercised in a way which is prohibited by Article 82.[18]

The Court of First Instance also stressed that it is enough in order for Article 82 to be applicable that the abusive conduct is capable of affecting trade between member states. No present and real effect on such trade is requested.[19]

The *Magill* cases went on to be appealed before the Court of Justice.[20] The main problem with the approach taken by the Commission and the Court of First Instance is that it could suggest that once an undertaking occupies a dominant position, the simple refusal to grant a licence could constitute an abuse of that dominant position (Haines, 1994, p. 401). This cannot be a correct interpretation of Article 82. As suggested in *Volvo* and *Renault*, the interpretation of Article 82 develops along the lines of the interpretation of Articles 28 and 30. This is the approach we advocated above in relation to the free movement of goods and it was also the approach taken by Advocate-General Gulmann in his conclusion which was delivered in June 1994.

In a controversial judgment, the wording of which strongly resembles the *Commercial Solvents* line of thought,[21] the Court of Justice declined to overrule the Court of First Instance. The reasons given by the Court and the implications of the judgment require some careful examination though (Stamatoudi, 1998, p. 153). The main principle is that a refusal to licence intellectual property rights can contravene Article 82 in 'exceptional circumstances'. In those cases compulsory licensing is an available remedy.[22]

When it established that the broadcasters occupied a dominant position, the Court indicated first of all that it accepted that the relevant product and geographical market should be defined as the market in comprehensive TV listings guides in Ireland and Northern Ireland. The Court went on to confirm that the mere ownership of an intellectual property right, here the copyright in the programme listings, does not confer a dominant position.[23] That dominant position did however exist in the particular circumstances of the case. This was derived from the fact that the broadcasters were the only source of the basic programming information, that they had a *de facto* monopoly over the raw material which that programming information constituted[24] and that they could therefore prevent effective competition in the secondary market of weekly TV magazines.[25]

Even so, the question remained whether the refusal to licence amounted to an abuse of that dominant position. The existing case law pointed towards the fact that the mere existence of the intellectual property right and its use that stays within the specific subject-matter of the right cannot amount to an abuse. If the possession of the immaterial right is to have any value, its owner must be free to decide under which circumstances and under which financial conditions he is pre- pared to grant a licence. A right to refuse to grant a licence must be part of such a system and must therefore come within the specific subject-matter of the right. In normal circumstances such a refusal can therefore not be in breach of Article 82. However, there may be circumstances where the intellectual property right is used improperly and to serve purposes that have nothing to do with the real purpose and essential function of the right. If the right is abused, the refusal to grant a licence is no longer used to implement the essential function of the right and, just as anything else in relation to an exclusive or monopoly intellectual property right, exposes itself to the sanction of Article 82. This approach is endorsed by the Court's judgment. The Court argued that a refusal might in exceptional circumstances constitute an abuse.[26] These exceptional circumstances involved the following in this case. The broadcaster's main activity is broadcast- ing; the TV guides market is only a secondary market for them. By refusing to provide the basic programme listing information, of which they were the only source, the broadcasters prevented the appearance of new products which they did not offer and for which there was a consumer demand. The refusal could not be justified by virtue of their normal activities. And, by denying access to the basic information which was required to make the new product, the broadcasters were effectively reserving the secondary market for weekly TV guides to themselves. The use of copyright to block the appearance of a new product for which the copyright information is essential and to reserve a secondary market to oneself is an abuse and cannot be said to be necessary to fulfil the essential function (reward and encouragement of the author) of copyright. This is especially so if one is the only source of the copyright information or material. Especially the latter element is of vital importance. It may not be part of the abuse, but the availability of other sources for the material would take away the element of dominance. And without dominance there can simply be no abuse of a dominant position.

Looking at it this way, the Court has allayed the fears that had arisen on the basis of the problematically worded judgment of the Court of First Instance. It is also clear that the Court's judgment in *Magill* is by no means a departure from its existing case law. It is rather an application of that case law in an extreme set of circumstances. All intellectual property rights still have their role in a free market economy, but as we explained earlier that role is restricted to their capacity to enhance overall levels of competition. This means that intellectual property rights can only be used to fulfil their essential function. This point has been overlooked on too many occasions and the specific subject-matter of a right has too often been seen as a list, written in stone, of things that the rightholder is allowed to do. Refusing a licence had to be on that list. *Magill* has shown that that list is by no means written in stone and that the items on there are only there in as far as they fulfil the essential pro-competitive function of the intellectual property right involved. They will be caught by the operation of competition law if they are (ab)used for other purposes. This will be the case in what the Court described as 'exceptional circumstances' and the essential facilities doctrine which is so prominently present in the judgment provides just one, but admittedly a poignant, example of exceptional circumstances in which the use of an intellectual property right falls outside what is required for the fulfilment of the essential function of the intellectual property right concerned.

One can find criticism of the fact that the UK and Ireland grant copyright to basic programme information listings that have such a low level of originality between the lines of the *Magill* case. This point will have to be addressed though by the member states concerned or by means of a Parliament and Council Directive. The Court has no power to interfere with issues such as what is original enough to attract copyright or in trade marks terms, with the point whether there is *de facto* confusion between two trade marks. It made this clear in the *Deutsche Renault vs Audi* case.[27] These issues of substantive law are part of the sovereign powers of the member states in the absence of Community harmonisation measures on the points concerned.

It must be obvious that these exceptional circumstances will rarely be found and that the operation of the rule in *Magill* will be restricted to unusual and special cases. The essential function is by no means a narrow concept. *Magill* must also be seen against the background of the fact that a weak copyright was involved. Most other member states would not even have given copyright in the basic programme information concerned. Basic information is more easily an indispensable raw material for new products than the more traditional highly creative personal expressions of certain ideas by authors. This means that the Magill rule will more easily bite in the former cases. The more original the work is, the more creative expression that has gone in a particular expression of an idea, the more unlikely it is that a refusal to licence will be an abuse. The refusal to grant a licence for the TV listings became abusive, among other things, because without the licence Magill could not publish any guide. The whole market and the emergence of a new product were blocked. A refusal to grant a licence to turn a novel into a movie is clearly not in the same league. Plenty of other films can be made and the monopolisation of any secondary market is simply not present.

Ladbroke

The conclusion that *Magill* needs to be confined to a small number of extreme cases is also supported by the Court of First Instance's judgment in one of the many *Ladbroke* cases.[28] This case was concerned with the question whether a refusal by the French copyright owners to license sound and pictures of French horse races to a Belgian betting agency amounted to a *Magill*-style abuse of a dominant position (Fitzgerald, 1998, p. 154). The emphasis lies in this case squarely on the issue of abuse. That abuse must be found on the relevant geographical market and any activity or decision outside that market is irrelevant. The Court of First Instance ruled that no *Magill*-style abuse could be found. It reached this conclusion for a couple of reasons.[29] First, Ladbroke was not prevented from entering another market by the refusal to licence. It was already an important player in the market concerned and it could not be argued that the French horse racing organisations reserved that betting market for themselves, especially since they were not even present in it. The pictures were not essential for the exercise of the activity in question. And second, the emergence of a new product was not blocked and in any case the sound and pictures were not the essential ingredient of such a product. Ladbroke rather wanted to offer an additional service to its clients for its main betting activity. Only a refusal to licence that concerned either a new product whose introduction might be prevented, despite specific, constant and regular potential consumer demand, or a product of service that was essential, due to the absence of a real or potential substitute, for the activity concerned, would fall foul of Article 82.

Ladbroke was also not excluded from a market in which the French horse racing organisations were operating by the refusal to licence and neither was it discriminated against on the Belgian market.[30]

IMS Health

Facts and issues

It has become clear from the discussion above that it is at least arguable that *Magill* had left open several issues.[31] These issues were primarily open to argument because it was not clear whether the decision on that point in *Magill* depended entirely on the facts of the case, that is, other facts could receive a different treatment, or whether they were necessary element from a legal point of view. One of the issues left open is the question whether a finding of exceptional circumstances required cumulatively the fact that the intellectual property right was linked to essential inputs for secondary markets on the one hand and that a new product had to be introduced in that market for which there was significant and unmet demand on the other hand. Do the conditions in Magill apply cumulatively (as was the case in Magill on its facts) or are they alternative conditions? The latter option would see the essential facilities doctrine apply to many more cases as there would be more exceptional circumstances. Magill also stresses the need for monopolisation of a secondary market. How secondary should that market be? Is it simply a separate or derivative market? And could the essential facilities doctrine apply if the competitor that was refused a licence wanted to compete on the rightholder's main market? In other words, how close to the core business of the rightholder can one come?

The IMS Health saga provided an opportunity to answer some of these questions. IMS Health is developing along two parallel tracks on the basis of the following facts. IMS Health is a major supplier of marketing data to pharmaceutical and other healthcare companies. In the German market it has established a structure of local geographic segments, 1,860 in total, called bricks, each containing a comparable number of pharmacies in order to collect standardised data without violating data protection laws that do not allow for the identification of individual pharmacies' data. That structure is protected by copyright under German copyright law. That point as such is not in dispute. However, there is more to it than pure copyright. From the user or consumer side there is a high demand for the data collected through use of the brick structure, which has become an impressive success on the market. The brick structure has *de facto* become the industry standard and its competitors asked for it to be licensed to them in order for them to be able to compete. The user is indeed only interested in data that are presented in a comparable fashion. When IMS Health's competitors NDC Health and AzyX Deutschland GmbH Geopharma Information Services applied for a licence covering the brick structure at various stages during the complex timeline and developments of the case, the details of which are not necessary for our present purposes, the grant of such a licence was refused by IMS Health and that resulted in the end in a complaint by NDC and AzyX to the European Commission for abuse of dominant position. In due course the Commission issued its decision, in which it went against IMS in a first stage but without reaching a final conclusion. Interim measures were imposed. That Commission decision was appealed and as a result followed the two Orders of the President of the Court of First Instance[32] and one Order from the President of the Court of Justice[33] that suspended those interim measures. In the light of that suspension and of the sceptical attitude that the President of the Court of First Instance and the President of the Court of Justice took towards the Commission's approach the Commission withdrew its interim measures decision.[34]

At the same time though IMS Health's competitors had decided to make use of the brick structure anyway, without waiting for the grant of the licence. IMS Health therefore brought copyright proceedings against them in the German courts. In the course of these copyright proceedings the German court referred the case to the Court of Justice for a preliminary ruling.[35] The Court has now given its judgment in that case. That means that the two elements that are still outstanding in this case are the final decision of the Commission on the competition issue and the judgment of the German court which will have to apply the guidance from the Court of Justice.

The Commission's approach

We will start by analysing the Commission's decision first. From it, the approach the Commission takes to the wider issue of the essential facilities doctrine in relation to IP rights will become clear. Afterwards we will move on to the decision of the Court of Justice. Let us therefore now first of all have a look at the process followed by the Commission in giving its decision[36] in order to find out how it interpreted and applied the essential facilities doctrine in this case. Following the standard provisions for any case in which the abuse of a dominant position is alleged the Commission first of all identifies the relevant geographical market. In its view that relevant geographical market is Germany,[37] whereas the relevant product market is the regional sales data services.[38]

As regards the position of dominance, IMS Health is found to be dominant after examining several factors, but the Commission primarily refers to the fact that IMS Health holds a high market share not only in Germany but also in Europe,[39] Germany being the country that has 'the largest market for regional sales data services in Europe'[40] it may therefore be regarded as a 'substantial part of the common market' in this respect.[41]

Let us now return to the relevant market for German regional sales data services. In order to understand the background to the case we need to know what these services are in this case and why they are needed. Pharmaceutical companies need the brick system and in particular the system put in place by IMS because this system enables them to gather data in which they can record sales of a particular drug, comparing the sales figures for each of their products with those for the products of their competitors and it also offers them a tool to measure the performance of their sales representatives.[42] In the brick structure these data are collected in each brick for a small number of pharmacies in a local area. This allows the pharmaceutical companies to obtain a detailed picture showing possible local differences, without at the same time infringing German Data Protection laws. The use of data relating to individual doctors or pharmacies would cause problems under these laws.

The Commission adopts the conclusion that IMS Health occupies a position of quasi-monopoly[43] and this is, according to the Commission, due to the fact that IMS Health owns the copyright in unique structure for recording sales data for pharmaceutical products and services and that in the relevant market there was simply no competition before the arrival on the market of NDC and AzyX. The Commission argues that IMS obtained this quasi- monopoly position through a close collaboration with the German pharmaceutical industry which lead them to the creation of a brick structure,[44] in the form of the 1,860 brick structure which is segmenting the German market in several sectors in which many data are collected including those of names of sales representatives, customers, doctors, and so on. The exact shape of the brick structure is therefore to a large part the outcome of that collaborative effort. That involvement of the primary customer in the establishment of the structure also helps to explain why this structure seems to be indispensable for other competitors that made enormous investment to enter into that market and that found it impossible to build a new structure due primarily to the unwillingness[45] of the pharmaceutical industry to switch to another structure, a process in which the industry would incur important additional costs.[46]

The Commission is further sustaining that the IMS brick structure is becoming a '*de facto*' industry standard or a 'common language' as defined by the Commission[47] in the sense that the common language of that structure is well known and it is commonly used. For the Commission the '1,860 brick structure is becoming a common language for communicating the information',[48] and all the pharmaceutical companies which assisted with its creation are in the end effectively 'locked in' that structure, even if one needs to add that they are locked in on a voluntarily basis. Everything turns around that structure[49] and the situation in Germany does not offer so much space for a substitution. The 1,860 brick structure is especially a great and unique source of information.[50] And here the Commission sees parallels with the *Magill* case, as this is what it happened in *Magill* where the information concerned was contained in the TV listings on the basis of which the broadcasters had indeed a unique source of information.[51]

The possibility to change the system for the collection of data exists, but despite the fact that competing companies tried it[52] this did not bring to a structure very different to the one put in place by IMS Health. But changing that structure will also mean changing other data[53] linked to that structure and therefore this will increase the costs and that will work as a deterrent for any such change. Also the relationship of the companies using the (new) structure with their sales representatives will be harmed, since also this relationship has been shaped around the 1,860 brick structure.[54] The Commission's analysis, despite the fact that in its defence IMS Health accuses the Commission on more than one occasion of not being precise enough,[55] has shown that IMS Health's brick structure became indispensable and the overall standard.

Moreover, there are 'technical and legal constraints'[56] which make it even more difficult and in the Commission's view even impossible for other companies to create a new structure for regional sales data in Germany that is able to compete with the 1,860 brick structure. The Commission concluded therefore that IMS Health should grant all its competitors a licence upon payment of a reasonable royalty for the use of its copyright work. The Commission justifies its conclusion as follows. There is an abuse that is due to the dominant position occupied by IMS Health and moreover IMS Health owns an essential facility that is impossible to substitute.

In its decision the Commission refers repeatedly to the essential facility doctrine, especially in the sense in which it was set out by the Court of Justice in the *Oscar Bronner*[57] case. *Bronner* was not a case concerned with intellectual property rights, but *Bronner* may be important because it is clearly a case about essential facilities. *Bronner* could therefore shed light on the correct interpretation of the essential facilities doctrine in European competition law. *Bronner* dealt with a system for the house to house distribution of newspapers in Austria set up by the major national newspaper. A smaller competitor argued that it should be allowed to make use of the system in order to be able to compete. In its view the system had become an essential facility. The Court of Justice followed the suggestion of its Advocate General Francis Jacobs to interpret the essential facilities doctrine restrictively and then ruled that it did not apply here. Important for our current purposes is the establishment of a test that a firm violates Article 82 where:

- 'the refusal of access to the facility is likely to eliminate all competition in the relevant market;'
- 'such refusal is not capable of being objectively justified; and'
- 'the facility itself is indispensable to carry on business, inasmuch as there is no actual or potential substitute in existence for that facility'.[58]

However, the Commission forgets to mention that *Bronner* is a case that can only show how the essential facilities doctrine can be applied in a European competition law context in general, being a case of pure competition rules application. It is indeed vital to recall that in a normal situation competition rules are the only set of rules used to regulate market behaviour. That is also so in the *Bronner* case.

The presence of copyright complicates things though. As copyright confers an exclusive right there is almost by definition also a possibility that such an exclusive right will be used in one way or another to restrict competition. There may therefore be a conflict between competition law on the one hand and copyright law on the other hand in a given situation (Furse, 2002, pp. 205, 214).

But in order to understand the nature of such a potential conflict better one needs to see how both regulatory systems, that is, copyright and competition law, operate. Copyright operates at a structural level. It puts in place a rewards and incentives structure that applies to all relevant cases and that aims to enhance competition at creation and innovation level by granting an exclusive right in the copyright work that restricts to some extent competition at the production level. In doing so copyright defines (intellectual) property rights. Competition law on the other hand operates in an entirely different way. It operates at the behavioural level and it does so almost on a case by case basis. It is therefore not the case that there is a conflict between two sets of rules that operate in the same way and at the same level (Ramello, 2003, p. 118). Copyright and competition law share the same objective, but they have ways of achieving it and they operate at a different level (Lemarchand *et al.*, 2003, pp. 17–19).

Competition law does not operate at the structural level and as such it does not interfere with the structure created by copyright to enhance creation and innovation at competition at that stage. What is true though is that it may wish to interfere at a later stage with some of the behaviour that flows from the grant of copyright. In more down to earth terms, copyright may be used or exercised in an improper way and such behaviour is then regulated and addressed by means of competition law. The factor which complicates matters is that it is to a fair extent the incentives and exclusive rights created at the structural level by copyright that facilitate or at least make possible the emergence of inefficient behaviour that might infringe competition law rules. What can be derived at this early stage is that a system that is designed to regulate behaviour should not operate in a way to undue the structural system put in place by a system such as copyright. The legislator has made a policy decision to put a structure such as copyright in place to enhance and reward creativity and innovation and that decision should be respected. In other words, competition law should restrict itself to its proper role which is to address anti-competitive behaviour, such as any use of copyright that is not pro-competitive as was envisaged when the structural system was set up (Whish, 2001, p. 676). This conclusion should not surprise anyone, as it should be kept in mind that it is competition law itself that allows for the grant of exclusive rights if on the one hand they are necessary and unavoidable to obtain the benefits which the rightholder brings about for the consumer and if on the other hand they do not lead to a complete elimination of competition (Lemarchand *et al.*, 2003, p. 19).

As we have demonstrated above, in intellectual property cases in general and particularly in copyright cases there is not just one set of rules that affects the market behaviour regulation point. Both intellectual property and copyright rules on the one hand and competition rules on the other hand set out to regulate competition conditions on the market and to steer certain forms of behaviour on the market. The presence of such a second set of rules must have an impact on the test that is used, otherwise its vital role is completely ignored. It is therefore submitted that it is not possible to transfer the test set out in the *Oscar Bronner*[59] case to intellectual property and copyright related cases without modifying it. This must mean that any strict reliance by the Commission on the *Bronner* case in its IMS Health decision must be misguided. The decision cannot be based solely and straightforwardly on the Court's judgment in the *Oscar Bronner* case.

To be fair to the Commission, it also argues that its decision follows from the judgments in *Magill*[60] and *Ladbroke*.[61]

The exceptional circumstances referred to by the Court in relation to the broadcasters' refusal to licence the programme listings in *Magill* come down to two elements. By refusing to make programme listings available to Magill under licence the broadcasters prevented the appearance of a new product that they did not offer, but for which there was a clear demand from the side of the consumer. It is important to add in relation to this first element that as a result of their exclusive copyright in the listings the broadcasters were the only source for any such information that is vital for anyone wishing to publish a weekly TV guide. The second element is that by denying access to that vital material without which the new product could not see the light of day, the broadcasters were effectively reserving the secondary market for weekly TV guides to themselves. The Court clearly emphasises the secondary market point by indicating that the broadcasters' main activity is broadcasting and that the prohibited activity therefore did not affect that primary activity but only the TV guides market that is only a secondary market for them. The refusal could not be justified by virtue of the broadcasters' normal activities.

At this stage one clearly sees the appearance of the essential facilities doctrine. As the broadcasters are the only source of the necessary copyright material and as that material is essential, that is, the TV guide cannot be produced without it, the copyright protected information concerning programme listings has become an essential facility for any company that wishes to operate on the relevant market. *Magill* can therefore be seen as an application of the essential facilities doctrine in a copyright case, whereas *Bronner* applies the same doctrine to a 'normal' non-intellectual property related case, as discussed above (Treacy, 1999, p. 501; Woolridge, 1999, p. 256; Stothers, 2001, p. 256). It is also important to highlight the fact that the Court emphasised that there was a clear and unmet demand on the consumers' side. Like all US essential facilities cases *Magill* also links the essential facilities doctrine to the benefit that arises for the consumer from its application (Areeda, 1989, p. 84).

When the Commission refers to the Court's judgment in *Magill*, it summarises the position adopted by the Court as follows:

> The Court therefore recognised that in exceptional circumstances the exercise of an exclusive right deriving from an intellectual copyright may be abusive even in the absence of additional abusive conduct when, *inter alia*, it prevents the appearance of a new product.[62]

This summary is causing problems in as far as the use of the term '*inter alia*' is possibly a misrepresentation of the Court's judgment in *Magill*. Indeed, the Commission seems to suggest that the appearance of a new product is not a necessary element and that other elements might replace it. In the Commission's view the appearance of a new product is just one of the exceptional circumstances to which the Court refers. It is submitted that it is wrong to use the term '*inter alia*' in this way and to give this interpretation to the judgment of the Court. Instead, it is submitted that the '*inter alia*' type of exceptional circumstances which the Court withheld in *Magill* amount to the fact that the information concerned had become an essential facility for the publishers of TV guides. The judgment in *Magill* supports the point of view that the application of the essential facilities doctrine in relation to intellectual property, that is, for there to be an abuse of the dominant position the possession of which is not an abuse *per se*, requires the presence of all elements, set out above. The prevention of the emergence of a new product is therefore a necessary component and not just an optional element as suggested by the Commission.

The Commission also argues that its point of view is supported by the judgment of the Court of First Instance in *Ladbroke*.[63] The Court of First Instance came to the conclusion that the facts of the *Ladbroke* case did not warrant the application of the rules set out in *Magill*. One could argue that the main reason for the Court of First Instance not to examine the point of the emergence of a new product is the fact that if one condition is not met, the case was bound to fail as the conditions apply cumulatively. But one could go further, as the Commission seems to be doing in its IMS Health decision, and highlight the Court of First Instances statement that the 'refusal to supply the applicant could not fall within the prohibition laid down by Article [82] unless it concerned a product or service which was either essential for the exercise of the activity in question, in that there was no real or potential substitute, OR was a new product whose introduction might be prevented, despite specific, constant and regular potential demand on the part of the consumer'.[64] Taken on its own this quote could suggest that there is no need to establish that the abuse takes place on a downstream market before *Magill* can be applied and even more importantly that the conditions found in *Magill* might be alternatives, which excludes the need for their cumulative application. It is submitted though that this is not a correct approach. The whole approach hinges on the literal interpretation out of context of the single word 'or'. If one puts in the context that interpretation becomes difficult. The Court of First Instance felt hardly any need to investigate the second point (Hull *et al.*, 2002, p. 37). They dismissed the case on the first ground.

Anything they said about the second point is therefore obiter. If they had seen the requirements as real alternatives, as the Commission suggests, they would have needed to deal with the second point in much more depth even if the truth is probably that the emergence of a new product was not blocked and that in any case the sound and pictures were not the essential ingredient of any such product.

The Commission's interpretation which dismisses the new product requirement that seemed so prominent in *Magill* is therefore based on flimsy grounds and reliance on the passage from the judgment of the lower European court in *Ladbroke* to achieve this is precarious. This is even more so since it disregards the economic analysis set out above. The approach may well work in a non-intellectual property context. The *Bronner* case which we discussed above showed how the essential facilities doctrine could work in this context. Similarly the *Commercial Solvents*[65] judgment leads one to the conclusion that there is an abuse of a dominant position on the sole ground of the monopolisation of a secondary market. In non-intellectual property cases that is an abuse as such even if a new product is not prevented from appearing on the market. Here the requirements do not need to be applied cumulatively. But we already explained that the presence of intellectual property rights and their competition regulative function change the picture dramatically. It is therefore submitted that the Commission is misguided in its reliance on *Ladbroke* for its views in the IMS Health decision (Hull *et al.*, 2002, p. 37).

IMS in the Court of Justice

The scepticism towards the broad interpretation of the essential facilities doctrine proposed by the Commission that has been expressed in the foregoing analysis was also reflected in the Orders of the President of the Court of First Instance and the President of the Court of Justice. It is therefore welcome to see that the Court of Justice adopted a much more careful and sensible approach in its judgment in case C-418/01 *IMS Health vs NDC Health*.[66] The Court first of all turned its attention to the vital question when in a copyright context a facility has become an essential facility.

The Court held that, in order to determine whether a product or service is indispensable for enabling an undertaking to carry on business in a particular market, it must be determined whether there are products or services which constitute alternative solutions. It does not matter in that respect that these alternative solutions are less advantageous, and whether there are technical, legal or economic obstacles capable of making it impossible or at least unreasonably difficult for any undertaking seeking to operate in the market to create, possibly in cooperation with other operators, the alternative products or services. The existence of economic obstacles will only be able to rule out an alternative solution if it is established, at the very least, that the creation of those products or services is not economically viable for production on a scale comparable to that of the undertaking which controls the existing product or service. This is a very strict interpretation of the essential facility point and as the existence of an essential facility is a prerequisite that must be met before even the issue of abuse can be addressed this will severely limit the number of cases where the exercise of copyright will be interfered with.

In the IMS case the Court advised the German Court that in applying the test account must be taken of the fact that a high level of participation by the pharmaceutical laboratories in the improvement of the 1,860 brick structure protected by copyright has created a dependency by users in regard to that structure, particularly at a technical level. The Court went on to say that

> In such circumstances, it is likely that those laboratories would have to make exceptional organisational and financial efforts in order to acquire the studies on regional sales of pharmaceutical products presented on the basis of a structure other than that protected by copyright. The supplier of that alternative structure might therefore be obliged to offer terms which are such as to rule out any economic viability of business on a scale comparable to that of the undertaking which controls the protected structure.[67]

The strong suggestion to the German Court is therefore no doubt that these additional circumstances have turned the block structure into an essential facility. Once it has been established that the facility, here the block structure as protected by copyright, is an essential facility the second step, that is, the issue whether there has been an abuse of a dominant position, here by refusing to license the block structure, can be addressed. The Court ruled on this point that three conditions have to be met cumulatively for there to be an abuse:

- the refusal is preventing the emergence of a new product for which there is a potential consumer demand;
- there is no objective justification for this refusal; and
- the refusal is such as to exclude any competition on a secondary market.[68]

This way the Court clearly adopts a very restrictive interpretation of its earlier dicta in *Magill* and *Bronner*. The Commission's suggestion that the criteria could be applied alternatively rather than cumulatively and in particular that the existence of separate markets was not required has been rejected straightforwardly. The point is now clear, all three requirements apply cumulatively if there is to be a finding of abuse.

The Court then went on to clarify each of the three requirements and their application to the IMS Health case. The third condition, relating to the likelihood of excluding all competition on a secondary market requires that it is possible to distinguish an upstream market, constituted by the product or service that forms the essential facility, for example, in *Bronner* the market for home delivery of daily newspapers and in *IMS* the market for brick structures, and a (secondary) downstream market, on which the product or service in question, that is, the essential facility, is used for the production of another product or the supply of another service, for example, in *Bronner* the market for daily newspapers themselves and in IMS Health the market for the supply of sales data.[69] The fact that the essential facility is not marketed separately is not regarded as precluding, from the outset, the possibility of identifying a separate market. It is indeed sufficient that a potential market or even hypothetical market can be identified (Benabou, 2004, p. 825). One of the positive aspects of the approach is that an abuse can also be found in those circumstances where the rightholder's behaviour does not simply hinder competition but where its behaviour completely excludes competition to such an extent that in reality no downstream market exists. Second, it is now clear that a secondary market does not have to be of secondary importance to the rightholder, as was the case on the facts in *Magill*. All that is required is the existence of two markets. Or in the words of the Court:

> Accordingly, it is determinative that two different stages of production may be identified and that they are interconnected, the upstream product is indispensable inasmuch as for supply of the downstream product.[70]

It is therefore possible that the applicant for the licence that is refused wanted to compete head on with the rightholder on the same market.

In practical business terms it will be relatively easy to determine the markets involved in those cases where there is a real existing market for the goods or services that allegedly amount to an essential facility, but things get more difficult when one is looking at the potential or hypothetical markets which the Court mentions and which are likely to represent the majority of cases. Indeed, the abuse complained of prevents the existence of a real market in business terms. The Court's approach is to argue that there is a potential or a hypothetical market if two conditions are met:

- the products or services must be indispensable in order to carry on a particular business, and
- there is an actual demand for them on the part of undertakings which seek to carry on the business for which they are indispensable.

In terms of the IMS Health case this means asking whether the 1,860 brick structure constitutes, upstream, an indispensable factor in the downstream supply of German regional sales data for pharmaceutical products, coupled with the demand on the part of the competitors of IMS.[71]

The approach adopted by the Court refers back to the criteria used to determine whether or not a facility is indeed an essential facility. One could allege that it is therefore a circular reasoning. More importantly though this may well be a workable solution. Admittedly, copyright itself is narrowly associated with its exploitation, for example, IMS only created the brick structure in order to be able to supply the sales data and the brick structure and the copyright in it have little or no value outside the sales data business. The distinction between two markets for the creation of the copyright work and the right and the work on the one hand and for the exploitation of the work on the sales data market on the other hand may therefore seem artificial. But this is a peculiarity of copyright and one should resist the temptation to argue that the creation of two somewhat artificial markets in this way opens the door for the application of the essential facilities doctrine in a vast number of cases to the detriment of copyright (Benabou, 2004, p. 825).

It should indeed not be forgotten that two additional requirements need also to be met before the essential facilities doctrine can be applied.

It is to these two other requirements that we now turn. The first condition relates to the emergence of a new product. The Court clarified in this respect that in the balancing of the interest in protection of copyright and the economic freedom of its owner, against the interest in protection of free competition the latter interest can only prevail over the copyright interest where refusal to grant a licence prevents the development of the secondary market to the detriment of consumers. There is therefore a need for the applicant for a licence to offer a new and different product and to show consumer demand for such a product. The consumer interest point is therefore of vital importance. Copyright is indeed not granted to stop the emergence of new and different products for which there is a demand. Any use of copyright to that end must amount to an abuse of right.

The final requirement is that the refusal to license must be unjustified. This means simply that the court is to examine whether the refusal of the request for a licence is justified by objective considerations.

Microsoft

For our current purposes it can be said that the Commission's decision in the *Microsoft* case is an application of the *Magill–IMS Health* line of cases. The Commission indeed insists on Microsoft being obliged to compulsory license its communication protocols for its Windows software. In the eyes of the Commission, Microsoft's behaviour meets all the requirements set out in the *Magill–IMS Health* line of cases. Microsoft, obviously, disagrees.

A first point raised by Microsoft is that the intellectual property concerned is not indispensable for the purposes of carrying on a business as a supplier of work group server operating systems. In other words, it is not an essential facility for these purposes. In Microsoft's view interoperability can be achieved in other ways and consumers have no complaints about the degree of interoperability that has been achieved despite Microsoft's refusal to license certain intellectual property. Several competitors have entered the market irrespective of the refusal.[72] The Commission disagrees with this assessment, because in its view, making some information available does not demonstrate that the refusal to make all further information available does not amount to an abuse that can be qualified as withholding an essential facility.[73] The Commission also argues that Microsoft has for years been enjoying such a dominant position that it effectively sets the standards of interoperability. As such interoperability with the Microsoft standard has become an essential facility.[74]

The second point follows logically in Microsoft's view. Indeed, the emergence of a new product for which there is an unsatisfied consumer demand has not been prevented. There is no evidence to support this and the evidence shows on the contrary that Microsoft's competitors simply want to replicate the existing Microsoft products.[75] The Commission instead emphasises that not making the specification available hinders the emergence of interoperable products that may be quite different in nature.[76] Innovation has been stifled and consumer choice has been limited.[77]

Third, Microsoft's policy to retain its intellectual property has not had the effect of eliminating competition on a secondary market. The growth of Linux can be seen as evidence in this respect.[78] But the Commission argues that Microsoft's refusal puts its competitors at such a strong competitive disadvantage that there is a real risk that competition will effectively be eliminated.[79]

Microsoft's fourth argument is that the company is able to objectively justify its refusal to license its technology. Unlike in *Magill* and *IMS Health*, the intellectual property involved was not in the public domain, but it was instead secret and valuable. Taken in combination with Microsoft's positive impact on innovation in the field, this must offset any negative impact on competition and be seen as an objective justification not to license the technology.[80] The Commission again disagrees. In its view any disadvantage to Microsoft is in these exceptional circumstances offset by the benefit of the positive impact on the level of innovation of the whole industry of the granting of a compulsory licence.[81]

It will eventually be for the European Court to resolve this case, but even at present it demonstrates that many issues in relation to copyright works as essential facilities are still unresolved when it comes to the finer details. IMS Health was a major step forward, but we have not yet reached the end of the road.

Conclusion

In conclusion, despite the fact that we are at the end of the IMS saga and that a lot of points have been clarified in relation to the essential facilities doctrine and its application in relation to copyright (and IP rights in general) there are still a number of issues that need to be refined and clarified, as the Microsoft decision and the controversy surrounding it demonstrates. It is submitted that the Court's restrictive approach in IMS Health is to be applauded (for a critical analysis, Drexl, 2004, p. 788) as it does justice to the pro-competitive role of copyright (and other IP rights) and as it allows on the other hand competition law to stop any abuse for undue purposes of copyright (or other IP rights). Those cases where copyright (or IP rights in general) will be interfered with will be limited to a small number and it this may well be rightly so. The Court may not have ruled out all difficulties in applying the test in practice and further difficult cases, such as the Microsoft case, will no doubt arise, but at least did get the balance right in theory. Getting the economic theory entirely right and clarifying the detailed application of the concept of essential facilities in all circumstances will have to wait until the Microsoft decision of the Court or it may even only happen in later cases. There are still several chapters of the story that need to be written (and commented upon).

Notes

1 See in general the Speech delivered by Judge Bo Vesterdorf, President of the Court of First Instance, at the 'European Copyright Revisited' Conference, held in Santiago de Compostela, 16–18 June 2002, 'The Role of Copyright and Related Rights as a Policy as Compared to Other Policies', available on line at europa.eu.int/comm/ internal_market/en/ intprop/news/2002–06-conference-speech-vesterdorf_en.htm

2 On the issue of free-riders in relation to intellectual property see R. Benko, *Protecting Intellectual Property Rights: Issues and Controversies*, American Enterprise Institute for Public Policy Research (AEI Studies 453) (1987) at 17.
3 For a more detailed analysis of the economics of copyright see also R. Watt, *Copyright and Economic Theory: Friends or Foes?*, Edward Elgar (2000).
4 On the issue of inappropriability see Arrow, 'Economic Welfare and the Allocation of Resources for Invention' in National Bureau for Economic Research, *The Rate and Direction of Inventive Activity: Economic and Social Factors*, Princeton University Press (1962) at 609–625 and Lunn, 'The Roles of Property Rights and Market Power in Appropriating Innovative Output', [1985] *Journal of Legal Studies* 423 at 425.
5 Directive of the European Parliament and of the Council on the protection of databases [1996] OJ L77/20.
6 Case 53/87 *Consorzio Italiano della Componentistica di Ricambio per Autoveicoli and Maxicar vs Régie nationale des usines Renault* [1988] ECR 6039, [1990] 4 CMLR 265.
7 Case 238/87 *AB Volvo* vs *Erik Veng (UK) Ltd* [1988] ECR 6211, [1989] 4 CMLR 122.
8 Ibid., with reference to case 144/81 *Keurkoop BV vs Nancy Kean Gifts BV* [1982] ECR 2853, [1983] 2 CMLR 47.
9 Case 53/87 *Consorzio Italiano della Componentistica di Ricambio per Autoveicoli and Maxicar vs Régie nationale des usines Renault* [1988] ECR 6039, [1990] 4 CMLR 265; this quotation at [1988] ECR 6039, 6073.
10 Case 238/87 *AB Volvo vs Erik Veng (UK) Ltd* [1988] ECR 6211, [1989] 4 CMLR 122 at 6235.
11 Products protected by an intellectual property right may be sold at a higher price than similar unprotected products if the price difference forms a reasonable return of the investments made, see Case 24/67 *Parke, Davis & Co vs Probel, Reese, Beintema-Interfarm and Centrafarm* [1968] ECR 55, [1968] CMLR 47, confirmed in case 53/87 *Maxicar vs Régie nationale des usines Renault* [1988] ECR 6039, [1990] 4 CMLR 265.
12 Case 238/87 *AB Volvo vs Erik Veng (UK) Ltd* [1988] ECR 6211, [1989] 4 CMLR 122 and case 53/87 *Maxicar vs Régie nationale des usines Renault* [1988] ECR 6039, [1990] 4 CMLR 265.
13 Ibid. and see C. Bellamy and G. Child, *Common Market Law of Competition*, Sweet and Maxwell (1st Supp to 3rd edn, 1991) at 86. The Patents Court in London dealt with an application to patents in *Philips Electronics NV vs Ingman Ltd and the Video Duplicating Co Ltd* [1999] FSR 112.
14 Case T-69/89 Radio Telefis Eireann vs EC Commission (Magill TV Guide Ltd intervening) [1991] ECR II-485, [1991] 4 CMLR 586; case T-70/89 British Broadcasting Corpn and BBC Enterprises Ltd vs EC Commission (Magill TV Guide Ltd intervening) [1991] ECR II-535, [1991] 4 CMLR 669 and case T-76/89 Independent Television Publications Ltd vs EC Commission (Magill TV Guide Ltd intervening) [1991] ECR II-575, [1991] 4 CMLR 745.
15 Magill TV Guide/ITP, BBC and RTE decision (1989) OJ L78/43, [1989] 4 CMLR 757.
16 Case T-69/89 Radio Telefis Eireann vs EC Commission (Magill TV Guide Ltd intervening) [1991] ECR II-485, [1991] 4 CMLR 586; Case T-70/89 BBC and BBC Enterprises Ltd vs EC Commission (Magill TV Guide Ltd intervening) [1991] ECR II-535, [1991] 4 CMLR 669 and Case T-76/89 Independent Television Publications Ltd vs EC Commission (Magill TV Guide Ltd intervening) [1991] ECR II-575, [1991] 4 CMLR 745.
17 Case T-69/89 Radio Telefis Eireann vs EC Commission (Magill TV Guide Limited intervening) [1991] ECR II-485, [1991] 4 CMLR 586 at 618; similar rulings are found in the other Magill cases.
18 Compare R. Whish, *Competition Law*, Butterworths (3rd edn, 1993) at 648, differently: C. Bellamy and G. Child *Common Market Law of Competition/First Supplement to the Third Edition*. Sweet and Maxwell (1991) at 87 could not reconcile the Commission's decision with the *Volvo vs Veng* doctrine.

19 Case T-69/89 Radio Telefis Eireann vs EC Commission (Magill TV Guide Ltd intervening) [1991] ECR II-485, [1991] 4 CMLR 586; case T-70/89 BBC and BBC Enterprises Ltd vs EC Commission (Magill TV Guide Ltd intervening) [1991] ECR II-535, [1991] 4 CMLR 669 and case T-76/89 Independent Television Publications Ltd vs EC Commission (Magill TV Guide Ltd intervening) [1991] ECR II-575, [1991] 4 CMLR 745.

20 Joined cases C-241/91 P and C-242/91 P Radio Telefis Eireann and Independent Television Publications Ltd vs EC Commission [1995] ECR I-743, [1995] 4 CMLR 718.

21 See Case 6, 7/73 *ICI and Commercial Solvents vs EC Commission* [1974] ECR 223, [1974] 1 CMLR 309.

22 Joined cases C-241/91 P and C-242/91 P *Radio Telefis Eireann and Independent Television Publications Ltd vs EC Commission* [1995] ECR I-743, [1995] All ER (EC) 4161.

23 Ibid., at para 46.

24 Ibid., at para 53.

25 Ibid., at para 47.

26 Ibid., at paras 54 and 57.

27 Case C-317/91 *Deutsche Renault vs Audi* [1993] ECR I-6227, [1995] 1 CMLR 461.

28 Case T-504/93 Tiercé Ladbroke SA vs EC Commission (Société d'Encouragement et des Steeple-Chases de France intervening) [1997] ECR II-923, [1997] 5 CMLR 309. The same conclusion was also strongly emphasised in the UK courts in Philips Electronics NV vs Ingman Ltd and the Video Duplicating Co Ltd [1999] FSR 112. See also Case C-7/97 *Oscar Bronner GmbH & Co KG* vs *Mediaprint Zeitungs und Zeitschriftenverlag GmbH & Co KG* [1998] ECR I-7791; [1999] 4 CMLR 112.

29 See Case T-504/93 Tiercé Ladbroke SA v EC Commission (Société d'Encouragement et des Steeple-Chases de France intervening) [1997] ECR II-923, [1997] 5 CMLR 309 at paras 129 to 131.

30 Ibid. at paras 124 to 128 and 133.

31 See the discussion in paragraphs 88–105 and the conclusion in paragraph 106 that there is 'a very serious dispute' concerning these in the Order of the President of the Court of First Instance of 26 October 2001 in case T-184/01 R [2001] ECR II-3193. This Order was upheld by the Order of the President of the Court of Justice of 11 April 2002 in case C-481/01 P(R) [2002] 5 CMLR 44. See also *Intel Corp vs Via Technologies Inc* [2003] FSR 574 (CA).

32 Order of the President of the Court of First Instance of 10 August 2001 in case T-184/01 R [2001] ECR II-2349 and Order of the President of the Court of First Instance of 26 October 2001 in case T-184/01 R [2001] ECR II-3193.

33 Order of the President of the Court of Justice of 11 April 2002 in case C-481/01 P(R) [2002] 5 CMLR 44.

34 Commission Decision of 13 August 2003 (2003) OJ L268/59, based on the fact that urgent measures were no longer needed.

35 Case C-481/01 *IMS Health vs NDC Health* [2004] 4 CMLR 1543.

36 Commission Decision 2001/165/EC of 3July 2001 in Case COMP D3/38.044 – NDC Health / IMS Health: Interim Measures [2002] OJ L59/18.

37 At paragraph. 55 of Commission Decision 2001/165/EC.

38 At paragraph 51 of Commission Decision 2001/165/EC.

39 At paragraph 59 of Commission Decision 2001/165/EC, where the Commission refers on this point to the Court of Justice's judgment in Case C-62/86 *AKZO Chemie BV vs Commission* [1991] ECR I-3359.

40 At paragraph 60 of Commission Decision 2001/165/EC.

41 At paragraph 60 of Commission Decision 2001/165/EC.

42 At paragraph 93 of Commission Decision 2001/165/EC.

43 Paragraph 58 of Commission Decision 2001/165/EC.

44 See the first sentence of paragraph 83 and the first sentence of paragraph 86 of Commission Decision 2001/165/EC. See also paragraph 87 of the Decision and

the opinion expressed by some pharmaceutical companies. See also paragraph 185 of the Decision.

45 See final sentence of paragraph 86 of Commission Decision 2001/165/EC.

46 Especially it has been argued by the competitors of IMS that a change to the brick structure involves a change in working conditions under German labour law and that the additional costs therefore include the fact that the contract of service of the sales representatives has to be renegotiated using the German system of co-determination and that any such change to the brick structure used will therefore mean a long and costly procedure due to the involving the workers' council in the renegotiation procedure. See paragraph 115 of Commission Decision 2001/165/EC.

47 In paragraph 123 of Commission Decision 2001/165/EC and in paragraphs 86 and 89 in response to the defence of IMS Health (in paragraph 88) regarding the legal requirements for something to be considered an industry standard.

48 At paragraph 89 of Commission Decision 2001/165/EC.

49 Also marketing campaigns and market research are organised according to the data in this structure.

50 Paragraphs 102, 103, 104 of Commission Decision 2001/165/EC. Also data companies as well as software companies make use of the brick structure and deliver their products in it. All the other data effectively follow the 1,860 brick structure.

51 The crucial fact in *Magill* is that the monopoly was a monopoly over information and that information happened to be the raw material required by a third party. Therefore *Magill* is now not any longer the only case to be remembered for its unusual facts: the unusual protection of copyright of factual information.

52 See the comments in paragraphs 124 and 128 of Commission Decision 2001/165/EC.

53 At paragraph 100 of Commission Decision 2001/165/EC.

54 At paragraphs 107 and 108 of Commission Decision 2001/165/EC. Pharmacia also stated that 'each restructuring of sales force destroys customers' relationships with our reps, which means that we would lose significant numbers of sales at the end of the day', as reported in paragraph 107 of Commission Decision 2001/165/EC. See also paragraph 114 of Commission Decision 2001/165/Ec, where the loss of the special relationship between doctors and sales representatives in case of a change of the brick structure is highlighted.

55 At paragraph 122 of Commission Decision 2001/165/EC.

56 At paragraph 124 of Commission Decision 2001/165/EC.

57 Case C-7/97 *Oscar Bronner GmbH &Co KG vs Mediaprint Zeitungs und Zeitschriftenverlag GmbH & Co KG* [1998] ECR I-7791, [1999] 4 CMLR 112.

58 Ibid.

59 For a complete analysis of the case see Treacy, 'Essential Facilities – Is the Tide Turning', [1999] IPQ 501 and Stothers, 'Refusal to Supply as Abuse of a Dominant Position: Essential Facilities in the European Union', [2001] *Eur. Competition L. Rev.* 256.

60 Case T-69/89 Radio Telefis Eireann vs Commission (Magill TV Guide Ltd intervening) [1991] 4 CMLR 586; case T-70/89 *British Broadcasting Corporation and BBC Enterprises Ltd vs Commission (Magill TV Guide Ltd intervening)* [1991] 4 CMLR 669 and case T-76/89 *Independent Television Publications Ltd vs Commission (Magill TV Guide Ltd intervening)* [1991] ECR II-575, [1991] 4 CMLR 745.

61 Case T-504/93 *Tiercé Ladbroke SA vs Commission (Société d'Encouragement et des Steeple-Chases de France intervening)* [1997] ECR II-923, [1997] 5 CMLR 309.

62 Paragraph 67 of Commission Decision 2001/165/EC.

63 Case T-504/93 *Tiercé Ladbroke SA vs European Commission (Société d'Encouragement et des Steeple-Chases de France intervening)* [1997] 5 CMLR 309. For a complete overview of the case see Fitzgerald 'Magill Revisited: Tiercé Ladbroke SA vs The Commission' [1998] EIPR 154.

64 Paragraph 68 of Commission Decision 2001/165/EC.

65 See *ICI and Commercial Solvents vs Commission* [1974] ECR 223.

66 [2004] 4 CMLR 1543.
67 Ibid., at 1577.
68 Ibid., at 1579.
69 Ibid., at 1580.
70 Case C-418/01 *IMS Health vs NDC Health* [2004] 4 CMLR 1543, at 1580.
71 Ibid.
72 See the Order of the President of the Court of First Instance of 22nd December 2004 in case T-201/04 R, *Microsoft vs Commission*, at paragraphs 100–103.
73 See Commission Decision of 24th March 2004 in case COMP/C-3/37.792 Microsoft, at recital 563.
74 Ibid., at recital 779.
75 See the Order of the President of the Court of First Instance of 22nd December 2004 in case T-201/04 R, *Microsoft vs Commission*, at paragraph 104.
76 See Commission Decision of 24th March 2004 in case COMP/C-3/37.792 Microsoft at recital 631 and see also recital 702.
77 Ibid., at recital 782.
78 See the Order of the President of the Court of First Instance of 22nd December 2004 in case T-201/04 R, *Microsoft vs Commission*, at paragraph 105.
79 See Commission Decision of 24th March 2004 in case COMP/C-3/37.792 Microsoft, at recital 589 *et seq.*
80 See the Order of the President of the Court of First Instance of 22nd December 2004 in case T-201/04 R, *Microsoft vs Commission*, at paragraph 106.
81 Commission Decision of 24th March 2004 in case COMP/C-3/37.792 Microsoft, at recital 783.

References

Anderman, S. (1998) *EC Competition Law and Intellectual Property Rights: the Regulation of Innovation*, Oxford: Oxford University Press.
Areeda, P. (1989) 'Essential Facilities: An Epithet in Need of Limiting Principles', 58 *Antitrust Law Journal*, 84.
Arrow, K. (1962), 'Economic Welfare and the Allocation of Resources for Invention', in National Bureau for Economic Research, *The Rate and Direction of Inventive Activity: Economic and Social Factors*, Princeton, NJ: Princeton University Press, 609–625.
Bellamy, C. and Child, G. (1991) *Common Market Law of Competition/First Supplement to the Third Edition*, London: Sweet and Maxwell.
Bénabou, V.-L. (2004) 'Chroniques: Transversales', *Propriétés Intellectuelles*, 807.
Benko, R. (1987) *Protecting Intellectual Property Rights: Issues and Controversies*, Washington, DC: American Enterprise Institute for Public Policy Research (AEI Studies 453).
Cooter, R. and Ulen, T. (1988) *Law and Economics*, Glenview: Harper Collins.
Drexl, J. (2004), 'IMS Health and Trinko – Antitrust Placebo for Consumers Instead of Sound Economics in Refusal-to-Deal Cases', *International Review of Industrial Property and Copyright*, 788.
Fitzgerald, D. (1998), 'Magill Revisited: Tiercé Ladbroke SA vs The Commission', *European Intellectual Property Review*, 154.
Furse, M. (2002) *Competition Law of the UK and the EC*, 3rd edn, Oxford: Oxford University Press.
Haines, S. (1994), 'Copyright Takes the Dominant Position: The Advocate-General's Opinion in Magill', *European Intellectual Property Review*, 9, 401.

Hull, D., Atwood, J. and Perrine, J. (2002) 'Intellectual Property – Compulsory Licensing', *European Antitrust Review*, 36 (A Global Competition Review Special Report).

Korah, V. (1988) 'No Duty to Licence Independent Repairers to Make Spare Parts: the Renault, Volvo and Bayer Cases', *European Intellectual Property Review*, 12, 381.

Landes, W. and Posner, R. (1989) 'An Economic Analysis of Copyright Law', *Journal of Legal Studies*, 18, 325.

Lehmann, M. (1989) 'Property and Intellectual Property – Property Rights as Restrictions on Competition in Furtherance of Competition', *International Review of Industrial Property and Copyright*, 1.

Lemarchand, S., Fréget, O. and Sardain, F. (2003) 'Biens informationnels: entre droits intellectuels et droit de la concurrence', *Propriétés Intellectuelles*, 11.

Locke, J. (1970) 'The Second Treatise', Section 27 in Laslett, P. (ed) *Two Treaties of Government*, Cambridge: Cambridge University Press.

Lucas, A. and Lucas, H.-J. (2001) *Traité de la propriété littéraire et artistique*, 2nd edn, Paris: Litec.

Lunn, J. (1985) 'The Roles of Property Rights and Market Power in Appropriating Innovative Output', *Journal of Legal Studies*, 423.

Mackaay, E. (1991) 'Economic and Philosophical Aspects of Intellectual Property Rights', in Van Hoecke, M. (ed.), *The Socio-Economic Role of Intellectual Property Rights*, Brussels: Story-Scientia, 1–30.

Maskus, K. (2000) *Intellectual Property Rights in the Global Economy*, Washington, DC: Institute for International Economics.

Neumann, M. (2001) *Competition Policy. History, Theory and Practice*, Cheltenham: Edward Elgar.

Nozick, R. (1974) *Anarchy, State and Utopia*, Oxford: Basil Blackwell.

OECD (1989) *Report on Competition Policy and Intellectual Property Rights*, Paris: OECD.

Ramello, G.B. (2003) 'Copyright and Antitrust Issues', in Gordon, W.J. and Watt, R. (eds) *The Economics of Copyright: Developments in Research and Analysis*, Cheltenham: Edward Elgar, 118.

Shapiro, C. (2000) 'Competition Policy in the Information Age', in *Foundations of Competition Policy*, London: Routledge.

Silva, F. and Ramello, G.B. (2000). 'Sound Recording Market: the Ambiguous Case of Copyright and Piracy', *Industrial and Corporate Change*, 9, 415–442.

Spector, H. (1989) 'An Outline of a Theory Justifying Intellectual and Industrial Property Rights', 8 *European Intellectual Property Review*, 270.

Stamatoudi, I. (1998) 'The Hidden Agenda in Magill and its Impact on New Technologies', 1 *Journal of World Intellectual Property*, 153.

Stothers, C. (2001) 'Refusal to Supply as Abuse of a Dominant Position: Essential Facilities in the European Union', *European Competition Law Review*, 256.

Torremans, P. (2001) *Holyoak and Torremans Intellectual Property Law*, 3rd edn, London: Butterworths.

Treacy, P. (1999) 'Essential Facilities – Is the Tide Turning', *Intellectual Property Quarterly*, 501.

Watt, R. (2000) *Copyright and Economic Theory: Friends or Foes?*, Cheltenham: Edward Elgar.

Whish, R. (1993) *Competition Law*, 3rd edn, London: Butterworths.

Whish, R. (2001) *Competition Law*, 4th edn, London: Butterworths.

Woolridge, F. (1999) 'The Essential Facilities Doctrine and Magill II: The Decision of the ECJ in Oscar Bronner', *Intellectual Property Quarterly*, 256.

10 The treatment of marital assets

Common-law property rights and EU harmonization

Antony W. Dnes

Introduction

Article III-170 of the EU Draft Constitution expressly places family law with cross-border implications within the realm of legislative competency of the Council of Ministers.[1] Should this Constitution develop further, the implication is that the competency not only involves international civil procedure and conflict rules, but may also concern substantive family law institutions. Policy aimed at harmonizing EU family law has generated considerable debate. This discussion is characterized by anxiety in England that common-law traditions will be lost. A good case can in fact be made, from a British perspective that there is a need for some form of statutory reform of the law affecting ancillary relief following divorce, partly because of recent attempts to introduce a rebuttable presumption of equal division by case law.[2]

Ancillary relief is mostly concerned with division of the whole pool of assets in a failed marriage. In particular, there is a need to harmonize EU law in the area of pre-nuptial agreements. Some EU member states are better than others at establishing clear principles governing agreements, where 'better' refers to the likelihood that the spouses' welfare is enhanced by agreements.[3] It might be said that England is particularly out of line in relation to pre-nuptial agreements. This paper concentrates on assets and is not directly concerned with spousal maintenance payments.

Harmonization is desirable in EU marital law to avoid forum shopping, expensive conflict and associated opportunistic behaviour. Forum shopping already occurs in more general international terms. Americans sometimes claim English residency in order to divorce under a needs-based approach traditionally associated with low awards to women in 'big-money' cases, rather than in a US jurisdiction like California that uses a pretty strict 50–50 division of marital property. Englishmen have been known to divorce in South Africa, which has an even more wealth-protecting history than England (clearly the Americans do not realize this – they are in the wrong place).

People may shop around in order to avoid meeting promises implied by the system of marital law under which they were married. There are two possibilities to prevent such opportunism within the EU: either we can create a degree of uniformity across member states, or we can require courts to enforce agreements from other jurisdictions as though the parties were still in those jurisdictions. The latter route will cause problems as courts deal with unfamiliar matters. Therefore, uniformity appears to be the only real approach. A lack of uniformity can reduce the attractiveness of marriage. It can also cause inefficient 'breach' of marital contracts relative to the original promises, if they are not enforceable owing to forum shopping.

The starting point is an examination of the wide discretion traditionally afforded to the courts in England and the impact this has on incentives for divorcing parties and their legal representatives. Two specific reforming measures have been proposed to reduce this judicial discretion. First, a mathematical formula, such as a rebuttable presumption to divide equally the whole pool of assets upon divorce, could be used. Such a formula would be a variant of a system of community property similar to the one used in Scotland, in some US jurisdictions, and elsewhere in the EU. Such a rule usually operates by default in the absence of a pre-nuptial, marital, or separation agreement between the parties dividing assets. Rebuttal might still allow judicial discretion over what is usually described as 'equitable distribution' (although equity is really an elusive concept). Second, legal enforceability could be accorded to pre-nuptial agreements.

Giving legal enforceability to pre-nuptial agreements could, in turn, support a move to community property. The default rule (equal shares) would then only operate in the absence of such an agreement. This approach is broadly what happens in many community–property jurisdictions, for example, Germany, Denmark and the community–property American states. This route would be the most obvious one for achieving a consistent approach across the EU. In some ways it is simply an argument that England, as the odd one out, should get into line – given the dominance of the contract-governed community–property approach prevalent throughout the EU. England did in fact recently move in *case law* (*Cowan vs Cowan*) hesitantly in the direction of equal division of what amounted in practice to community property.[4] There are also some English proposals to introduce enforceable pre-nuptial contracts reported in Thorpe, 1998.

In an earlier paper (Dnes, 1998) I argued that marital law can easily create incentives for opportunistic behaviour (essentially cheating relative to earlier promises) by marriage partners.[5] This will occur if transfers of property (or alimony) following divorce are set too low for at least one partner, relative to earlier promises (to an ex-spouse) of providing a certain lifestyle. I shall examine the proposals for community property and enforceable pre-nuptial agreements in terms of whether they enhance or reduce incentives for opportunism.

Generally, reducing the incentives to cheat on marriage promises might be expected to enhance the attractiveness of marriage compared with a less reliable environment (Dnes, 2005). The uncertainty attached to the value of marriage would be reduced. There is some statistical evidence (e.g. Brinig and Crafton, 1994) that increasing contractual uncertainty in marriage, which might be expected to increase incentives for opportunism, does indeed deter marriage. Brinig and Crafton found that the introduction of no-fault divorce in US states significantly reduced the number of marriages, after controlling for population and other trend effects.[6] They are correct in testing the effects of divorce-law reform on *marriage*: introducing no-fault divorce may well only have temporary effects on *divorce* rates as marriage rates adjust to the new rules (Zelder, 1993; Smith, 1997). However, Binner and Dnes (2001) found in a time-series model that marriage rates increased, controlling for other factors, following the introduction of no-fault divorce in England. Binner and Dnes suggest that increased freedom to divorce may cause less caution in marrying.

The structure of the paper follows the questions raised above. I begin with a brief comparison between England and Germany as a less discretionary EU juris-diction. This comparison is followed by an analysis of the incentives discretion creates for opportunistic and adversarial divorce. I then assess the impact moving to a system of community property might have on divorcing couples and on the costs imposed on the courts. In assessing the impact, I make use of the idea of property versus liability rules (Calabresi and Melamed, 1972), borrowed from the economic analysis of conflict over property rights (normally applied to the law of nuisance) to compare clear property rules with court discretion. I conclude that England's changing to community property and enforceable agreements should be welfare improving but would need to be forward looking and applied to marriages, rather than divorces, from a well-defined date. This in turn suggests a statutory route rather than changes in case law as the basis for effecting the change.

Discretionary vs formulaic approaches

In England and Wales, contemporary divorce law, for example, as reflected in the Family Law Act 1996 or the Matrimonial and Family Proceedings Act 1984, embodies a mixture of approaches focusing on expectations, rehabilitation and the needs of the parties. There is a dominant, statutory requirement to meet the needs of dependent children. The law (Hoggett *et al.*, 1996) is based on separate ownership of property within the marriage and gives considerable discretion to be exercised by the courts in dividing assets upon divorce. Successive governments have had many opportunities to move towards, in particular, a community-property system and to establish firm rules of property division but have not done so. Parliament opted instead, as Thorpe LJ recently noted in an earlier case, 'for a wide judicial discretion that would produce a bespoke solution to fit the infinite variety of individual cases'.[7]

Notable characteristics of the law in practice are the trading of asset transfers within a settlement and the trading of assets for maintenance payments. The non-housing needs of children have come to be treated separately following the Child Support Acts of 1991 and 1995, under which Child Support Payments are channelled from absent parents through the Child Support Agency (CDA).

Divorce law in England has never operated to enforce the material side of marital promises (Dnes, 1998). To do so would be to treat marriage contractually, award-ing (expectation) damages for breach of contract and denying support or capital payments to a breaching party. Even in the days of fault-based divorce, for example, under the parliamentary procedure, the cost to a husband of divorcing, for example, an adulterous wife, would include making some support provision for her (Hoggett *et al.*, 1996, p. 295). Historically and for the most part, divorcing parties with means have not been permitted to leave divorced parties destitute. The twentieth-century liberalization of divorce law is associated with a move to no-fault divorce procedures, provision of legal aid for petitioners, development of the court's ability to transfer assets, and the focusing on a mixture of expectations, needs, restitution and rehabilitation standards of awards. Note also that no-fault divorce may still be equivalent to breach of contract, for example, when a husband divorces his wife without her consent after abandoning her for five years.[8]

Several reasons can be given for avoiding an expectation–damages standard when dividing marital assets on divorce. It is inconsistent with the modern development of divorce law that increasingly emphasizes the 'rehabilitation' and independence of abandoned spouses (although most of the problems that might be cited, have really arisen in the context of life-time support obligations not based strictly on an expectation–damages approach). The Law Commission (1982) concluded that the duty to place the parties in the position they would have been had the marriage not broken down, imposed by the Matrimonial Causes Act 1973, was 'not a suitable criterion'. The conclusion was based largely on a perceived movement in public opinion against the idea of lifetime support. However, examination of their earlier analysis (Law Commission, 1980) shows that this was not really an attack on expectation damages but on the practice of the courts. In particular, the standard was not to be operated only in cases of breach of the marital contract but was more of a lifetime support obligation (hence, 'parties'). In Dnes (1998b) and (1999) I argued for fresh thought to be given to the use of an expectations standard that would penalize breach of contract, owing to its deterrence of opportunistic behaviour.

The main alternatives (other than need) to expectation damages are approaches based on restitution or reliance, which are often confused with each other. The reliance approach compensates an ex-spouse for the opportunities foregone in entering the failed marriage and has been criticized for being tough on poor women who married wealthy men (Trebilcock, 1993). Reliance is also difficult to calculate: the principle (as the *status quo ante*) was put forward by Gray (1977) but rejected by the Law Commission (1980) as requiring too much speculation about what might have happened in the distant past. In Dnes (1998b) I show that reliance will generally be less than expectation damages and this difference can cause an incentive for opportunistic divorce (essentially, divorce may be too 'cheap' as the petitioner for divorce will not be required to compensate for lost promises).

In a restitution framework, divorcees are compensated, at market value, for investments made in the other party's career or business (Carbone and Brinig, 1991). The principle is one of the elements in the current discretionary basis to divorce law in England and Wales, as for example, in the case of *Conran vs Conran*.[9] Restitution is only relevant where there is a market value to divide, is difficult to calculate, and is not likely to be as high as expectation damages as it will not cover the entire expected benefits from the marriage (Dnes, 1998a). Again, a restitution standard invites opportunistic behaviour as divorce may become cheap, relative to meeting promises made earlier in the marriage. Furthermore, there may be the problem of negative restitution: the ex-spouse may have hindered the petitioner's career or business.[10]

A further approach, that of viewing marriage as a partnership analogously with the business partnership, potentially fits in with a community–property rather than separate–property regime. A point worth noting is that if partnership is the modern expectation in marriage, equal sharing could potentially give the same result as an expectation–damages standard for dividing marital assets, and therefore might fare better than most standards in deterring opportunism. EU jurisdictions with equal-sharing presumptions embedded in their family law codes, typically make a rebuttable presumption in favour of equal division of the property acquired during marriage. This presumption reflects a form of (deferred) community property, even if it is sometimes referred to as a separate property regime.

Germany is an interesting example of such a property approach. The *Equality Act 1957* created a statutory marital property regime designated 'community of surplus'. This means that property acquired before or during the marriage remains separate property. However, the management of property acquired by either party during the marriage requires the informed consent of the other spouse. In the event of divorce, the property acquired during the marriage is equalized between the spouses. The statutory scheme is therefore representative of deferred community property, albeit applying to property rather than to income earned during the life of the marriage.

Couples in Germany have the option of avoiding the statutory property scheme by entering into enforceable pre-nuptial or postnuptial agreement. This might be used to establish separate property for the spouses, as is often the case for self-employed persons, and to limit spousal obligations to those of maintenance. Limits are applied by the state, in that certain choices are not permitted: one could not use a foreign-law regime, and nor could one avoid child maintenance obligations. The restrictions are consistent with those in other countries, where frequently one finds limits imposed on freedom of contract in marital or cohabitation matters.

Another German choice is a more conventional community–property regime, where income earned and assets acquired during marriage can become community property. In practice this will have little difference from the community of surplus. This is because income will either be spent or turned into assets. However, the community–property option gives the opportunity to *exclude* assets from the community of property.

Thus, in general, couples in Germany have the benefit of a clear regime that has applied to new marriages from a specified point in time. In addition, they can tailor their property affairs to avoid the statutory scheme if it does not reflect the promises they wish to have enforced in the event of divorce. This is a system embodying a great deal of freedom of choice. It would be hard for spouses to make promises and then avoid them under the German regime.

In contrast, in the English system divorce could be either too 'cheap', if a needs-based award does not embody the full value of promises made, or too expensive if, post *Cowan*, a high-proportion division occurs when it was never expected. Spouses might easily end up behaving opportunistically in the English system. Marriage involves costly long-term promises. There is therefore a real danger that failing to enforce promises will create an incentive for divorce among some people whenever they see a preferred relationship and realize that they need not fully meet their earlier financial obligations.[11] In Dnes (1998b) I describe this as leading to a form of opportunistic behaviour most likely affecting wealthy men that I called the 'greener-grass' effect. It is also possible to identify a further adverse incentive encouraged by the current law. As awards are often made without any or much regard to fault, damages are not linked to breach of contract. A possible consequence is that a party might petition for (no-fault) divorce in anticipation of receiving a substantial share of the marital assets. Again, this would be deterred if damages were restricted to victims of breach. In principle, the petitioner can sometimes be bought off by reworking the implied terms of the marriage in his/her favour. However, reworking may not be possible where the benefits to individual marriage partners (e.g. enjoyment of association with the children) are not transferable between them (Zelder, 1993).

To conclude these brief comments on the existing judicial discretion over asset division, there is a problem that adverse incentives are created over the decision to divorce. The problem is caused by divergence from a contractual ideal in which expectation damages would be awarded for breach of contract. It is however difficult to see how the variety of marital expectations could be enforced (either as performance or as compensation) owing to problems of identification as nothing in the current law aids identification. The relevant observation is that it is possible that the setting of a statutory norm (equal shares) together with an opportunity for the couple to indicate their expectation over assets if it differs from the norm (using a pre-nuptial agreement) may overcome the problem of identifying marital expectations. This is broadly the system to be seen in a number of EU jurisdictions, for example, Germany.

Community property: the importance of pre-nuptial agreements

Dividing the assets of a marriage at divorce is a question of defining property rights or possibly of resolving conflict over property rights. Earlier work in the economics of law has generated several insights into sensible ways to settle conflict over property rights. Such conflicts frequently occur in cases of nuisance, which are usually characterized by ill-defined entitlement to make a particular use of land. The area is a long way from marriage but the principles may be borrowed as it turns out there is little logical difference between conflict over use and conflict over ownership.

According to Calabresi and Melamed (1972) conflict over property rights can be solved by adopting either a 'property' or a 'liability' rule depending on the bargaining costs likely to arise between the parties. Thus, in a simple case of nuisance spilling over between two neighbouring landowners a property rule may be followed because bargaining costs are likely to be low as there are just two parties involved.

Under a property rule, the entitlement to create the nuisance can, as one possible solution, safely be given to the neighbour generating the nuisance. If the 'victim' values freedom from the nuisance more than the 'generating' neighbour values the entitlement to create the nuisance, money will change hands as the victim will bribe the generator to stop. Thus, the 'entitlement' will end up in the ownership of the hands of the neighbour who values it most highly.

It is equally efficient for the entitlement to be given to the victim, who would then obtain an injunction stopping the nuisance. If the generator of the nuisance is the highest valuing party, money will again change hands and the generator will effectively bribe the victim to condemn the injunction. With low bargaining costs, from the point of view of economic efficiency, it does not matter who has the entitlement (an application of the Coase (1960) theorem) as bargaining will ensure that the entitlement goes to the highest valuing user. Therefore, the courts can avoid costly determination of issues in such cases by issuing or denying an injunction depending on their views of distributing benefits between the parties, secure in the knowledge that bargaining will take care of efficiency.[12] For completeness at this point, note that it would be worthwhile for courts to follow a liability rule and become involved in valuing nuisance and imposing damages to create a deterrent to the nuisance where bargaining costs are high: typically when damages are diffused across populations.

In the case of ancillary relief, the problem is not nuisance but, rather, one of determining who owns what from the point of divorce onwards. Marriage is clearly a case where bargaining costs are low in that two people are involved who can be expected to communicate, at least in a technical sense. Thus, a property rule should be appropriate, as it should be possible to rely on couples forming their precise marital expectations based on the existence of that rule. In a sense, it should not matter much what exactly the rule is as the important point is simply to give some focus to bargaining.

One could as easily start from a presumption that divorcees will split marital assets equally as from a different assumption. Presumptions that assets might be split in other proportions would not cause problems. Knowing what the rebuttable presumption is (e.g. take an extreme case like 100 per cent to one party) a couple would negotiate a pre-nuptial agreement to produce the division (e.g. equal shares) they actually wanted. Negotiation would be straightforward: the parties would agree what would happen in the event of divorce. As long as the presumptive rule was well known in advance of marriage and people were free to negotiate enforceable contracts around it, bargaining should result in optimization for individual cases.

The proposal for a presumptive rule of equal shares coupled with enforceable pre-nuptial agreements can be seen as one application of a property rule. The pro-posal is likely to support the welfare of married and divorcing couples providing it results in a clear presumptive rule and given that the use of pre-nuptial agreements allows bargaining to occur. This line of reasoning would support the continental EU approach, which is emerging in English case law. However, the rule should be forward looking and apply to new *marriages*, rather than *divorces*, from a certain date onwards. Such a forward-looking approach would allow couples to find their optimal asset plan knowing exactly what they must do to achieve this if they do not like the presumptive rule. However, imposing the rule on divorces at a point in time (which seems to be the position in *Cowan*) would be confusing: unless the couple happened to have a pre-nuptial agreement (unlikely, as these were unenforceable previously) they would be forced into the presumptive rule. Newly marrying couples would not be forced into the presumptive rule, as they would have a clear opportunity to enter a pre-nuptial agreement. There is an argument for statutory introduction of the rule.

Enforceable agreements?

In view of the above, it is appropriate to think of the proposal to establish a rebuttable presumption of equal shares and enforceable pre-nuptial agreements as a move to a (community) 'property rule'. The pre-nuptial agreement would allow people to deviate from the presumption of equal shares in a clear manner and is needed to support the implied or explicit bargaining upon which the property-rule approach to conflict over property rights relies. The courts would thereafter pay attention to such agreements, or enforce the presumption of equal shares, or consider arguments for exceptions to be otherwise made.

If the presumptive rule and the enforceability of pre-nuptial agreements is widely recognized, we could be sure that marriages were established on terms that reflected the interests of both husband and wife. All the standard arguments concerning the gains from trade under voluntary exchange in regular markets would carry over into the 'marriage market'. A corollary is that the incentive towards opportunism under current divorce law would be attenuated. Individuals would know what the rules of asset division were and that these could not be distorted, and that, therefore, a divorce settlement would bear close relation to initial marital promises concerning assets. Generally then, the worries raised earlier about 'inefficient' (opportunistic) divorce would be allayed by the change to a community–property rule.

The considerations just raised suggest that courts should be firm in their enforcement of the new property rule, which needs to be utterly transparent. This would involve firm enforcement of pre-nuptial agreements or of the presumption of equal shares. If routes are introduced through which agreements might be overturned retrospectively, or that could cause deviation from the equal-shares presumption, the incentive to be litigious would grow accordingly. Furthermore, there would be the danger that current levels of discretion would be returned to the courts 'by the back door'. The reason for firm enforcement is similar to that which may be given in the economic analysis of contract law for not supporting contract modifications (Aivazian *et al.*, 1984; Dnes, 1995). It is not easy to distinguish between desirable adjustments and opportunistic ones (e.g. based on duress). The long-term effect of the contract uncertainty that could be created by enforcing modifications that might not have been agreed *ex ante* might be to undermine the attractiveness of contracts (marriages) that would otherwise be of mutual benefit to the parties concerned.

Post-nuptial agreements and contract modification

The literature on contract modifications is extremely pessimistic over the prospect of welfare gain from enforcing *mutually agreed and compensated* modifications (Jolls, 1997). This is because of the difficulty of distinguishing between genuinely beneficial revisions and those resulting from opportunistic behaviour, which can amount to duress. Consider the difficulty in marriage contracts in distinguishing between a genuine modification (because a party now has improved prospects) and the case where a party threatens to make their spouse's life hell unless certain terms are agreed. Such an example is actually a simple one, and I have already noted the problems of opportunism in divorce, following the 'greener-grass' and Black-Widow models. Thus, we might well wish to enforce highly flexible pre-nuptial agreements but generally not to enforce post-nuptial agreements.

Contract modifications (post-nuptial agreements) will not set up incentives for opportunism if, in the context of unforeseen events, (i) it is not clear who is the lowest-cost bearer of the risk, (ii) the events were judged of too low a value to be worth considering in the contract or (iii) it was infeasible for either party to bear the risk.[13] Generally, the view that supporting all modifications is desirable because there appears to be a short-term gain is unsound: there may be undesirable long-term instability as a result, as already noted in the previous subsection, since fewer people will make contracts if it is difficult to protect them from opportunism.[14]

The idea that modifications can be legally supported when events unfold for which it would not have been clear early on who should have benefited or borne a fresh cost does give a clue to a rôle for the court. It can determine whether some change was foreseeable and whether the attendant risk would have been clearly allocated, for example, one's wife's ageing is not a reason for scooting off without compensating her, on the other hand mutually tiring of each other would have been hard to allocate to *one* party.

Compared with simple, classical contracting, a more appropriate fundamental model of the marriage contract would be as a relational contract (Scott and Scott, 1998). Macneil (1978) has suggested that complex long-term contracts are best regarded 'in terms of the entire relation, as it has developed [over] time'. Special emphasis is placed on the surrounding social norms rather than on the ability of even well-informed courts to govern the relationship (Macneil calls governance that emphasizes third-party interpretation 'neo-classical' contracting). An original contract document (e.g. marriage vows) is not necessarily of more importance in the resolution of disputes than later events or altered norms. Courts are likely to lag behind the parties' practices in trying to interpret relational contracts.

A relational contract is an excellent vehicle for thinking about the fundamental nature of marriage but it may be of limited help in designing practical solutions to divorce issues unless it is possible to fashion legal support for the relational contracting process. Crucially though, the idea emphasizes flexibility. Many of the problems associated with the division of marital assets arise because social norms change but the individual marriage partners fail to match the emerging marital norm. Therefore, a possible approach to divorce law is to enforce pre-nuptial agreements or the equal-shares rule to guard against opportunism but to allow the interpretation of expectation to be governed by differing 'vintages' of social norms.

The law could help in this process by indicating a range of possible forms of marriage and associated pre-nuptial agreements. Laying out several alternative contracts to capture changing or differing marital norms, from among which couples can choose, would help people to visualize the possibilities. This would seem to be a useful role for the state and it accords with the idea of enforcing pre-nuptial agreements. The argument is that it may be asking people to do a lot if we expect them to draft comprehensive marital contracts *ab initio*. It is probably more realistic to expect them to make a reasonable match when models are presented to them, covering at least the principal cases (e.g. traditional marriage, equal-shares partnership and separation of property).

As long as expectations are clarified, inefficient and opportunistic breach of marital contracts could be broadly suppressed. Providing usable models of pre-nuptial agreements would assist in this clarification. It would also help to avoid the problem that appears to have arisen in Scotland, where the presumption of equal shares has resulted in courts preferring to maintain discretion.

Conclusions and summary

There are strong arguments, in the case of England, in favour of removing judicial discretion in favour of a presumptive rule of awarding equal shares of marital assets to divorcees. The presumption could be rebutted by the existence of a pre-nuptial agreement, and might indeed be expected to put parties on notice to state their expectations at an early stage. The presumptive rule would represent a move to community property and would require the scope of marital property to be carefully defined, and to include items like human capital and pensions. The move is already beginning in a haphazard way in the English case law.

The presumption would not so much be rebutted by requirements to meet the needs of children, or even of dependent ex-spouses, as it would be required to work around such socially imposed obligations. There is no necessary conflict between needs-based obligations and a negotiated property rule: people would take the obligations, and the presumptive rule, into account in framing their own pre-nuptial agreements. This does not mean that the existence of obligations following divorce has no effect: weaker marriages should be deterred as people become increasingly aware of their obligations.

The presumption of equal shares is a property rule of the kind likely to be success-ful in solving conflict over property rights in small-numbers bargaining cases.

The courts at present try to assign liability when this is not necessary and may well be a relatively costly approach. Given the small numbers (two-party bargaining) in a marriage, a clear statement of a default rule should be enough to drive people to tailoring pre-nuptial agreements to their marital expectations. These agreements would prevent opportunistic divorce, otherwise caused when promises can be avoided and divorce effectively becomes too cheap. They would also provide less incentive to become litigious. Overall, the proposal to move to a community–property rule may be judged to be a good idea from the perspective of the economic analysis of law. Incentive structures would improve compared with judicial discretion.

It does not matter too much exactly what the property rule is, although a presumption of equal shares may well accord with contemporary expectations. The aim should really be to drive people into forming their own agreements. To this end, it could be useful for a range of standard models to be provided (e.g. traditional marriage, partnership marriage and so forth) from which people could select an appropriate agreement. Such standards might naturally arise in solicitor's offices. It is more important to define the scope of the rule, in terms of the assets covered, comprehensively.

A final very important conclusion is that the presumptive rule should not be applied retroactively. This means that it should be applied to marriages from a certain date rather than to divorces. There is a case here for the changes to be made by statute, which tends to be forward looking, rather than through case law, which is retroactive. Otherwise, there is a danger that inappropriate marital expectations will be imposed in many cases, which would distort the incentives to divorce. EU-generated reforms would likely be forward-looking statutes and could give an opportunity to stabilize spousal expectations over property division.

Notes

1 http://european-convention.eu.int/docs/Treaty/cv00850.en03.pdf
2 White vs White (2001) 1 AC 596 (Thorpe LJ changes his view on the desirability of equal division as a starting point, given current directions in social change). The presumption is rebuttable and drew on existing elements of the Matrimonial Causes Act. There has been subsequent guidance from the House of Lords clarifying the position of couples and making clear that there has not been full move to equal property division (a retreat from Lambert vs Lambert (2002) 3 FCR 673. Recent proposals from the Law Commission (2005) have also made it clear that moves towards a property rule would need the court to retain some discretion in 'small money' cases.
3 Welfare maximization is understood here to mean maximizing the joint wealth of the parties. Nonpecuniary issues are ignored as romance is assumed to be dead by the time the parties arrive in court.
4 Cowan vs Cowan, Court of Appeal 17 May 2001; White, supra Note 2.
5 The arguments are also developed in Dnes (1998b).
6 They also found introducing no-fault divorce significantly reduced birth rates and significantly increased violence towards spouses, again after controlling for other likely influences. The story on births is that women may be less willing to make highly marriage-specific 'investments' like child raising if vulnerable to divorce at will (their re-employment prospects are poor). On violence, the penalty for egregious

behaviour becomes lower when the financial consequences of divorce are not affected by behaviour.

7 Dart vs Dart (1996) 2 FLR 286 (appraising the applicant's reasonable requirements in a high-value case).

8 Brinig and Crafton (1994) take a different line, arguing that marriage was viewed contractually (in US jurisdictions) prior to the introduction of no-fault divorce.

9 Conran vs Conran (1997) 2 FLR No. 5 (assessing reasonable requirements in relation to past contribution).

10 The Scottish Law Commission (1981) noted this problem.

11 In terms of the economic analysis of law, it would be efficient (wealth maximizing) for the divorce to go ahead if, having compensated the ex-spouse for lost expectation, the petitioner for divorce still wished to proceed.

12 This result assumes that there is no technical advantage (e.g. an abatement-cost advantage) in giving the entitlement to either party.

13 As explained fully in Dnes (1995).

14 The literature on contract modifications is complex. The fundamental problem alluded to is the high cost of distinguishing between 'genuine' changes that allow a move to a jointly preferred position and opportunistically contrived changed circumstances.

References

Aivazian, V., Trebilcock, M. and Penny, M. (1984) The law of contract modifications: the uncertain quest for a benchmark of enforceability, 22 *Osgoode Hall Law J.* 173.

Binner, J. and Dnes, A. (2001) Marriage, divorce and legal change, *Economic Inquiry*, 39, 298–306.

Brinig, M. and Crafton, S. (1994) Marriage and opportunism, 23 *J. Legal Studies* 869.

Calabresi, G. and Melamed, A. (1972) Property rules, liability rules and inalienability: one view of the cathedral, 85 *Harvard Law Rev.* 1089.

Carbone, J. and Brinig, M. (1991) Rethinking marriage: feminist ideology, economic change, and divorce reform, 65 *Tulane Law Rev.* 953.

Coase, R. (1960) The problem of social cost, 3 *J. Law & Econ.* 1.

Dnes, A. (1995) The law and economics of contract modifications: the case of *Williams vs Roffey*, 15 *International Rev. Law & Econ.* 225.

Dnes, A. (1998a) *The Division of Marital Assets Following Divorce With Particular Reference to Pensions*, Research Series No. 7/97, Lord Chancellor's Department: London.

Dnes, A. (1998b) The division of marital assets following divorce, *J. Law & Society*, 25, 336–364.

Dnes, A. (1999) Applicationss of economic analysis to marital law: concerning a proposal to reform the discretionary approach to the division of marital assets in England and Wales, *International Review of Law and Economics*, 19, 533–552.

Dnes, A. (2005) *The Economics of Law: Property, Contracts and Obligations*, Mason, Ohio: Thomson South Western.

Gray, K. (1977) *The Reallocation of Property on Divorce*, Abingdon: Professional Books.

Hoggett, B., Pearl, D., Cooke, E. and Bates, P. (1996) *The Family, Law and Society: Cases and Materials*, London: Butterworths.

Jolls, C. (1997) Contracts as bilateral commitments: a new perspective on contract modification, 26 *J. Legal Studies* 203.

Law Commission (1980) *The Financial Consequences of Divorce: the Basic Policy*, Cmnd 8041, London: HMSO.

Law Commission (1982) *The Financial Consequences of Divorce*, London: HMSO.

Law Commission (2005) *Financial Provision in Matrimonial Proceedings*, London: HMSO.

Law Society (1991) *Maintenance and Capital Divission on Divorce*, London: Law Society.

Macneil, I. (1978) Contracts: adjustment of long-term contractual relations under classical, neoclassical and relational contract law, 72 *Northwestern Univ. Law Rev.* 854.

Scott, E. and Scott, A. (1998) Marriage as relational contract, 84 *Va L. Rev.* 1225.

Smith, I. (1997) "Explaining the Growth in Divorce in Great Britain," 44 *Scottish Journal of Political Economy* 519.

Thorpe, A. (1998) *Report to the Lord Chancellor by the Ancillary Relief Advisory Group*, London: Lord Chancellor's Dept.

Trebilcock, M. (1993) *The Limits of Freedom of Contract*, Cambridge, MA: Harvard University Press.

Zelder, M. (1993) Inefficient dissolutions as a consequence of public goods: the case of no-fault divorce, 22 *J. Legal Studies* 503.

11 Intellectual property rights and judge-made law

An economic analysis of the production and diffusion of precedent

Sophie Harnay and Alain Marciano

Introduction

One of the most important economist's contributions to the understanding of legal phenomena lies in the assumption that judges act as rational, utility maximising agents; or as Posner noted, that judges 'maximize the same thing everyone else does' (Posner, 1994). Judges are indeed no 'titans' or 'saints' (ibid., p. 4) but human beings, so to speak. Accordingly, their behaviour must be apprehended in their 'ordinariness', just like the behaviour of any other agent.

Undoubtedly, economic assumptions help to gain insight on certain aspects of judges' behaviours. However, other dimensions of judicial decision making and in particular, the attitude of judges towards existing rules – that is, precedents – remains intriguing and controversial: why do judges comply with existing rules while the latter do not necessarily reflect their personal preferences or ideology? Or, by contrast, why do judges accept to incur the costs of innovating and creating new precedents while the probability of a rejection of their innovation is non-negligible? More precisely, the questions are made difficult by the fact that precedents are modelled as collective goods upon which it is impossible to ascertain property rights. Free riding, a seemingly rational behaviour, remains rare among judges. In other words, judges attitudes towards non-binding precedents illustrates the paradox of collective action.

The argument put forward in this article is that standard law and economics analyses put too much emphasis on the 'market analogy' and on the private incentives that possibly guide judicial decision making. We argue that the judicial community is actually governed by distinctive norms, customs and institutions that differ from those that characterise other market transactions. More precisely, we claim that the rules of judicial governance within common law regimes shape the conditions of an open-knowledge community and we analyse judicial decision-making and the production of judge-made law as a specific instance of knowledge creation. Briefly, our core argument is that the functioning and continuity of *stare decisis* relies on the intertwining of private and collective dimensions in judicial innovation that is typical of collective invention situations. From this perspective, a judge may be willing to share a decision with the others – to give it away as a precedent – because he or she expects private benefits from this release, while other judges may be willing to follow the precedent because, through practice and incremental innovation, they can contribute to its improvement.

The second section of the paper deals with the features of judge-made law and presents the precedent as a kind of 'informational commons' possibly plagued by the 'tragedies' that are associated with commonality. The third section develops a functionalist analysis of the judiciary as an open-knowledge community governed by specific rules ensuring that individual contributions to the collective output occur. The fourth section checks that the judicial objectives traditionally put forward by the standard law and economics approach are congruent with an open-knowledge logic. The fifth section provides some brief elements of conclusion.

The features of judge-made law, or: why contribute to 'informational commons'?

The precedent as a kind of 'informational commons'

An informational good

Standard law and economics models compare the formation of judge-made law with capital formation (see in particular the pioneering article by Landes and Posner, 1976). The set of existing precedents is viewed as a stock of capital goods. More precisely, precedents are described as informational goods conveying low cost information to judges as well as to litigants. Precedents are depicted as 'a stock of knowledge that yields services over many years to potential disputants, in the form of *information* about legal obligations' (Posner, 1986, p. 509; emphasis added)[1] Let us note that this perspective derives from the standard neo-classical definition of information: information – and precedents as information – is defined at the same time as a 'stock' and as an 'increment' to the stock.[2] Precedents, information equated with a form of knowledge 'reduced and converted into messages that can be easily communicated among agents' (Dasgupta and David, 1994, p. 493).

Accordingly, the initial production of a precedent by a judge – formalisation and codification of implicit rules into formal legal knowledge – consists in the transformation of the information privately held by the judge into data that then are more easily transmittable to and usable by other agents in other instances. In other words, a precedent, as an informational good, has to be considered both as an output – resulting from the decision made by a judge – and as an input into the resolution of conflicts and disputes for the different agents that are involved in the conflict to be solved – that is both litigants and other judges. In effect, the latter both produce precedents and use them, thereby contributing to the incremental development of legal knowledge. Producers are thus also users, although all users may not be producers. For instance, some judges may limit themselves merely to the use of precedents made by others, without adding any 'novelty' of their own to the body of precedents. In a similar way, litigants can also be considered as a specific group of users playing a role of co-production of legal ideas and decisions, but unable to produce judicial innovations and to enrich the body of precedents without the actual help or intervention of a court.

A collective good

Being reduced to its informational content, a precedent obviously possesses the properties of a collective good (Nelson, 1959; Arrow, 1962), such as indivisibility, non-rivalry and non-excludability of the beneficiaries. Thus each judge can consume the precedent entirely, a judge can use a precedent or a legal ideal without decreasing the use for other judges, and legal information contained in the precedent is not depleted when shared, the service provided by a precedent is not excludable, as no individual can be prevented from using a precedent that others do benefit from. The information embodied in the precedent is used jointly by as many as care to do so, the incremental cost of an additional user is very low, and the body of precedents eventually represents a pool of shared information.

A by-product of the resolution of disputes

Another particularly important characteristic of the process of production and diffusion of judicial information resides in the fact that any decisions made by a judge, is considered a by-product of the resolution of private conflicts.

Law and economics analyses of the production of precedent mainly focus on the demand-side and the interest of parties in precedents. In a one-shot game, litigants are not interested in the production of a favourable precedent, but only in the resolution of the current dispute.[3] Therefore, they do not demand judge-made law *per se*, but judicial rulings derive from the normal process of the resolution of conflicts by judges. In other words, judges issue judicial decisions as a by-product of their activity of dispute resolution – intentionally . . . or not.

From the judiciary's standpoint, it is worth questioning the implication of the by-product argument for the supply-side of the market for precedents. The relevant point here is that a judge is not allowed to elude the demand for precedent, but is obliged to match the resolution of a dispute with a rule that will become a precedent. This 'unavoidable' production of precedents is the consequence of the choice of parties to resort to a public trial. By contrast, their choice to settle their case – through an arbitrator or a private judge – rather than to bring their dispute before a public court would not lead to the production of a precedent.

Therefore, the distribution of precedential innovation can be realised without incurring a dramatic increase in the general cost of production and diffusion of the resolution of disputes. Since the public enforcement of the resolution of a dispute – as well as the social recognition of the respective rights of the parties it entails – requires the issue of the trial to be made public knowledge, the diffusion of the pertaining precedent does not dramatically increase the cost of publicisation. Or, whatever the cost of the resolution of conflict, the cost of distributing the corresponding precedent is comparatively very low – as is the cost of reuse. In this respect, the situation is very reminiscent of that of scientific research, where the costs associated with initial research may be very high while the costs of the dissemination of the results may be very low.

A network good

Like other forms of knowledge that are also inherently social and related to specific collective contexts, a precedent has a higher value in the social context in which it was produced and for individuals who share common social references.[4] The body of precedents constitutes thus a special type of informational collective resource that benefits from *increasing returns from the number of users*. In this view, judicial decision-making can be seen as a kind of networked activity with which *direct adoption externalities* are associated. More precisely, the compliance with a common rule delineates a 'legal club' whose members share a common pool of legal information. This sharing of a common legal resource promotes confidence between members, increases legal certainty, and reduces the transaction costs incurred by each member in the interactions with others. From this perspective, belonging to a same legal community provides *litigants* with the benefits usually associated with legal certainty. *Judges* also benefit from direct adoption externalities when they comply with a same precedent. Namely, a single precedent has no value – or a lower value than a precedent that has been strengthened by an accumulation of decisions dealing with the same question. By contrast, it is more valuable when it is adopted and endorsed by a large number of judges. If one accepts that a judge derives positive satisfaction from solving a case in accordance with his or her own private preferences and from having further cases solved accordingly as well, it comes that a judge will have an interest in having his or her decision endorsed by others. Then, the adoption of the innovative decision by the judicial community means first enhanced resistance of the innovation against reversal and, therefore, an increase in the inherent value of the precedent. Second, it also implies positive satisfaction from an 'adequate' resolution of cases dealing with the same question. The larger the size of the judicial community adopting the judicial innovation, the larger the individual utility of the judicial innovator.

Furthermore, like most other intellectual activities, precedents are not produced *ex nihilo*, but are rather the outcome of 'a substantial extent of a recombination of conceptual and physical materials that were previously in existence' (Ramello, 2005a, p. 5). A precedent is an input that can be incorporated into more or less sophisticated legal reasoning by other judges. Thus, the acceptation of a precedent by the judicial community may not be restricted to the channel of its mere adoption and reuse in further cases. Another important dimension of the acceptation is that the other members of the community may not simply ground their own decisions on the precedent, but may actually build upon the precedent in order to produce further innovations themselves. While doing so, they extend the scope of the precedent and to the enlargement of the set of compatible or interoperating precedents. The analogy of the precedent with a *system good* comes straightforward, with the consequence that positive club externalities will arise from a higher number of compatible decisions.

This social conception of the precedent and the corresponding emphasis put on associated network externalities do not plead towards a relativistic conception of law nor imply that a precedent or a legal rule has no value at all outside its 'natural circle'. However, this means that the value of a precedent may decrease when transplanted outside of its social context, in a framework where network externalities could not be realised. This conception of judicial decision-making as a networked activity also sustains the idea of some kind of systemic efficiency of law, rather than the line of the divisibility of legal systems.

The impossibility to appropriate precedents privately

Considering the patterns of judge-made law, the body of precedents can be conceived as a form of informational commons. The specific organisation of the judicial community, including the impossibility to appropriate legal ideas on a private basis, prevents some versions of the 'tragedy of the commons' to take place. Yet, the absence of classical appropriation leaves the questions of the production and diffusion of precedents unanswered.

No classical way of appropriation

The informational, collective good and by-product nature of judge-made law justify the absence of classical appropriation of a precedent. Obviously, a judge does not retain individual property rights on his or her decisions or ideas. No classical system of private appropriation – under the form of rewards or compensation for innovative activity – is at work within the judicial community. Patents, copyright, trade secret or trademark cannot be used to ground individual property rights. Other forms of compensation aimed to honour inventive activities generating spillover effects, in the scientific or artistic fields, are not available either in the legal field – no mention of a Nobel prize to a judge or a legal scholar.

Furthermore, the assignment of property rights would be made still more complicated by the co-production situation at work in the judicial setting. Assigning property rights over precedents would thus require to grant parties with part of the bundle of rights, taking into account that, in most cases, a judge cannot issue a decision if litigants do not decide to sue their case before a court. In other words, through their choice to size a court or to settle, litigants play a gatekeeping role in the production process of judge-made law which may entitle them to claim appropriation over precedents.

Neither the 'tragedy of the commons' nor the 'tragedy of the anticommons'

Considering the features of judge-made law and the absence of private appropriation, the neoclassical theory logically predicts that the contribution of individual judges to the system of precedent should be affected by various types of market failures.

A first failure of the market refers to the well-known situation of the 'tragedy of the commons' in which overexploitation of the common resources occurs as a consequence of the absence of private property rights (Hardin, 1968). However, the absence of rivalry between judges prevents the overexploitation of the precedents: the precedent is not depleted when more agents use it; one may even add that, to the contrary, the network dimension of precedents yield higher benefits for any user as they comply with a same legal rule. Except when some asymmetries of information between agents occur, leading to excessive inertia and lock-in in inefficient rules, adoption behaviours and bandwagon strategies are socially profitable (Harnay and Marciano, 2004).

A second form of market failure affecting a common resource is pointed out by Heller (1998), when the establishment and management of a complex system of rights discourages those activities that cannot afford these new costs, yielding therefore to the 'tragedy of the anticommons'. Information and creative commons appear especially vulnerable to and threatened by this form of market failure, with the consequence that 'since inventive activities are usually incremental by nature, meaning that the downstream research embodies the upstream researches, the anticommons dynamics can have a considerable negative impact on the knowledge creation and the total welfare' (Ramello, 2005b, p. 81). Since legal ideas and judicial precedents are not privately appropriated, the under-exploitation of the body of precedents is not a relevant problem in the judicial setting.

However, while the patterns and non-appropriability of precedents prevent their overexploitation and underexploitation as a common resource, some puzzles remain concerning the individual contribution to the system of precedents. Judicial compensation and incentive to innovate appear paradoxical in many respects.

The twin paradoxes of judicial innovation and adoption.
Or, why contribute to the precedent principle?

A third type of market failure that may affect the production of judge-made law concerns the initial contribution to the body of precedents. Why should a judge contribute individually when he or she expects that no personal reward will be derived from contributing and that the benefits of judicial decisions will accrue to the society as a whole? Judicial under-supply of precedents and under-investment in legal ideas are the expected consequences of the divergence between private and social returns to the production of precedent. At the extreme, no judicial invention should take place where obviously some is observable. What triggers, thus, judicial innovation?

A fourth problem that has been highlighted in the law and economics literature concerns the free-riding problem that might affect the production of judicial decisions. One may expect that the absence of intellectual property rights over judicial decisions would induce judges to draw from the common resource to make their decisions. However, *a precedent may not be binding.*[5] In addition, judges may have *heterogeneous individual preferences* over a case, due to differences in their ideological preferences or private backgrounds for instance. They may thus be tempted to systematically *replace* the existing precedent by their own decision, made in accordance with their own private preferences, without consideration of the precedent (i.e. of the preferences of the others or of some social prevailing norm). Doing this, they avoid bearing a private loss from the *falsification of their preferences* (Kuran, 1995). However, they undermine the whole system of *stare decisis* as well, since nobody would longer accept to comply with a precedent if he or she expects that the other judges will not. Typical of a Prisoner's Dilemma, the lack of coordination allowed by the decentralisation of judicial decisions brings about *under-exploitation of the common resource.* Now, this kind of under-exploitation differs from the one associated with anti-commons since, despite the intentional and voluntary disclosure of information by the inventor, potential adopters may lack the will to reuse the innovation fur-ther rather than be prevented to do so. Insufficient adoption results subsequently in a duplication of costs associated with judicial decision-making, increased legal uncertainty, and prevents network externalities to be realised.

Finally, one may wonder why opportunistic behaviours are not observed more frequently and why the precedent system functions at all. The next section develops an analysis grounded in the notion of collective invention. It argues that the judicial community functions according to an open-knowledge logic. Treating the produc-tion of judge-made law by analogy with other forms of intellectual production, we show that this organisation of the judicial community precisely serves the purpose of the production and diffusion of precedents. This functionalist approach is sustained by the actual institutions that prevail in common law countries.

A functionalist view of the judicial institution: the judicial community as an open knowledge community?

This section analyses how judicial institutions are specifically designed and oriented towards remedying the absence of classical forms of compensation for individual contributions. The purpose is to show that the prevalence of specific institutions actually makes the production and diffusion of precedents possible and is intended to serve the goal of the society at the dynamic level. We first describe the judicial community as following an open-knowledge logic based on expectations of generalised reciprocity. Second, the modes of collective governance and self-regulation are analysed. We conclude that the conditions for collective invention to occur are satisfied.

The judicial community as an open knowledge community

The precedent system relies on free exchange of information

Specific patterns of production and diffusion of information can be identified in judge-made law, in relation with the very functioning of the precedent mechanism.

One of the most important is the free exchange of information within the judicial community. Namely, the functioning and survival of *stare decisis* and precedent in common law systems relies first on the *revelation of their innovation* by individual judges. Second, it also relies on the *adoption and reuse* of the disclosed information by other judges. Here, the logic at work is reminiscent of Merton's communalistic rule of disclosure in the *Republic of Science* (1973) – in both cases, an individual willing to have his or her decision recognised by the community has no choice but to release it publicly and the initial release of the innovation is a precondition for further exploitation. In that sense, the commonality rule in the judicial field fosters the conditions of cooperation in the 'Republic of Law', as it does among scientists.

The compliance with the rule of disclosure is reliant on both an individual interest in releasing information and an individual interest in using the information released by others. On the one hand, an innovating judge who has issued a decision bears *no disutility* from the use of the decision by the others, due to *non-rivalry* in consumption. Thus, he or she has no incentive to retain it privately and to conceal it from the others. On the contrary, as a consequence of the positive *network externalities* associated with the adoption of a common rule by judges, an individual judge has an incentive to have his or her innovation adopted by the others. He or she also has a private interest to the production by others of decisions that are compatible with his or her own legal invention.

On the other hand, judge may also find an interest in the adoption of another judge's decision. One of the most commonly admitted reason for such an adopting behaviour in the law and economics literature is the corresponding saving in the individual *costs of judicial decision-making*, since the adoption of a precedent – rather than the production of an innovative decision – enables a judge to 'avoid having to rethink the merits of a particular legal doctrine' (Macey, 1998, p. 71), thereby reducing individual workload. This simple view provides a straightforward basis for the analyses of precedent as informational cascade – or 'precedential cascades', as termed by Talley (1999). From this perspective, judges may choose to use past rules as inputs into their own decisions – and therefore, to substitute the decisions of their colleagues to their own – because they believe that the others are more or better informed than they are themselves (Daughety and Reinganum, 1999). The adoption of a precedent appears thus to be a variant of herding behaviours. This capacity to use the information provided by the others may bring an individual to balance the individual gains derived from the reduction in the costs of decision-making with the loss associated with the falsification of his or her private preferences.

The disclosure of the details of the production process

The release of the judicial information is not limited to the mere outcome of the judicial decision. It also concerns the very production process of decisions, that are made public through the display of the set of considerations that has finally resulted in the individual decision. First, the tradition in common law systems is for judges to write their opinions carefully and to detail the motivations and grounds of the judicial decisions in the *ratio decidendi*. This is the case when they make original decisions that depart from the precedent or for which no precedent already exists – they have then to explain why the case precisely differs from former ones or why no precedent does correspond to the present case. The thorough writing of judicial opinions is also the tradition in cases where judges actually follow a precedent – the purpose is then to justify why the case is similar to the precedent. Second, the *ratio decidendi* may be backed up by a range of incidental considerations that shapes the *obiter dictum*, and that also contains relevant information about the conditions of the decision, possible comparisons with other cases or even overall remarks in relation to the issue. Third, even *dissenting opinions* are also considered as informative and deserving publication and communication. Common law countries recognise that judges issuing a decision collegially may not agree with each other. Dissenting opinions from the prevailing opinion – albeit not binding – should thus be written for their informational content, as possible 'archive materials' for future decisions. In particular, the pragmatic conception of law prevailing in common law countries does not preclude future reversal *ex ante* nor incorporation of dissenting opinions in the grounds of future decisions. Even, dissenting opinions are seen as possibly preparing the field for future evolutions. This is to be compared with the style of judicial decisions in civil law countries, that is much more succinct and formalist, and less informative as well than in common law countries.

This importance granted to judicial communication goes beyond the borders of (common law) countries. The circulation of judicial ideas does not only take place at the domestic level, but also between foreign courts, allowing for a larger pool of judicial precedents to be drawn from when no local precedent exists. For instance, Supreme Courts in common law countries frequently refer to each other. Canada, Australia, New Zealand are traditionally very receptive to British decisions. This facilitates the migration of judicial innovations and the corresponding realisation of network externalities, while at the same time foreign decisions remain non-binding. This attention brought to the diffusion of judicial information also explains why common law countries also resort to the forms of informational dissemination that are typical of civil law countries, such as codification or collections of judicial decisions. While codification in common law countries may not have the same significance as in civil law regimes (Harnay, 2002), it pursues the imputed purpose to complement the spontaneous exchange of judicial decisions that under some circumstances may be flawed by coordination failures.

A system based on generalised reciprocity expectations

We have seen that the precedent is based on free exchange of information among judges and that several institutional arrangements exist within and among common law countries so as to ensure an efficient communication and sharing of judicial ideas. The exchange of precedents is made possible because it ensures the mutual satisfaction of individual interests on the basis of generalised expectations of reciprocity.

The reversibility of roles

The release and adoption of information depend on a reversibility of roles assumption. Namely, a judge issuing an innovative decision in the current period expects that he or she may find himself in the situation of an imitator in the future, over other cases. He expects then to take benefit from the future release of information by the others, so as to be able to freely use their information and expertise. Similarly, a judge who accepts to follow a precedent today expects that he or she may act as an innovator tomorrow – and expects that the others will follow then. Since judges are aware that their respective roles are not set rigidly once and for all, they are more willing to cooperate.[6] As a consequence, the expectation of generalised reciprocity coupled with the reversibility of roles *fosters cooperation* among agents. More precisely, it ensures that cooperation will exist and that the legal network will develop, so that the adoption externalities associated with the use of common legal references will be realised. On the contrary, if judges did not expect reciprocity, they would have no incentive to contribute from the very outset and the adoption externalities associated with a precedent could never be realised.

Expected gains from reciprocity

Judges do cooperate because they expect gains from reciprocity.

First, reciprocity is expected to yield *enlargement* of information. By releasing information to other judges, a judge imparts information that will be useful to other agents. But in exchange, he or she learns a larger volume of legal information than the one given away. Reciprocity and the sharing of information clearly appear advantageous at the individual level, since the flow of information that an individual can derive from his or her participation in the judicial network exceeds from far his or her own contribution.

Second, reciprocity is fed by the *improvement* of judge-made law that it makes possible and that will benefit to individuals and to the society as a whole. First, in a way that is quite close to what can be observed in other open knowledge situations, such as in the scientific or open source software communities, initial innovators derive a *positive feedback* from releasing information and from the reuse of their ideas. Second, the incentive of *followers* to adopt a precedent derives thus from the *possibility to improve* the rule in a sense that suits their personal needs. As a consequence, judge-made law may improve strongly through repeated interactions and feedbacks from users–innovators providing *incremental* innovations to the initial precedent. For instance, as most judicial rules are by nature incomplete, judges filling gaps in the body of precedents and refining former legal reasoning contribute to the improvement of the quality of judge-made law through incremental innovation and a trial and error process

(Kornhauser, 1989; Macey, 1989). Learning-by-doing effects for users also bring about positive feedbacks for the innovator, who can obviously benefit from the release by others of an improved version of the original innovation. This positive effect on the initial innovator, through incremental innovation, can be interpreted as an *indirect network externality* positively affecting the quality of the service provided by the original precedent.

Third, in the judicial field, reciprocity increases the *value of a precedent.* Namely, when judges accept to adopt and enforce a precedent, its resistance against reversal increases – *ceteris paribus.* Thus, the accumulation of decisions issued in accordance with a precedent increases its value, in the sense that it brings more legal certainty and conveys 'stronger' information. In that sense, accumulation leads to a self-enforcing cumulative process that reinforces the value of the original innovation. From this perspective, the adoption of a precedent by the judicial community plays a reinforcing role that the duplication and verification of an information in other knowledge communities may not actually play. For instance, although the duplication of an experiment may also entail positive value in the eyes of the scientific community, the intrinsic value of the discovery is not increased when the discovery is made several times. From this perspective, because it provides a means to strengthen precedents, reciprocity also provides society with valuable legal certainty.

Self-governance and collective regulation of the judicial community

A system of reciprocal disclosure of judicial decisions enables all members of the community to screen and evaluate individual contributions. As it is the case in other open knowledge communities, judicial findings are *peer-reviewed* according to a collective or collegial evaluation process. The judicial community collectively assesses the contributions to the body of precedent and determines which contributions are valuable to the whole community and should therefore be incorporated into judge-made law. If a decision is perceived as improving law, it will be endorsed by the judicial community. Otherwise, it will not be adopted but will be reversed. Since the decisions and improvements more likely to be praised and accepted are those that may provide useful help and satisfy the needs of the peers, self-governance and collective regulation of the judicial community provide the *conditions of a cumulative shift towards higher quality.* From this point of view, peer reviewing by the judicial community plays a social role. As the public at large are unable to check the quality of judicial decisions and to screen judges by their innate abilities, the judicial community plays the role of an agent for the society.[7]

The sanctions exerted by the community on individual behaviours in open knowledge communities are often claimed to be managed by 'invisible colleges'. In the judicial framework, judges who are likely to adopt the position of followers constitute this 'invisible college' that might thus refer to the horizontal competition existing among courts. However, the 'disciplinary' role of this 'invisible' college may also be complemented by the action of a 'visible' college, under the form of a vertical evaluation by the judicial hierarchy. Namely, the hierarchical organisation of courts formally organises an evaluation of the decision of lower courts and recognises the formal leadership of some leaders (Courts of Appeal, Supreme Courts) on the other judicial decision-makers. In this respect, Posner (1986, p. 512) recalls that the structure of appellate review keeps the free-rider problem in check. In other words, just as some programmers are sometimes in charge of checking the contributions of the others in Open Source Software (OSS) communities, higher courts are in charge of the evaluation of individual contributions to judge-made law.[8] This task may entail the harmonisation and cohesiveness of the body of precedent as a whole.

In relation with this twofold dimension of the collective regulation, sanctions may be more or less formal or informal. Very often, the sanction exerted on a judge by peers located at the same level of hierarchy will take the form of non-adopting the decision. The sanction may thus remain quite informal, for instance taking the form of a kind of professional 'ostracism' and criticism. When issued by a higher court, the sanction may take 'harsher' – more 'visible' – forms, such as the absence of promotion to a higher job.

A collective invention situation

As a consequence of both the characteristics of judge-made law and of the organisation of the judicial community as an open-knowledge community, the production of precedents can be seen as the result of a collective invention situation, whose conditions of occurrence are clearly met.

Collective invention is the fourth form of inventive institution put forward by Allen (1983) besides invention by firms, individual inventors and invention by non-profit institutions such as universities or government agencies. It characterises situations in which important discoveries cannot be attributed to any single inventor or firm, but are the outcome of a specific form of invention that Allen labels 'collective invention' and that he defines as an accumulation of incremental improvements driven by the free exchange of information between competing firms. In this setting, knowledge is divided and dispersed (Machlup, 1984) and related to the local situations in which it is produced. Specific innovations are not appropriated through patents or any other classical system, but private agents freely reveal their innovations that can be reused by others very easily. Firms can exploit technical knowledge that they have not discovered personally and build on the experience of other firms openly by adopting changes that have proved to be profitable elsewhere. The sharing process allows a rapid diffusion of the successful innovation – following a trial and error process (Allen, 1983, p. 4) – and the improvement of the innovation as well, as soon as the conditions for all agents to learn and develop innovations further are fulfilled. Furthermore, firms do not engage in formal research effort and do not allocate resources to invention directly, since 'the new technical knowledge [is] a by-product of normal business operation' (ibid., p. 2).

Obviously, these conditions are fulfilled in the setting of judge-made law. First, as it was the case in the very specific sector studied by Allen – the blast furnace industry in Britain's Cleveland district in the nineteenth century – judicial innovation results from the *investment of private resources* by agents in order to produce a collective good. Second, the production is *decentralised* and dispersed among judges and courts. Third, it is the outcome of a process of *incremental innovations* undertaken by judges and that shape a trial and error process. Fourth, these innovations are *not privately appropriated* through a classical property rights approach. While a decision may be originated by an identifiable individual, the functional exchange of decisions among judges and the free exploitation and recomposition of past precedents allows for the *collective improvement* of the precedent to occur. Judicial innovation is not identified with the activity of single individual, but seen as the outcome of the joint effort of the judicial community as a whole. Fifth, as a consequence, the compensation for private contribution to the collective production has both *individual and collective dimensions*, under the form of an improved product that serves the individual and collective goals better. Judges do contribute to the production of the collective good individually because they are aware that they contribute to networked activity and expect positive feedbacks from their cooperative behaviour. Sixth, judge-made law clearly satisfies the condition of collective invention that is that the community itself *evaluates* the value of contributions and which contributions it is worth to accept.

Finally, the free exchange and sharing of judicial information can no longer be assimilated to a kind of intellectual 'plundering' made possible by the absence of traditional intellectual protection. On the contrary, full disclosure of information, its reuse and adoption appear to be driving forces in the precedent dynamics with which they are consubstantial. In a functionalist view, the specific rules, customs and practices governing the whole system of precedent are no longer a puzzle or a paradox in the terms of neoclassical self-interested rationality. They have their own internal coherence and logic well-suited to serve their imputed purposes and provide the conditions for judicial innovation and adoption to occur, despite the absence of individual compensation. In a dynamic view, they ensure that the production of judge-made law will not be prevented in the future by the private appropriation of precedents on the current period. Furthermore, they organise the congruence of individual incentives to contribute to the collective mechanism of precedent with the collective interest.

The reward structure of judges: the congruence of the standard law and economics objective function with the open knowledge reward structure

The preceding section has shown that the judicial community is governed by specific rules and customs that create the conditions of a collective invention of judge-made law. The question now concerns the motivation underlying the decisions of individual judges privately contributing to a collective production – as judicial innovators and adopters – and therefore providing them with the incentive to behave in a socially responsible way. The open knowledge literature has addressed this problem by identifying benefits that are exclusive to private contributors and from which potential free-riders are excluded. Accordingly, contribution appears self-rewarding and only those judges whose satisfaction is greater when contributing than when free-riding will choose to contribute.

In this section, we utilise the distinction between extrinsic and intrinsic motivation to compare the description of judicial objectives by the law and economics literature with the reward system at work in open knowledge communities. Interestingly, we find that both analyses are congruent with each other, supporting the view that information-sharing and disclosure are actually implemented by judges because they further not only the interest of the community but also their self-interest. In particular, the distinction between extrinsic and intrinsic motivation that has been widely used to account for the prevalence of non-market-based incentives in open knowledge communities is also frequently used in the law and economics literature. In other words, the situation of collective invention is made possible by incentive mechanisms that substitute to intellectual property rights so as to allow the individual contribution to the production of judge-made law as well as its diffusion. Judicial motivations at work are twofold, of an extrinsic and intrinsic form.

Extrinsic motivation in law and economics

The irrelevance of monetary motives

The most obvious external incentive to which judges may be responsive is pecuniary, consistently with Posner's assumption that judges are self-interested rational maximisers. From this perspective, they may be motivated at least partly by pecuniary and career rewards, such as increases in salary and future promotion likely to result themselves in increased salaries. Higgins and Rubin (1980), Kimenyi *et al.* (1985), Cohen (1991, 1992) build on such judicial objectives. Similarly, Toma (1991) establishes a positive correlation between the level of the budget received by the US Supreme Court and the proximity of its decisions with the political preferences of the Congress, which might suggest a pecuniary motivation in judicial decision-making. However, most law and economics analyses show that non-monetary objectives prevail in the determination of judicial behaviours. For instance, Greenberg and Haley (1986) utilise US data to show that a judge would obtain higher salaries in the private than in the public sector; they interpret their finding as the consequence of a judicial motivation mainly driven by non-monetary arguments – rather than the clue of high risk aversion. They conclude that judges make a trade-off between money and other forms of compensation, such as power or status. Several other studies carried out on the issue of judicial independence also sustain this interpretation, since no clear correlation between salaries and the decisions made by courts appears systematically. For instance, Anderson *et al.* (1989) find a positive correlation between the independence of judges and the level of their salaries. The prevailing view is that the insulation of judges from traditional budgetary incentives prevents the production of a partial decision in exchange for a monetary compensation.

Reputation motives

Thus, monetary rewards do not provide a totally convincing argument to account for private contribution to a collective good such as a precedent. Alternative motivations have then to be considered. Reputational motives also belong to the set of extrinsic motivations that are put forward by both the open-knowledge and law and economics analyses. In both cases, namely, individuals are assumed to be motivated by the desire of recognition and esteem by peers and the society. In the scientific field, the corresponding effects of reputation usually take the channel of eponymy, prizes, publication and citations (Stephan, 1994, p. 1201). In OSS communities, reputational gains are also attached to the recognition of individual contributions. These gains can be individually realised through the kind of signalling effect described by Lerner and Tirole (2001), according to which private contributions can be seen as an investment activity allowing an individual to signal the quality of his or her own human capital, therefore allowing him or her to private marketplace rewards subsequently.

Reputation plays a decisive role in judicial decision making. Recent studies have insisted that judges appear strongly motivated by the search for the approval of the legal community, either narrowly defined as the group of judges or, more broadly, as the judicial audience, including advocates, litigants, other judges, legal scholars (Miceli and Cosgel, 1994; Bueno de Mesquita and Stephenson, 2002; Harnay and Marciano, 2004). As a consequence, personal motives of a judge may not be the only variable explaining his or her attitude towards precedent, but he or she may also pay much attention to the reception of his or her decision. More precisely, a judge issuing a decision that is recognised and accepted by the judicial community as a valuable one and is therefore followed by other judges will benefit from positive rewards in terms of reputation, popularity and prestige. These reputational rewards may even yield monetary gains, through a promotion and an increase in salary. By contrast, individual disutility is associated with a decision that is criticised and reversed by other judges. The corresponding loss in satisfaction may then take the form either of formal sanctions, such as the absence of subsequent promotions, or of informal professional sanctions, such as 'bad reputation'. Judicial decision-making may thus be determined not only by personal preferences, but also by reputational concerns whose importance in the judges' eyes is attested by the importance granted to quotation (Posner, 2000).

Intrinsic motivations in law and economics

In addition to extrinsic motivation, law and economics also identifies judicial intrinsic motivation – that is, a motivation derived from activities that are valued for their own sake. This intrinsic motivation parallels the intrinsic motivation of contributors in open knowledge communities. However, law and economics also points out some sources of intrinsic satisfaction that might be specific to judges and their production.

Intellectual satisfaction and the pure consumption value of the judicial decision

Just as contributing to other open knowledge communities may provide an individual with positive satisfaction, a judge may derive positive utility from contributing to the precedent system. When a judge innovates, he or she may feel the same kind of personal or intellectual gratification that an individual derives from creative activities. Where a scientist derives positive utility from a scientific discovery or an artist from his or her creation, a judge similarly derives satisfaction from the resolution of an intellectual 'puzzle' of legal nature. Indeed, according to Posner (1994, p. 18), the judicial decision may be 'a source of satisfaction, or even of exhilaration, akin to that experienced by creative people. Artists make works of art that sometimes change sensibility; judges make decisions that sometimes change social or business practices'. Furthermore, 'for the handful of judges who today still write their own opinions', judges derive 'additional utility, akin to that which a literary or scholarly author obtains, from being a published author. There is also the intrinsic pleasure of writing, for those who like to write, and of exercising and displaying analytical prowess or other intellectual gifts, for those who have them and want to use them' (ibid., p. 19). A pure consumption value is therefore associated with judicial decision-making, which refers to enjoyment-based motivation.

In relation with such intellectual satisfaction, and with their twofold role of producers and users, judges may also derive positive utility from a kind of 'self production' akin to that obtained from extended functionality by contributors in OSS communities. In the same way as OSS contributors gain non-pecuniary benefits from tailoring the software to their own needs, judges contributing to the production of judge-made law also favour the production of precedents that are of specific use for them. Coupled with the reciprocity principle, this may thus provide them with a further incentive to contribute to the precedent system.

Ideology and power

Another source of intrinsic motivation put forward by law and economics is the ideological satisfaction that a judge can derive from imposing his or her private ideological views upon society. According to Posner (1986, p. 506), again,

> the principal explanation for judicial behaviour must lie elsewhere than in pecuniary and political factors. One possibility that is consistent with the normal assumptions of economic analysis is that judges seek to impose their personal preferences and values on society. This may explain judges'

sensitivity to being reversed by a higher court: the reversal wipes out the effect of the judge's decision both on the parties to the immediate case and on others, similarly situated, whose behaviour may be influenced by the rule declared by the judge.

As a consequence, if judges are actually motivated by the search for power, defined as the capacity to impose one's own ideological preferences upon society, this may explain why they intentionally disclose their innovations to the rest of the community. Namely, the disclosure of information is obviously a precondition for its reuse by others. This reuse by others, and the incorporation of a precedent into future decisions, enlarges the initial impact of an individual decision. As a consequence, the ideological satisfaction that a judge derives from making a decision in accordance with his or her own ideological views is increased when these ideological views 'contaminate' other cases. The disclosure of a judicial innovation that is subsequently endorsed by the judicial community is thus expected to have a positive feedback on the private utility of the innovator, whose ideological satisfaction is then directly correlated with the number of other adopters.

In addition, this cumulative effect of adoption on ideological satisfaction might also interact with the reputational dimension of judicial motivation. Namely, when other judges comply with a precedent, the reputation of the innovator increases. Again, positive adoption externalities are associated with the adoption of the precedent by the judicial community, that may provide him with increased professional rewards.

Whereas this ideological motivation of judges may not have direct counterpart in other open knowledge communities – if one sticks to the idea of an 'objective' science, for instance, it nevertheless provides a further reason for a self-interested judge to divulge his or her decision to the rest of the community.

Moral considerations and public interest

Open knowledge communities – among others the open source community – are sometimes depicted as grounded in a gift culture instead of an exchange culture. Altruistic motivations are then assumed to induce gift behaviours by individual contributors who will 'spontaneously' take the welfare of the community into consideration and enter it into their preferences. Transposed to judicial interactions, this assumption means that judges believe that the right thing is to give their legal reasoning away and to follow the precedents issued by others, because – for some reason, moral and ethical considerations, a high degree of concernment for the public good, their attachment to legal values and so on – this contributes to the good of the legal community.

Standard law and economics seems quite reluctant to admit such altruistic motivation explains judicial behaviours, but usually dismisses them as irrelevant and inconsistent with the basic assumption that judges do maximise 'the same thing everybody else does'. From this perspective, the consideration that the promotion of public interest and moral concerns may drive judicial decision-making may as well be seen as a disguised attempt to restore the assumption of a superior morality and disinterestedness of judges that the standard law and economics research precisely challenges.

Finally, judge-made law shares many of the features of open knowledge in the way it is functionally organised and in the motivations underlying individual contributions to the construction of the body of precedents as well. In particular, if monetary arguments do not provide any persuasive argument to account for judicial behaviours and for judicial interactions that are crystallised around compliance and non-compliance with the precedent, the analyses of the functioning of open knowledge communities suggest self-rewarding contributions that are very close to those highlighted by the law and economics literature and that are relevant to account for the transformation of the social dilemma of knowledge-sharing into a coordination game in which judge-made law can be produced.

Conclusion

Building upon the specificities of judge-made law as an informational commons and judicial decision-making as a network activity, this paper attempts to provide an explanation of the puzzle of individual contribution to the system of precedent in a framework characterised by the absence of any classical (individual) means of appropriation. The puzzle is twofold. First, the question of the individual incentive to innovate and to give away the outcome of one's private effort remains paradoxical within the assumptions of the standard neoclassical law and economics approach. Second, the diffusion of a precedent – that is, its adoption by judges who have not issued it directly and whose private preferences about a case may differ from those having commanded of the production of the precedent – also remains difficult to account for in this analytical framework. We find that the institutional arrangements, norms and customs that govern the judicial community in common law countries share a lot with so-called 'open-knowledge communities'. In particular, at the very basis of the precedent system, free exchange of judicial information is regulated by generalised expectations of reciprocity that are themselves reliant on collective regulation and self-governance by the community. This provides the conditions for judge-made law to be produced, as an expression of collective invention.

Our contribution is to emphasise the centrality of cooperative behaviours that are largely dismissed as irrelevant or marginal by standard law and economics models. We claim that the production of judge-made law cannot be explained without understanding of such behaviours that are central to the functioning and survival of the precedential mechanism. An crucial point is that our analysis does not invalidate the traditional judicial utility function retained by the law and economics approach. On the contrary, we check that the rich range of judicial motivations that have been gradually incorporated into law and economics analyses are fully compatible with the array of motivations displayed by actors in open knowledge communities. Borrowing from the latter, we show that judicial compliance with the precedent system is largely fed by self-rewarding contributions.

At a further level, our analysis builds upon a more realistic conception of the precedent as an incremental innovation, at odds with the 'all-or-nothing' approach prevailing in most of the law and economics literature. In particular, our analysis allows us to account for the cumulative effect of adopting decisions on the social value of the precedent.

Further research requires to analyse the impact of a collective invention process on the content and evolution of judge-made law. In particular, the assumption of heterogeneous judges requires to be questioned further, in relation with the coordination problems that may arise among judges and result in legal path-dependence and lock-in situations.

Notes

1 The depreciation rate of a precedent is a function of changes in the environment and of the uncertainty that affects economic, social, and legal conditions. Overall, precedents with a high degree of generality can be expected to depreciate more slowly than precedents with a high degree of specificity, and the legal production of competing decision-makers – under the form of statutory regulation for instance – also tends to discount the value of a precedent more rapidly.
2 See Faulkner and Runde (2004).
3 See Bailey and Rubin (1994) for an analysis of the demand of judge-made law in a repeated game. They consider the case where litigants may have an incentive to demand a precedent when they expect to be involved in a similar dispute in the future again. The anticipation of a repetition of the game gives parties an incentive to engage litigation expenditures so as to induce the judicial production of a favourable precedent.
4 In that view, its value might also be related to the tacit knowledge shared by judges of a same legal community. The debate between tacit and codified knowledge is beyond the scope of this article.
5 A judge cannot be prevented from using a precedent to make his or her own present decision. But he or she cannot be forced to adopt it too, as long as the precedent is not binding. By contrast with some other collective goods, and from the judge's standpoint, the precedent is not always characterised by the *obligation d'usage* and it may thus not be a pure public good. Some precedents are binding while some others are not. When a precedent is not binding, a judge can choose whether to adopt it or not. Theoretically, he or she is allowed to depart from the existing precedent as soon as the decision of dissidence is motivated and subsequently accepted and followed by the other judges.
6 The introduction of explicit vertical competition among courts partially invalidates the reciprocity principle.
7 David and Dasgupta (1994, p. 505) issue the same remark as for scientists and the appreciation of scientific discoveries by the public at large.
8 A difference with open source software communities resides in the fact that in most systems a superior judge has to be seized by a litigant to be able to express his or her opinion.

References

Allen, R.C., 1983. 'Collective invention', *Journal of economic Behaviour and Organization*, 4, 1–24.

Anderson, G., Shughart, W., Tollison, R., 1989. 'On the Incentives of Judges to Enforce Legislative Wealth Transfers', *Journal of Law and Economics*, 32, 215–228.

Arrow, K.J., 1962. 'Economic Welfare and the Allocation of Resources for Inventions', in R.R. Nelson (ed.), *The Rate and Direction of Inventive Activity: Economic and Social Factors*, Princeton University Press, Princeton, NJ.

Bailey, M., Rubin, P.H., 1994. 'A Positive Theory of Lagal Change', *International Review of Law and Economics*, 14, 467–477.

Bueno de Mesquita, E., Stephenson, M., 2002. 'Informative Precedent and Intrajudicial Communication', *American Political Science Review*, 96, 4, 755–766.

Cohen, M., 1991. 'Explaining Judicial Behaviour or what's "Unconstitutional" about the Sentencing Commission?', *Journal of Law, Economics, and Organisation*, 7, 183–199.

Cohen, M., 1992. 'The Motives of Judges: Empirical Evidence from Antitrust Sentencing', *International Review of Law and Economics*, 12, 13–30.

Dasgupta, P., David, P.A., 1994. 'Towards a New Economics of Science', *Research Policy*, 23, 487–521.

Daughety, A.F., Reinganum, J.F., 1999. 'Stampede to Judgment: Persuasive Influence and Herding Behaviour by Courts', *American Law and Economics Review*, 1, 1–2, 158–189.

Faulkner, P., and Runde, J., 2004. 'Information Knowledge and Modelling Economic Agency', in J. Davie, A. Marciano and J. Runde (eds), *The Elgar Companion of Economics and Philosophy*, Edward Elgar, Cheltenham, UK, Northampton, MA.

Greenberg, P.E., Haley, J.A., 1986. 'The Role of Compensation Structure in Enhancing Judicial Quality', *Journal of Legal Studies*, 15, 417–426.

Hardin, G., 1968. 'The Tragedy of the Commons', *Science*, 162, 3859, 1243–1248.

Harnay, S., 2002. 'Was Napoleon a Benevolent Dictator? An Economic Justification for Codification', *European Journal of Law and Economics*, 2002, 14, 237–251.

Harnay, S., Marciano, A., 2004. 'Judicial Conformity *versus* Dissidence: An Economic Analysis of Judicial Precedent', *International Review of Law and Economics*, 23, 4, 405–420.

Heller, M., 1998. 'The Tragedy of Anticommons: Property in the Transition from Marx to Market', *Harvard Law Review*, 111, 621–688.

Higgins, R., Rubin, P., 1980. 'Judicial Discretion', *Journal of Legal Studies*, 9, 129–138.

Kimenyi, M.S., Shughart, W.F., Tollison, R.D., 1985. 'What Do Judges Maximize?', *Economia Delle Scelte Pubbliche*, 181–188.

Kornhauser, L.A., 1989. 'An Economic Perspective on *Stare Decisis*', *Chicago-Kent Law Review*, 65–1, 63–92.

Kuran, T., 1995. *Private Truth, Public Lies. The Social Consequences of Preference Falsification*, Cambridge, Harvard University Press.

Landes, W., Posner, R., 1976. 'Legal Precedent, A Theoretical and Empirical Analysis', *Journal of Law and Economics*, 249–313.

Lerner, J., Tirole, J., 2001. 'The Open Source Movement: Key Research Questions', *European Economic Review*, 45, 819–826.

Macey, J., 1989. 'The Internal and External Costs and Benefits of *Stare Decisis*', *Chicago-Kent Law Review*, 65–1, 93–113.

Macey, J., 1998. 'Precedent', in P. Newman (ed.), *The New Palgrave Dictionary of Law and Economics*, McMillan Reference Limited, 71–76.

Machlup, F., 1984. *Knowledge, its Creation, Distribution, and Economic Significance*, vol. 3, Princeton University Press, Princeton, NJ.

Merton, R.K., 1973. 'Singletons and Multiples in Scientific Discovery', in N.W. Storer (ed.), *The Sociology of Science: Theoretical and Empirical Investigations*, University of Chicago Press, Chicago, IL, 343–370.

Miceli, T.J., Cosgel, M.M., 1994. 'Reputation and Judicial Decision-Making', *Journal of Economic Behaviour and Organization*, 23, 31–51.

Nelson, R.R., 1959. 'The Simple Economics of Basic Scientific Research', *Journal of Political Economy*, 67, 3, 297–306.

Posner, R.A., 1986. *Economic Analysis of Law*, Little, Brown and Company, Boston, MA and Toronto, 2d ed.

Posner, R.A., 1994. 'What do Judges and Justices Maximize? (The Same Thing Everybody Else Does', *Supreme Court Economic Review*, 3, 1–41.

Posner, R.A., 2000. 'An Economic Analysis of the Use of Citations in the Law', *American Law and Economic Review*, 2, 2, 381–406.

Ramello, G., 2005a. 'Private Appropriability and Sharing of Knowledge: Convergence or Contradition? The Opposite Tragedy of the Creative Commons', in L. Takeyama, W. Gordon and R. Towse (eds), *Developments in the Economics of Copyright: Research and Analysis*, Edward Elgar, Cheltenham, UK, Northampton, MA.

Ramello, G., 2005b. 'Intellectual Property and the Market of Ideas', *Review of Network Economics*, 4, 2, 68–87.

Stephan, P.E., 1996. 'The Economics of Science', *Journal of Economic Literature*, 34, September, 1199–1235.

Talley, E., 1999. 'Precedential Cascades, an Appraisal', *Southern California Law Review*, 73, 1, 87–137.

Toma, E., 1991. 'Congressional Influence and the Supreme Court: The Budget as a Signaling Device', *Journal of Legal Studies*, 20, 131–146.

12 Failing property rights – the problem of *sleeping owners* in the city

A preliminary analysis of one aspect of the German unification treaty[1]

Jürgen G. Backhaus

Introduction

Take it as a given that between 6 and 9 percent of the territory[2] of the new German federal states are the property of *sleeping owners*. The term is designed to describe an economic agent who owns property but has no incentive to use it. This lack of incentives may be inherent or due to the restrictions on his realm of choice that are not deprivations of the property rights as such. Any visitor in the new federal states, who strolls through the downtowns in an idle moment, will find a peculiar occurrence that is hard to find in other geographical areas. In Buenos Aires, you find entire historical structures rather or more simultaneously and intentionally declining (Backhaus, 1998). In the new federal states, provided there is a historical structure[3] still remaining, you walk leisurely looking for what the city has to offer. Beautiful refurbished buildings stemming from the Renaissance, Baroque, Rococo, Founders, Arts Nouveau, and even Bauhaus Style can be admired and yet, as if there were missing teeth, you find dilapidated buildings located on what should be valuable, even choice property – with no apparent sign or evidence of work, activity, or intention. Are the owners asleep? This is the topic of the chapter.

The chapter has three parts. The first part offers a description of the little known, but economically and socially important phenomenon. The next part contains the analysis. The economic analysis of property rights, land rents, and opportunity costs are all needed in order to render an explanation of the phenomenon. The final part, followed by the conclusion, contains suggestions for relief and policy alternatives.

Describing the phenomenon

Property according to Roman Law is typically defined in three terms. *Usus* refers to actually working with something, such as driving a car or working the land. This activity obviously is designed to serve a purpose and *usus fructus* is the right to actually harvest the fruit of the labor. Looking at it, one may draw the conclusion that the effort could be better organized or scheduled. *Abusus* hence refers to the right to totally restructure the effort, corporation, enterprise, or firm. If these owners are appearing as if they were asleep, something in this system must be amiss. A straightforward effort is therefore to simply check one category after the other.

Sleeping ownership: property rights, land rents, and opportunity costs

A piece of real estate which lies idle nevertheless is not a negligible entity in city life. Literally, tiles and bricks may fall from the roof and hurt passers-by. This causes liability claims to which the owner has to respond. By implication, the owner either has to insure his property against such claims, or he is somehow immune from liability claims. This can be the case either by virtue of law, an owner could, for instance, be exempt because of his or her incorporation under public law, or second, because the owner is extraterritorial, or third, due to shallow pockets, illiquidity, or bankruptcy. In all other cases, leaving property unused creates costs to the owner. Idle property also can create costs to neighbours. To start with, unattended property is likely to be visited by vagrants, both human and nonhuman. This causes externalities, both physical and in terms of value. Most of these externalities tend to be negative. This implies that a piece of idle property does not only cause costs to the owner, unless he can avoid them, but also imposes costs on the owners of adjacent property; if the purported value of a piece of idle property is x, and the loss to the owner due to its idleness is therefore r times x *per annum*, where r is the standard interest rate, the total must obviously be the net present value of r times x. The cost to the adjacent owners is composed of the sum over all neighbours, of the decrements in their property values Δv, where v stands for property value, again discounted as the net present value over the relevant period. Under the *Coase theorem* (Coase, 1960), the second sum, if it exceeds the first, would drive the reallocation of resources in the absence of transactions costs. Since over time the second sum necessarily has to exceed the first at some point, in the presence of idle property 15 years after reunification either the purported property values are high (which is unlikely), or the externalities are relatively low (which is equally unlikely), or transactions costs are significant. This would therefore have to be the focus of political action.

It is not inconceivable that the lack of using property in real estate nevertheless creates a benefit to the owner. If an area grows with a particular rate g, and g is greater than r, then leaving the property idle still renders the speculative gain

$$\frac{v}{(g - r)} = 0$$

which, in principle, can even be liquidated by mortgaging the property. If growth continues, this liquidation could, in principle, go on indefinitely, and this would constitute an equilibrium in the absence of policy intervention. Of course, this equilibrium would have a siphoning effect on economic growth, and, in fact, operates like imposing a tax on the adjacent property values, a benefit which the owner of the idle property derives from his neighbors by doing nothing. Such a scenario is only possible under very peculiar circumstances, which can be described with precision. The equilibrium can be readily upset by political action. If such action is not forthcoming, in the presence of continuous damage being imposed on the neighbourhood, the political process itself has to be made the focus of economic analysis.

The opportunity cost of not using a piece of real estate is the loss of using the capital, which it embodies. The opportunity cost then is zero, if for some reason, *abusus*, that is, the sale or conversion of the property, is not an available option. This can be the case, if either the title is uncertain, or not transactional, or the benefit structure of the owner is constrained, for instance if only the fruit can be gained and not the value of the property itself. For instance, a piece of property can be institutionally devoted to a particular purpose such as worship. Indeed, the case occurs that church property remains idle. Yet, for the case under consideration, this is not a significant portion of the real estate under review. In the new federal states, the church is exposed to dramatically shrinking attendance in a secular environment. Less than a fifth of the population are active members, who pay their dues. Increasingly, church property is marketed; the Catholic Church even has its own real estate agency for conversion of ecclesiastical buildings. Hence, the church has found ways to operate efficiently even in a difficult environment. The sleeping owners must be located elsewhere.

Basic land rents consist of on the one hand the locational land rent, and on the other hand the improvements. An owner, who allows the property to deteriorate, can do so only, assuming he acts economically, if deterioration of the improvements is offset by a more than commensurate increase in the basic land rent, that is, the value of the unimproved land. For instance, a castle in the countryside, if located in an agricultural area with extensive farming, has basic land rents only more or less equal to unimproved farmland in the vicinity. Even intensive farming cannot increase the land rent, since the side of the castle cannot be used for farming, once the castle has been erected there. Also, such a castle has few alternate use values, is likely demarcated as a historical landmark, and offers the owner only few options.

Different is the case of a building of similar size, perhaps even of similar age surrounded by active urban development. Here, the owner can extract a premium by increasing the land rent of the adjacent properties, which would reflect on his own simultaneously. The improvement value is not directly affected by this development, but the total site value plus improvement can increase in the presence of declining improvement values only, if the site value of the land is larger without the historical improvement and a clean slate for urban development. For a private property owner, this "clean slate" is hard to accomplish, since it requires either rezoning or building permits, affecting often historic housing stock.

The strategy of acting like a *sleeping owner* is therefore the more likely, the stronger the probability of reaping benefits from adjacent developments. This can in particular be accomplished, if the *sleeping owner* is close to the political zoning process. In any event, this process of increasing the site value by simultaneously decreasing the value of the improvement and still reaping a net benefit is time consuming and the more costly (and unlikely), the higher the interest rate and the higher the tax rate for the property tax. Only such owners are likely to employ the strategy, who face no opportunity cost of capital and no tax liability.

Policy options

The standard policy options, if one encounters an inactive property owner, who exposes negative externalities on his neighbours, are the following:

1   On the basis of an existing zoning ordinance, a construction order can be imposed. This order typically carries a date, at which the owner has to file for the respective construction permit (to be checked against the zoning ordinance), a second date at which construction has to begin at the latest, and a sanction, such as a fine, in case any of these dates are missed. The fines tend to be progressively increased, if the owner remains inactive, and ultimately the city can seize the property in order to redeem the accumulated fines plus interest.
2   In addition, as the case may be, delinquent property can be entered into a publicly supervised auction as a distress sale. The city then collects back taxes plus interest, fines plus interest, and the auction fees, and remits any remainder to the owner.
3   Property taxes can be based on different bases for assessment. If economic development is the primary purpose, property taxes can be based on the yield that can be reaped from a fully developed piece of property on the site in question. The tax then can be the entire land rent, forcing the owner to maximize the yield from the improvement. This is an approach, which has on occasion been used with great success.[4]

All these policy options fail, if the property owner in question somehow cannot or will not be the addressee of any of these possible policies that the municipality can apply. Particular properties may be exempt from zoning. Owners may be immune to sanctions or they may be tax-exempt. This is certainly the case, if the city is herself the owner. In this case, since the city is not likely to sanction itself, the problem has *no policy solution* at the local level.

Any solution at a different level first requires an explanation of such bizarre behavior in a democratically structured environment. The *sleeping owner* obviously displays a very low time preference, far below the prevailing interest rate, and hence at odds with any type of an economic theory of democracy. In a democracy, officeholders, who strive for re-election, have a high time preference, since their term of four to five years is at the same time their relevant time horizon. All the benefits of any conceivable policy that a democratically elected officeholder will entertain, have to exceed the costs occurring during the term at the end of which re-election is thought. In this scenario, it is quite possible that the net present value of such a policy is low or even negative provided the costs occur in later periods. In the case under review, here, however, the city as a *sleeping owner* incurs the costs upfront in terms of lost revenues from developed property and lost revenues due to the externalities imposed on neighboring properties, let alone general effects of dissatisfaction caused by the obvious neglect.

The only remaining theory that can explain the case, is Tullock's theory of bureaucracy (1965), in which he distinguishes four different types of bureaucrats. Here, we have the *zealot*, who wants to fulfil the mission of his office, because it coincides with his own preferences; the *powerbuilder*, who maximizes his power irrespective of the mission; the *elder Statesman*, who wants to be seen in charge of a large empire, but left alone with respect to work and responsibility; and the *shirking bureaucrat*, who minimizes his work effort and the area of his responsibility by sharing it with others. (Today, we call this the network or matrix approach.) He displays a highly risk-adverse behavior and conceals the cost of his inactivity, thereby causing substantial slack in the bureaucracy. Interestingly, the behavior of the city as a non-acting sleeping property owner is compatible with all four types of bureaucratic behavior.

The *zealot* wants to retain all options of city planning, and is certain of a speculative gain in the long run – although the market does not share his optimism. This discrepancy in the respective outlooks plays into the *zealot's* hands as the city accumulates more and more underperforming property. The *powerbuilder* shares the zealot's acquisitive impulse as he is convinced that property entails power, for whatever purposes it can ultimately be used. This is, why he plays his cards with a cautious hand, keeping the big items for later. The *elder Statesman* is happy to preside over large tracts of lands, different options, for which he is constantly weighing different options in front of the public, receiving permanent attention. And the *shirker*, finally, is happy to preside over decaying property with minimal effort, responding belatedly to whatever problem it may cause, but ultimately doing part of what needs to be done in order to avoid liability claims. None of these bureaucrats has to consider in his behavior the opportunity costs of capital and the revenues foregone.

An alternative explanation, which is compatible with the first, explaining the peculiarly low time preference of the *sleeping public owner* with a combination of path dependence and the peculiarly German system of Savings and Loans banks (S & L's). These S & L's also serve as the cities' banks. Each major city tends to operate its own. They are combined in large associations, typically spanning several federal states, which serve as their lender of last resort. When the city acquires a piece of property, it can resort to credit expended by its S & L. The assessment of the property value is subjected to negotiation between the representative of the bank's owner, that is, the city, and the credit manager. This is also true, when the city returns to the bank in order to increase the mortgage. This route is a partial observation for the observed soft budget constraint.[5]

The acquisition drive financed in this way is only reversible, if property values exceed the assessed value on the basis of which the mortgages have been written.

When, on the other hand, the real estate market is in distress, city officials are credible as they claim that they cannot find a buyer for their dilapidated real estate. They cannot, because a sale would reveal the difference between the book value and the market value of the property in question.[6]

Conclusion

In conclusion, cities depend in their budget partly on own revenues, and to a larger part on revenues from the state. The state can calculate the revenue subsidy in terms of what the city could have earned in revenue, given the city structure, and only transferring the remainder. If the city revenue is R, the city expenditures E, and the revenues foregone F, the transfer should not exceed

$$E - R - F$$

It is easy for the state court of audit to calculate the revenues forgone, F. The court will be happy to have an additional task.

Notes

1 Helpful comments by Alexander Ebner, Jürgen Geilfuß, Jens-Uwe Mangold, and Gerhard Scheurer are gratefully acknowledged.
2 This is likely an underestimate. Precise data are hard to come by, serious efforts notwithstanding.
3 Many cities, of course, were razed during the *Second World War*. For details, see: Groehler (1990).
4 Andelson (1997) gives an international overview. For a study of what may be considered the most spectacular and successful case, see Backhaus (1997 and 2004).
5 " 'Soft budget constraints' – the refinancing of loss-making state-owned enterprises – have been portrayed as a major inefficiency in centrally planned economies, most notably by Janos Kornai (1979, 1980)" (Bolton and Dewatripont, 2005, p. 384; the authors refer to Kornai's pathbreaking work: "Resource-Constrained versus Demand-Constrained Systems," 1979, and *Economics of Shortage*, 1980). As the case shows, soft budget constraints do not only occur in centrally planned economies. The scenario considered shows that free-market economies provide amply opportunity for ingenious politicians to create soft budgets as well.
6 For residential property, which the city owns through housing cooperatives – they are no cooperatives except by name, rather typically they are in the form of limited liability, wholly and exclusively owned by the city. See Backhaus (2005).

References

Andelson, R.V. (ed.) (1997) *Land-Value Taxation Around the World*, New York: Robert Schalkenbach Foundation (2nd edition), Malden, MA: Blackwell Publishers, 2000 (3rd edition).

Backhaus, J. (1997) "Tsingtau 1997," paper presented at a conference on *Henry George*, Maastricht University, October 29.

Backhaus, J. (1998) "Das kulturelle Umfeld einer entwickelten Marktwirtschaft" (The Cultural Landscape of a Developed Market Economy). *Wirtschaftsgesellschaft und Kultur*. Gottfried Eisermann zum 80. Geburtstag. Zürich: Haupt, 79–94.

Backhaus, J. (2004.) "From Tsingtau to Qingdao: A Remarkable Story in Economic History." Unpublished Manuscript.

Backhaus, J. (2005) "Living it off or living it down: the economics of disinvestments." In: Alain Marciano and Jean-Michel Joselin (eds) *Law and the State. A Political Economy Analysis*. Cheltenham, UK: Edward Elgar, 399–403.

Bolton, P. and Dewatripont, M. (2005) *Contract Theory*. Cambridge, MA: MIT Press.

Coase, R.H. (1960) "The Problem of Social Cost." *Journal of Law and Economics*, 3, 1–44.

Groehler, Ol. (1990) *Bombenkrieg gegen Deutschland*. Berlin: Akademie-Verlag.

Kornai, J. (1979) "Resource-Constrained versus Demand-Constrained Systems." *Econometrica*, 47, 801–819.

Kornai, J. (1980) *Economics of Shortage*. Amsterdam: North Holland.

Tullock, G. (1965) *The Politics of Bureaucracy*, Washington: Public Affairs Press.

Index

For Product Safety Concerns and Information please contact our
EU representative GPSR@taylorandfrancis.com Taylor & Francis
Verlag GmbH, Kaufingerstraße 24, 80331 München, Germany